EDITORIAL

Labour history research reached a worldwide peak in popularity during the sixties and seventies. The prevailing "Old Labour History" with its institutional focus gradually made way for a *social* history of labour. This new trend disavowed the view that labour history was a highly specialized field and attempted to place this type of historical research in the context of society as a whole. Without ignoring the role of unions and other labour organizations, a variety of new approaches gained ground that established links with subdisciplines such as women's history, cultural history, the history of mentalities, and urban history, and applied insights from sociology and anthropology.

The field rapidly grew so diverse and complex that coherent synthesis became desirable. Unfortunately, the discipline's decline set in before anything could be accomplished towards this goal. This setback was especially serious in advanced industrial societies. Verity Burgmann provides a characteristic description of this development in Australia:

Labour history became progressively marginalised, increasingly regarded as irredeemably specialist, guilty of all the sins of the more traditional sub-disciplines, such as intellectual history or constitutional history. [. . .] Within history departments, labour history fell into desuetude, joining religious history as an outmoded sub-discipline consigned, if not to the rubbish bin of history, then at least to the laws of natural wastage so far as staff replenishment was concerned.[1]

While labour history's popularity did not always take such a dramatic turn for the worse, it certainly did end up on the defensive in many countries.

Labour history does not truly have itself to blame for its current nadir. The field has always welcomed new trends. Instead, the reasons appear to lie with external factors. First, the worldwide political constellation has undergone a metamorphosis that has caused the evanescence of the spirit of the 1960s, the collapse of 'socialism' in the Soviet Union and Eastern Europe, and the crisis of many working-class parties elsewhere. Second, the advanced countries have experienced a long-term shift in relevant standards and values. Work has "been objectively displaced from its status as a central and self-evident fact of life" and is consequently "also forfeiting its subjective role as the central motivating force in the activity of workers."[2]

These factors have turned historical research on labour relations and workers into an antiquarian field in the eyes of many. Both less politicized areas and new subdisciplines (such as environmental history) enjoy increasing popularity.

[1] Verity Burgmann, "The Strange Death of Labour History", in: Bob Carr *et al.*, *Bede Nairn and Labour History* (Sydney, 1991), pp. 69–81, 70–71.
[2] Claus Offe, *Disorganized Capitalism. Contemporary Transformation of Work and Politics* (Oxford, 1985), pp. 147–148.

International Review of Social History 38 (1993), pp. 1–3

T0349748

This collection of essays is a scholarly attempt to further the urgent integration of labour history in the broader discipline of social history and at the same time to highlight the field's undiminished vitality.

As previously mentioned, the plethora of perspectives from the past three decades still lacks a cohesion force, thereby creating an impression of fragmentation. Theoretical integration of the various approaches is necessary. This integrated social history of labour will have to deal with many obstacles. Some of the most important are the following:

(1) Geographical, spatial, and environmental circumstances of the developments in question have been neglected. Labour historians tend to view space as something "dead" (Michel Foucault) and therefore often fail to give ecological and locational influences on human actions the consideration they deserve.

(2) There is a contrast between the history of daily life and institutional history. It is necessary to bridge the gap between historical research on *objective* events such as labour processes, wages, and housing on the one hand and research on individuals' *subjective* experiences regarding these issues on the other. A true understanding of these developments is possible only when the objective and subjective aspects are viewed as interdependent.

(3) Research currently isolates the working-class and the workers' movement to the exclusion of outside influences. The theory that it is necessary to consider trends such as the history of entrepreneurs when writing about labour history should be applied in practice.

(4) Issues involving gender, race, ethnicity, and age are treated as separate subdisciplines. Although labour history research no longer appears to focus implicitly on young white male workers, it remains difficult to find a consistent approach to the plural identities of the working class.

(5) Misleading periodization persists. Two methods of exclusion by date have had an artificial and consequently distorting effect on labour history. Developments of the early modern period are all too often considered isolated incidents (although periods analysed are beginning to start around 1700 instead of around 1800). Labour historians are insufficiently aware of the importance of the development of merchant capitalism in places such as Florence during the *quattrocento* or the Republic of the Netherlands during the sixteenth and seventeenth centuries. Furthermore, analyses of very recent labour relations and labour movements from the past two decades are usually the domain of scholars from other fields (such as industrial relations or sociology).

(6) Labour history research overemphasizes core countries such as the United States, Canada, Western Europe, and Japan. The burgeoning labour history of the capitalist periphery merits the same consideration as the labour history of core countries. Whether developments occur in

Chile, Nigeria, India, or Malaysia, they deserve to be studied as events in their own right, rather than as early stages of or deviations from developments in highly developed countries.

The present collection of essays is a step towards carrying out this versatile programme. The authors use case studies to explore ways to integrate labour history with other historical perspectives. They focus on the first four points listed above. Topics include geography (Carville Earle), daily life (Alf Lüdtke), entrepreneurs (Gottfried Korff), race (Dave Roediger), gender (Sonya Rose), and households (Marcel van der Linden). Future publications will also examine the other issues.[3]

Marcel van der Linden

---

[3] The next *International Review of Social History* Supplement (December 1994) will deal with periodization.

Divisions of Labor: The Splintered Geography of Labor Markets and Movements in Industrializing America, 1790–1930

CARVILLE EARLE

Among the various methodological prescriptions of Anthony Giddens, perhaps the most useful for labor history are his advisories on social change, on the anxieties and tensions attending a society's transition from one geographical scale to another.[1] Labor's experience in the United States offers a case in point. The nation's transformation from a preindustrial to an industrial society entailed, in addition to the inexorables of accelerated urbanization, industrial expansion, and market extension, certain fundamental changes in the conditions of labor. Industrialization restructured the geography of labor markets, revised principles of wage determination, fomented sectarian division in the ranks of labor, and soured the relations between labor and capital. These structural changes led, in turn, to the inevitable responses of, among others, worker combination, protest, industrial violence, and a splintering in the ranks of labor.

Although the contours of these momentous social changes are well known, thanks to the diligence of labor historians, we know next to nothing about their geographical particulars, about the evolving geography of labor and labor markets.[2] And for good reason since the methodological directives of American labor history have privileged one or another of two scalar extremes. These directives fasten inquiry either on microscale case studies of community and locale or on macroscale studies of national institutions – the axis, not coincidentally, of older and newer approaches to institutional and social labour history, respectively.[3] Only on rare occa-

---

Any synthesis of the sort attempted here does a disservice to the literatures on which it depends for the simple reason that space precludes comprehensive citation. I trust, therefore, that my abridged set of references offers a hint of the richness of this literature and of my rather sizable debt to historians, sociologists, economists, and geographers, cited and not.

[1] Anthony Giddens, "Structuration Theory: Past, Present and Future", in Christopher G.A. Bryant and David Jary (eds.), *Giddens' Theory of Structuration: A Critical Appreciation* (London, 1991) pp. 201–221.

[2] Among others, Herbert Gutman, *Work, Culture and Society in Industrializing America* (New York, 1976); David Montgomery, *Workers' Control in America: Studies in the History of Work, Technology, and Labor Struggles* (Cambridge, 1979); and John R. Commons, *History of Labor in the United States* (4 vols.; New York, 1935).

[3] David Brody, "The Old Labor History and the New: In Search of an American Working Class", *Labor History* 20 (1979), pp. 111–126. On scales of analysis, various essays in Jeffrey C. Alexander, *et al.* (eds.), *The Micro-Macro Link* (Berkeley, 1987); Charles Tilly, *Big Structures, Large Processes, Huge Comparisons* (New York, 1984).

International Review of Social History 38 (1993), pp. 5–37

sions do these inquiries abandon scalar extremism and attend to the richly textured middle ground (mesoscale) of an as yet unwritten historical geography of American labor.

This methodological preoccupation with the very small or the very large is especially ironic for students of social change since, as Giddens reminds us, most great transitions, and certainly the transition from preindustrial to industrial worlds, run directly through the middling scales of metropolis and region. Yet save for the pioneering efforts of Shorter and Tilly, Hobsbawm and Rudé, and a few others, students of labor history seem disinterested in this coaxial zone of mediation and translation.[4] Eschewing mesoscale mappings of wages, worker protests, unionization, labor force, and the like has its consequences, however. And not the least of these is the obliteration of spatial context and subtext when inquiries are conducted, respectively, at micro (community) and macroscales (national institutions) of analysis.

Consider the microscale methodology of labor history. Community case studies, however insightful on matters of strategy, constraint, and action, rarely address their aptitude for inquiry. Is the case representative of all places and times, or of certain classes of places in time? Or is it a revealing anomaly? These are questions simultaneously of context and conditionalization – of positioning a case in periodic time and regional space, of typicality.[5] Herbert Gutman, the late dean of American labor history, forthrightly addressed these issues in proposing the hypothesis of an inverse relation between a community's level of modernity and its propensity for worker protest. His strategy provided at once argument – the declension of labor power in the course of modernization – and context – a specification of discrete microscale communities in their systematic mesocale geography.[6]

At the opposite extreme, consider the surreality of macroscale interpretations of labor history, divorced as they are from spatial and temporal particulars. In cobbling together coarsely drawn state and national statistics, institutional trends detached from the places that shaped them, and anecdotal data from highly varied places and times, these interpretations obscure systematic (regional) and particular (local) variances in strategy, constraint, and action. The problem with treating macroprocesses in this fashion is that it overlooks the spatially recursive nature of social change; to be sure, macroscale processes shape events at local and regional scales,

---

[4] Edward Shorter and Charles Tilly, *Strikes in France, 1830–1968* (New York, 1974); E.J. Hobsbawn and George Rudé, *Captain Swing: A Social History of the Great English Agricultural Uprising of 1830* (New York, 1968); and Herbert Gutman, "The Workers' Search for Power: Labor in the Gilded Age", in H. Wayne Morgan (ed.), *The Gilded Age: A Reappraisal* (Syracuse, N.Y., 1963), pp. 38–68.
[5] Carville Earle and Leonard Hochberg, "Varieties of Geohistorical Social Science", in *Geographical Perspectives on Social Change* (Stanford, forthcoming).
[6] Gutman, "The Workers' Search for Power", pp. 38–68.

but they are also shaped by these events.[7] The origins of the American Federation of Labor in the 1880s offers a telling case in point. The beginnings of this most important macroscale trade-union organization simply cannot be understood independently of mesoscale responses to the general strike of 1 May 1886 and the Haymarket "Riot" three days hence.[8]

Recall the scene as a handful of trade unionists in the Federation of Organized Trades and Labor Unions (FOTLU) formulated plans for and carried through with a general strike of all workers on behalf of the eight-hour day. The strike's geography taught several mesoscale lessons for macroscale trade-unionist strategy. Not the least of these was the location of loyal trade-unionist constituencies in the large industrial cities in the northeastern quadrant of the nation. In short order thereafter, FOTLU's overtures to the Knights of Labor ceased, and visions of a unified working class were abandoned. Trade unionists embraced instead their loyalist urban constituency and (for other spatial reasons soon revealed) embarked on a parochial and decentralized policy of "pure and simple" trade unionism – a policy formally ratified with the founding of the AFL in December 1886, less than nine months after the general strike. Ironically, labor history has paid little heed to the role of the general strike in enabling this momentous shift in the ranks of labor. That oversight, I submit, has a great deal to do with a methodology *in extremis*, a methodology which privileges micro and macroscales of inquiry. In the case of the general strike, however, the one is too particular and the other too general for rehearsal of the mesoscale spatial lessons which decisively deepened the schism in the ranks of American labor.

The dilemma of labor historiography, therefore, is that it sees the forest and the trees, while missing most everything in between. And it is this space in between – at the mesoscale of metropolis and region – which constitutes the peculiar domain in geography. And as it turns out, these mesoscale spaces also constitute the translational domain of social change, where national (macroscale) strategies intersect with microscale (local) actions, where structure and agency meet, and where individuals in locales creatively maneuver amidst a field of structural constraints. Which is to say that labor's actions in place are problematic; they cannot be deduced from the macroscale structures that bind them; nor generalized from unconditionalized case studies at the microscale.[9]

---

[7] Giddens, "Structuration Theory", pp. 20–21; Allan Pred, *Place, Practice and Structure: Social and Spatial Transformation in Southern Sweden, 1750–1850* (Totowa, 1986), pp. 5–31; Derek Gregory, "Contours of Crisis? Sketches for a Geography of Class Struggle in the Early Industrial Revolution in England", in A.R.H. Baker and D. Gregory (eds.), *Explorations in Historical Geography: Interpretative Essays* (Cambridge, 1984), pp. 68–117.

[8] The spatial lessons of the general strike are examined in some detail later in the essay; citations are reserved to that discussion.

[9] On the limits of cross-scalar inference, see Gillian Rose, "Locality Studies and Waged Labour: An Historical Critique", *Transactions of the Institute of British Geographers*, N.S. 14 (1989), pp. 317–328.

All is not contingency, however, in societal-cum-scalar transitions. Modernization and industrialization, for example, are not purely chaotic and disruptive processes; their advance, on the contrary, hinges on institutions which abstract and distance social relationships and thereby facilitate transitions to the mesoscale. Of the various institutions available, the market is the most obvious and perhaps the most powerful. The market is, above all, a spatial abstraction, a means for mediating the exchange of goods and services (an invisible hand, as it were) among producers and consumers unknown to one another and disjunct in space. This process of spatial abstraction, what Giddens' calls distanciation, traces its origins to Western European capitalism and the sixteenth-century ascendance of the market, or more precisely, a triad of markers – for products, for capital, and for labor.[10] For reasons which remain unclear, the market for labor evolved more slowly than the others. Not until the nineteenth century did the pace quicken, but once underway labor markets advance swiftly through three stages of a half century more or less. A word on each is in order.

In the first of these three stages, lasting perhaps from the sixteenth to the early nineteenth centuries, rural economy sets the tone. Agrarian hegemony translates into labor markets which are dual and asymmetric. Rural labor markets are large and powerful; urban ones are small and weak. In these asymmetric markets, wages of unskilled urban workers are determined, more or less, by rural earnings and the transfer wage. The latter equals the wage which is required to induce rural workers into unskilled urban employment, and its level is defined by opportunities in the vastly larger rural labour market and by the incomes workers could earn therein. These earnings, in turn, are established by the seasonal demands for labor of the staple crops produced within the encompassing agrarian region. Put succinctly, the transfer wage varies inversely with the seasonality of labor demand in the regional agrarian system, that is, wages are low in agrarian regimes which are highly seasonal, and high in regimes reliant on labor the year round. When a low transfer wage prevails, the ranks of labor are often riven as skilled labor fears displacement by cheap, unskilled workers and machine production; when the transfer wage is high, these fears are allayed and skilled workers make common cause with their well-paid but unskilled brethren.[11]

[10] Giddens, "Structuation Theory", pp. 201–221; *idem, The Constitution of Society: Outline of the History of Structuration* (Berkeley, 1984); John Urry, "Time and Space in Giddens' Social Theory", in Giddens' *Theory of Structuration*, pp. 160–175. On markets and the rise of capitalism, Karl Polanyi, *The Great Transformation: The Political and Economic Origins of Our Time* (Boston, 1957), pp. 163–219; Douglass C. North and Robert P. Thomas, *The Rise of the Western World: A New Economic History* (Cambridge, 1973).

[11] On early-modern markets and their contemporary analogues, Carville Earle, *Geographical Inquiry and American Historical Problems* (Stanford, 1992), pp. 173–235; Stanley Lebergott, *Manpower in Economic Growth: The American Record Since 1800* (New York, 1964); W. Arthus Lewis, "Reflections on Unlimited Labour", in Luis Eugenio DiMarco (ed.), *International Economics and Development: Essays in Honor of Raull Prebisch* (New York, 1972),

As industrialization advances, labor-market evolution enters its second stage. This stage is characterized by the emergence of autonomous and crudely segmented urban labor markets. It begins in large urban and industrial centers, where labor markets secure their independence from the rural economy. Having achieved autonomy, these markets subdivide into two distinct classes – the first, a highly competitive market for unskilled labor employable in a wide variety of urban industries; the second, an imperfectly competitive market for skilled workers whose specialized skills bind them to one (monopsony) or at most a few (oligopsony) firms. In the former, wages are determined eventually by marginalist economic principles; in the latter, by exercises of raw power pitting "combinations" of skilled workers against the relevant firm or firms. These radically divergent strategies of compliance and resistance, in turn, reinforce the schismatics inherent in urban labor markets in this, unskilled labor's "golden age".[12]

Industralization's triumphant dominance of the economy signals the third stage in labor-market evolution. In this stage, the debate over market perfection or imperfection is joined. Skilled workers continue their struggle to eliminate market imperfections (monopsony and oligopsony) through the collective actions of "combination" and protest. Entrepreneurs, meanwhile, seek to extend these imperfections into industries with large through-put. This they do by balkanizing the labor market, by parsing the task of unskilled and skilled labor into an infinitely expansible hierarchy of semiskilled, firm-specific jobs. In accordance with the latest principles of scientific management, their aims were nothing less than the transformation of the workplace, the imperfection of unskilled labor markets, and an end to unskilled labor's "golden age". That their actions inspired resistance among unskilled workers – a resistance modeled on the venerable repertoire of strategies and tactics previously developed by skilled workers – is testimony to the scope and power of managerial invasion into the American industrial system.[13]

Note, contra Giddens, that the historical process of labor-market evolution involves a narrowing of the spatial extent of labor markets. The abstraction of the market is progressively particularized (instantiated) to

---

pp. 75–96. And more generally, Friedrich Lenger, "Beyond Exceptionalism: Notes on the Artisanal Phase of the Labour Movement in France, England, Germany, and The United States", *International Review of Social History* 36 (1991), pp. 1–23.

[12] Of the several stages of labor-market evolution, the second is the least well known. This story of unskilled labor's golden age therefore is pieced together from a variety of sources later cited in full.

[13] I am prepared to argue that labor markets were transformed by the advent of new managerial practices in response to large-scale industrial production; that does not imply assent, however, to a model of societal transition from industrial to monopoly capitalism. See Richard Edwards, *Contested Terrain: The Transformation of the Workplace in the Twentieth Century* (New York, 1979); David F. Noble, *America by Design: Science, Technology, and the Rise of Corporate Capitalism* (New York, 1977).

highly specific places, firms and tasks – first in agrarian regions, next in autonomous and insular urban labor markets, and last in particular tasks in a particular place in a particular firm. And it is these spatial transitions from meso to microscales which constitute the changing field of action and reaction for workers as well as for industrial entrepreneurs and managers.[14]

The historical geography of American labor nicely illustrates these several stages in labor-market evolution during the course of economic development, 1790–1930. These mesoscale transformations would unfold in the nation's northeastern quadrant – in what was to become known as the "American Manufacturing Belt" – over three periods of a half century more or less. For ease of exposition, these periods or stages divide as follows:

> (1) 1790s–1830s — frontier expansion and industrial revolution: rural hegemony over asymmetric labor markets;
> (2) 1840s-1890s — frontier closure and economic involution; the emergence of autonomous urban labor markets, more or less perfect;
> (3) 1890s-1930s — preindustrial and industrial worlds: radical labor politics, scientific management, and the imperfecting of labor markets.

These several stages constitute a scaffolding for the geography of American labor history. Indeed, the stages are themselves constructed about a set of geographic processes which define mesoscale fields of action – that changing constellation of places, small and large, in an expansive industrializing nation – as well as the abstract means (the changing structure of labor markets) for articulating, however imperfectly, demand and supply. In all this there is a double irony. The first of these is that labor-market evolution has more to do with market constriction than with market dilation; more to do, in other words, with instantiated abstractions than with Giddensian mechanisms of distanciation. The second irony, which follows from the first, is that the search for perfection in labor markets was led by workers and not by entrepreneurs (or neoclassical economists). Towards that end, American workers engaged in a series of heroic struggles; these were countered, however, by entrepreneurial adversaries who adroitly deployed various mechanisms of market imperfection. Labor exploitation, as a consequence, endures as an uncomfortable fact for capitalism's apologists who would have us believe in (even as their actions discredit) the wonder-working powers of marginalism and perfectly competitive markets.

Frontier expansion and industrial revolution: the rural hegemony over asymmetric labor markets

No period of similar length in American history compares with the momentous changes which took place between 1790 and 1840. In that half

---

[14] These imperfections in product and labor markets are standard fare in neoclassical microeconomics and are discussed in most texts introducing that field.

century, population exploded outward toward the frontier at an annual rate of 2.5 percent, towns grew into cities in what seemed an instant of time, and the northeastern states embarked on an industrial revolution which would transform the nation. One wonders, however, if all of this dynamism might have melted into thin air had it not pivoted around a vast and productive rural economy. That economy, or more precisely series of economies, imposed its hegemony on the society as a whole. Its sheer size defined the parameters of urban labor markets everywhere but most especially in the nascent urban centers aborning in the northeastern states. These rural parameters at once regulated the level of urban wages and fixed them at levels which, in the case of the northern states, favored industrialization and urban growth. We begin, accordingly, with the industrial revolution and the asymmetric labor markets which facilitated, even permitted, this transformation.[15]

The American industrial revolution was probably premature. To be sure Alexander Hamilton and other Federalists did all in their power to stimulate infant industries, but the rise of factory production probably owed as much to a happy conjuncture of demand – the benevolent protection afforded by international warfare and an age of revolution – and supply – a dependable supply of cheap labor and the machines for them to use – as to explicit policy measures such as bounties, tariffs, and the like. Consider first the timing of the revolution. The "protectionism" afforded by three and a half decades of international warfare was a Federalist's dream come true. Napoleon's campaigns disrupted oceanic trade and sheltered infant industries in the United States as well as in England and on the Continent. And when in 1815 Napoleon was at last put to bed and the Anglo-American war came to a close, Americans hastened to replace the industrial protectionism afforded by Atlantic warfare with the controversial tariff of 1816.[16]

In this context of commercial chaos and economic uncertainty, American industry took root – but not everywhere, of course, for reasons which had more to do with supply than with demand. The geography of the new factories for making coarse cloth, the furnaces for making pig iron and castings, and the iron mills for rolling and slitting was lopsidedly concen-

---

[15] George Rogers Taylor, *The Transportation Revolution, 1815–1860* (New York, 1951); Douglass C. North, *The Economic Growth of the United States, 1790–1860* (Englewood Cliffs, N.J., 1961); Carville Earle and Changyong Cap, "The Rate of Frontier Expansion in American History, 1650–1890", in *Geographic Information Systems and the Social Sciences: A Handbook*, in Carville Earle, Leonard Hochberg, and David Miller (Basil Blackwell, forthcoming).

[16] On the macrohistorical paradox of protectionism in this period, see Earle, *Geographical Inquiry*, pp. 455–459. Paul A. David makes the neoclassical case against the benefits of tariff protection, albeit after 1824 when the foundations for industrialization were already in place; in "Learning by Doing and Tariff Protection: A Reconsideration of the Case of the Ante-Bellum United States Cotton Textile Industry", in *Technical Choice Innovation and Economic Growth: Essays in American and British Experience in the Nineteenth Century* (London, 1975), pp. 95–173.

trated in the northeast and, more precisely, on the outskirts and in the hinterlands of entrepôts such as Boston, New York, Philadelphia, and Baltimore. These "suburban" and rural locations held several advantages for budding industrial entrepreneurs including, of course, access to water power. To be sure water was important for textile manufacturers, but it was of lesser significance for iron producers and fabricators who refined their product along an extended spatial chain that stretched from the interior forests to the heart of the coastal cities.[17]

But nature's endowment was hardly the decisive factor in northeastern industrialization. More important than natural resources was the availability of a low-cost labor force which could be mobilized for industrial production. And on that front, the northeastern states enjoyed a special advantage. The region, as Hamilton observed in dismissing pessimistic opinions on the nation's industrial prospects, had four sources of inexpensive labor:

(1) children; (2) women; (3) immigrants; (4) seasonally unemployed farm laborers.

By 1840 American manufacturers had mobilized these supplies of unskilled labor – women in New England, women and farm laborers in the Middle States, and children in both.[18]

Mobilization occurred in various ways and combinations. Textile manufacturers, for example, combined cheap, unskilled labor with machines for spinning and weaving in mills on the outskirts of Boston (Waltham), Philadelphia (Manayunk), and Baltimore (Hampden, Ellicott City). The first of these used women and children; the others, women, men, and children. Iron manufacturers in Pennsylvania and Maryland similarly deployed cheap labor – in this case, seasonally unemployed farm laborers who were hired on for the winter tasks of chopping, hauling, and stacking cordwood for the collieries and iron furnaces.

But if Hamilton had successfully identified the sources of cheap American labor, he failed to provide a theoretical explanation for the paradox of cheap labor in the midst of land abundance. In theory, labor should have been dear owing to vast quantities of cheap land and a rapidly expanding frontier. And the absence of cheap labor, as Hamilton's critics averred, should have precluded industrialization.

The debate can be resolved, in Hamilton's favor, by tracing the sources of cheap labor to the workings of mesoscale labor markets in developing economies. Virtually everyone agrees on two points: first, that labor markets in these economies are dual and asymmetric, consisting of a large rural market and a much smaller urban one; second, that unskilled urban wages are determined largely by the annual earnings of rural workers.

[17] Curtis P. Nettles, *The Emergence of a National Economy, 1775–1815* (New York, 1962); Diane Lindstrom, *Economic Development in the Philadelphia Region, 1810–1850* (New York, 1978).
[18] Samuel McKee, Jr. (ed.), *Alexander Hamilton's Papers on Public Credit, Commerce and Finance* (New York, 1934), pp. 177–276, esp. pp. 206–208.

That is, the earnings of rural workers establish a transfer wage sufficient to bid them into unskilled work in the city. Disagreement arises, however, with regard to the level of rural earnings – and thus the transfer wage. Proponents of labor scarcity mistakenly project daily farm wages over a full year; doing so results in vastly inflated earnings, a high transfer wage, and excessively dear urban labor. Proponents of cheap labor, conversely, allow for the seasonality of rural work and they calibrate rural earnings accordingly, that is, multiplying the prevailing daily rural wage by the number of working days required in a crop's season.[19]

And in the wheat and corn belts of the Middle Atlantic states, seasonality was acute. Farmers there customarily hired labor for the "crop season" which lasted from corn planting in April through the harvest of small grains in June and July. Projecting rural earnings for the "season" rather than over the year leads to a dramatic reduction in the bidding level (transfer wage) for unskilled urban workers. Even allowing for supplemental earnings from by-employment in the off-season, rural earnings in these grain belts are a third to a half of the wages estimated by proponents of labor scarcity. In sum, the union of agrarian seasonality and asymmetric labor markets resulted in a low transfer wage which in turn facilitated industrialization based on cheap unskilled labor and machines.

This windfall for urban entrepreneurs disappears, however, as the agrarian season lengthens – as occurred in the American cotton belt and tobacco coast or even in the intensive mixed-farming systems in England. In these cases, where rural labor worked ten to twelve months per year, the cost of bidding them into nearby urban centers nearly doubled those in the grain-belt cities of Baltimore, Philadelphia, and New York. In these cities and their satellites, entrepreneurs housed cheap unskilled labor and machines in factories on the urban periphery, and there laid the foundations for industrial revolution as well as for schism between unskilled workers and the skilled craftsmen whom they threatened to displace.[20]

With minor amendment, the thesis of cheap labor as the basis for American industrialization can be extended from the Middle States to New England. The difference, of course, turns on New England's mobilization of young women for work in the textile mills of Waltham, Lowell, and Providence. A surplus of women seems to have arisen as the countryside was drained of young men who abandoned an unproductive agrarian system for the frontier. Male outmigration to New York and the upper Midwest left behind an imbalanced sex ratio which for many women meant the deferral of marriages for years or even a lifetime. Unable to marry and settle in the countryside, these young women regularly accepted the

[19] On the debate over cheap labor or dear, see Earle, *Geographical Inquiry*, pp. 173–236, 325–328, and 406–416; David, *Technical Choice Innovation*, pp. 19–91. For the social and political implications of wage structure, see the acute observations of David Montgomery, "The Working Classes of the Pre-industrial American City, 1780–1830", *Labor History* 9 (1968), pp. 3–22.

[20] Earle, *Geographical Inquiry*, pp. 173–236, 315–328, and 406–416.

blandishments of the textile mills which sprang up in the region. And while most women did not make a life of it, in the time allotted they provided industrial entrepreneurs with an inexpensive source of labor until the closure of the frontier in the 1840s displaced them with native and immigrant men.[21]

The odd coupling of cheap labor and hell-bent frontier expansion in the period 1790–1840 was not as paradoxical as economists would have us believe. In New England, frontier expansion cheapened the labor of women left behind. And in the middle American grain belt, a productive if seasonal agrarian system retained its males as it cheapened their labor for urban and industrial entrepreneurs. Cheap labor thus enabled an industrial revolution even as the nation extended its frontiers of settlement.

That revolution transformed society and economy in the northeastern states. Urbanization there rose from 8 percent to nearly 19 percent between 1790 and 1840. The pace was even faster in Massachusetts and Rhode Island, where city folk in 1840 made up 38 percent and 44 percent of the population, respectively. Industrialization and western trade equally stimulated expansion in the region's principal seaports, four of which exceeded 100,000 persons by 1840, led by New York's 360,000. And it was these places which were largely responsible for generating some $240,000,000 in manufacturing value added in 1839 – an impressive amount (worth roughly one-third of agriculture's contribution) for this youthful sector of the American economy.[22]

The industrial revolution in the northeast was well underway by 1840, yet it is important to keep these changes in perspective. Few of these new factories were really large. Probably no more than ten of them employed 100 workers or more; indeed, Baltimore and Boston had none. Moreover, the region and the nation remained predominantly rural and agricultural. Although American manufacturers made a sizable contribution to the American economy, that total paled in comparison to the increments provided by agriculture, commodity trade and transport, and the service sector.[23] And given the vast size of the rural economy, labor markets in the emerging cities and towns remained dependent on conditions in the

[21] Montgomery. "The Working Classes", pp. 3–22; *Historical Statistics of the United States from Colonial Times to 1970*, Part 1 (2 parts; Washington, 1975), pp. 24–37; U.S. State Department, *Digest of Accounts of Manufacturing Establishments in the United States, and of Their Manufacture* (Washington, 1823); Zachariah Allen, *The Science of Mechanics* (Providence, R.L., 1829), p. 347; Alexander J. Field, "Sectoral Shift in Antebellum Massachusetts: A Reconsideration", *Explorations in Economic History* 15 (1978), pp. 146–171; Thomas Dublin, *Women at Work: The Transformation of Work and Community in Lowell, Massachusetts, 1826–1860* (New York, 1979); and Jonathan Prude, *The Coming of Industrial Order: Town and Factory Life in Rural Massachusetts, 1810–1860* (Cambridge, Mass., 1983).
[22] *Historical Statistics*, Part 1, pp. 24–37.
[23] Paul A. Groves, "The Northeast and Regional Integration, 1880–1860", in Robert D. Mitchell and Paul A. Groves (eds.), *North America: The Historical Geography of a Changing Continent* (Totowa, N.J., 1987), pp. 198–217.

countryside. The wages of unskilled men continued to be determined by the transfer wage and the seasonal earnings of rural workers; and of unskilled women, by a combination of discrimination and a meager range of economic alternatives. And from these asymmetric labor markets issued a supply of cheap labor, which, in combination with machines and the "protection" of international warfare, launched an industrial revolution in the northeastern quadrant of the new nation. The ramifications were many, not the least of which were the emergence of divisions between, on the one hand, unskilled workers and the skilled workers whom they threatened to displace; and, on the other, between low-paid workers and the entrepreneurs who exploited them in the asymmetric labor markets of a developing economy.[24]

Frontier closure and economic involution: the emergence of autonomous urban labor markets

1840 marks a critical turning point in American history. The frontier, which since 1650 had expanded in long cycles of a half century more or less, suddenly came to close. Expansion henceforth ratcheted from the westward extension of settlement to the involutional pursuit of profits and opportunities eastward of the Great Plains. In the several regions – Northeast, South, and Midwest – high rates of return accelerated regional economic specialization, stimulated interregional exchange, and, in the north, initiated a fundamental restructuring of urban labor markets.[25] The latter embarked on the transition from asymmetric dependence on the rural economy to autonomous, if insular, independence. A half-century hence, urban wages would be determined by supply and demand under variable conditions of market perfection – conditions more nearly competitive for the unskilled and more nearly monopsonistic or oligopsonistic for the skilled. In response, skilled workers resisted market imperfections via "combination" and strike; the unskilled, by contrast, complied with economic forces, reaping thereby the benefits of a more less perfectly competitive market. And thus the wedge was driven even deeper into the ranks of labor.

Space precludes extended discussion of the involutional changes responsible for restructuring urban labor markets. Suffice to say that involution in the half century after 1840 stimulated regional economic

---

[24] On the fragility of skilled–unskilled alliances into the 1820s, see Cynthia J. Shelton, *The Mills of Manayunk: Industrialization and Social Conflict in the Philadelphia Region, 1787–1837* (Baltimore, 1986); Lenger, "Beyond Exceptionalism", pp. 9–10; Earle, *Geographical Inquiry*, pp. 400–445. More durable coalitions emerged in the 1830s (signaling, I suspect, the transition from asymmetric to autonomous labor markets); see Montgomery, "The Working Classes", pp. 21–22.

[25] Carville Earle and Changyong Cao, "Frontier Closure and the Involution of American Society, 1840–1890", *Journal of the Early Republic* 13 (1993), pp. 163–180.

specialization and, after the Civil War, the ascent of a hegemonic core region in the urban-industrial Northeast and Midwest. These core states dominated American manufacturing by 1860 when they accounted for over half the nation's establishments, three-fourths of its employees, and nearly three-fourths of its value added. Industrial advance was predicated, of course, on a legacy of cheap, unskilled labor and deployment in cotton textiles and metalworking. But to these industries were added firms producing boots and shoes and ready-made clothing along with a host of firms which processed the vast flow of agricultural commodities from the Midwest.[26]

Frontier closure and the involution of the American economy had several ramifications for industrial workers in the Northeast and Midwest. The first of these is that the agrarian South by and large dealt itself out of the industrialization process.[27] The second, and more decisive, is that the North experienced an unprecedented concentration of workers in industrial centers. In New England and the Middle States, city dwellers rose from less than 20 percent of the population in 1830 to nearly 35 percent by 1860 to over 60 percent by 1890. By the latter date, some thirty cities – twenty-four of which were in the northeastern quadrant of the nation – exceeded populations of 85,000, ten exceeded 250,000 and three exceeded a million. A half-century earlier, by contrast, only five cities had more than 85,000 people. These advances challenged rurality's hegemony over urban labor markets. By 1880, the agricultural sector of the economy was in retreat. Non-agricultural occupations exceeded agricultural ones in the labor force; and a decade hence, manufacturing's value added surpassed agriculture's. Neither situation would be reversed.[28]

These spatial and sectoral changes in the northern economy swiftly restructured northern labor markets. In a score or more cities, labor markets wrested free from rural hegemony – from dependence on agrarian economy, transfer wages, and asymmetric market structures – and installed in its place a series of increasingly autonomous and segmented labor markets. These segments consisted of: (1) a highly competitive market for unskilled labor reflective of the wide range of employment opportunities for these undifferentiated and interchangeable tasks; and (2) an imperfectly competitive market for skilled labor reflective of monopsony or oligopsony, that is, market dominance by one or at most a few firms (buyers). The first of these privileged marginalist wage determina-

---

[26] Richard F. Bensel, *Yankee Leviathan: The Origins of Central State Authority in America, 1859–1877* (Cambridge, 1990); Albert W. Niemi, Jr., *State and Regional Patterns in American Manufacturing, 1860–1900* (Westport, Conn., 1974).

[27] On the agrarian involution of the Southern economy after 1840, see Carville Earle, "The Price of Precocity: Technical Choice and Ecological Constraint in the Cotton South, 1840–1890", *Agricultural History* 66 (1992), pp. 25–60.

[28] *Historical Statistics*, Part 1, pp. 24–37, 134, 139; U.S., *Census of Population: 1950*, Vol.1: *Number of Inhabitants* (Washington, 1952), pp. 32–33.

tion, rising relative wages, reduced exploitation, and worker compliance; the second, submarginalist wage setting, falling relative wages, increased exploitation, and the reciprocal of worker protest.[29]

But these restructurings in labor markets were hardly instantaneous. One reason for the delayed reaction was the patchy advance of autonomous markets. Just a handful of large industrial centers satisfied the thresholds for market autonomy in 1840, and only about two dozen northern cities had qualified a half-century hence. But delay ensued even in these centers, which brings us to a second and more decisive cause. In these cities entrepreneurs vigorously resisted market realities. Unskilled wages remained low ('sticky" is the usual name applied to transitional lags between one market structure and another), and entrepreneurs attempted to keep them there. Workers countered by attempting the break "the cake of custom" and hasten the onset of autonomous labor markets.[30] Toward that end – albeit for quite different reasons – common laborers and skilled workers momentarily joined forces in a rising tide of worker protest and strategic "combination". But the alliance collapsed in the late 1870s and 1880s as the unskilled, having secured entrepreneurial obeisance to perfectly competitive labor markets, swiftly disengaged from the fray, complied with the market's dictates, and claimed the benefits of their "golden age".[31]

These awkward and difficult transitions in urban labor markets were played out in the historical geography of worker protest between 1840 and 1890. With the rise of autonomous labor markets in the 1840s and 1850s and war-time labor shortages in the 1860s, workers gained leverage in the workplace. Strikes, which had been sporadic before 1850, increased rapidly during the boom times of the 1850s and the early 1860s. Although protest erupted in various locations, the expansive metropolitan centers (and autonomous labor markets) of Boston, Philadelphia, and New York led the way (Figure 1). The end of the war and the ensuing recession

---

[29] The process of labor-market segmentation has its American origins in the rise of autonomous urban labor markets in the period 1840–1890; after 1890, segmentation involves the qualitatively different process of internalization of labor markets within the firm. See Edwards, *Contested Terrain*; Peter Doeringer and Michael Piore, *Internal Labor Markets and Manpower Analysis* (Lexington, Mass., 1971); and Allen J. Scott, *Metropolis: From the Division of Labor to Urban Form* (Berkeley, 1988), pp. 27–35.

[30] On lagged responses to labor markets, see E.J. Hobsbawn, "Custom, Wages, and Work-Load in Nineteenth-Century Industry", in his *Labouring Men: Studies in the History of Labour* (New York, 1964), pp. 244–270.

[31] It is ironic that the post-1870 advance in unskilled wages, rooted as it was in competitive labor markets, has generally eluded neoclassical economists who dwell instead on unionization, wage levelling, and the free rider. See, for examples, Lloyd Ulman, *The Rise of the National Trade Union* (Cambridge, Mass., 1955); Barry Eichengreen, "The Impact of Late Nineteenth-Century Unions on Labor Earnings and Hours: Iowa in 1894", *Industrial and Labor Relations Review* 40 (1987), pp. 501–515; and Paul H. Douglas, *Real Wages in the United States, 1890–1926* (Boston, 1930).

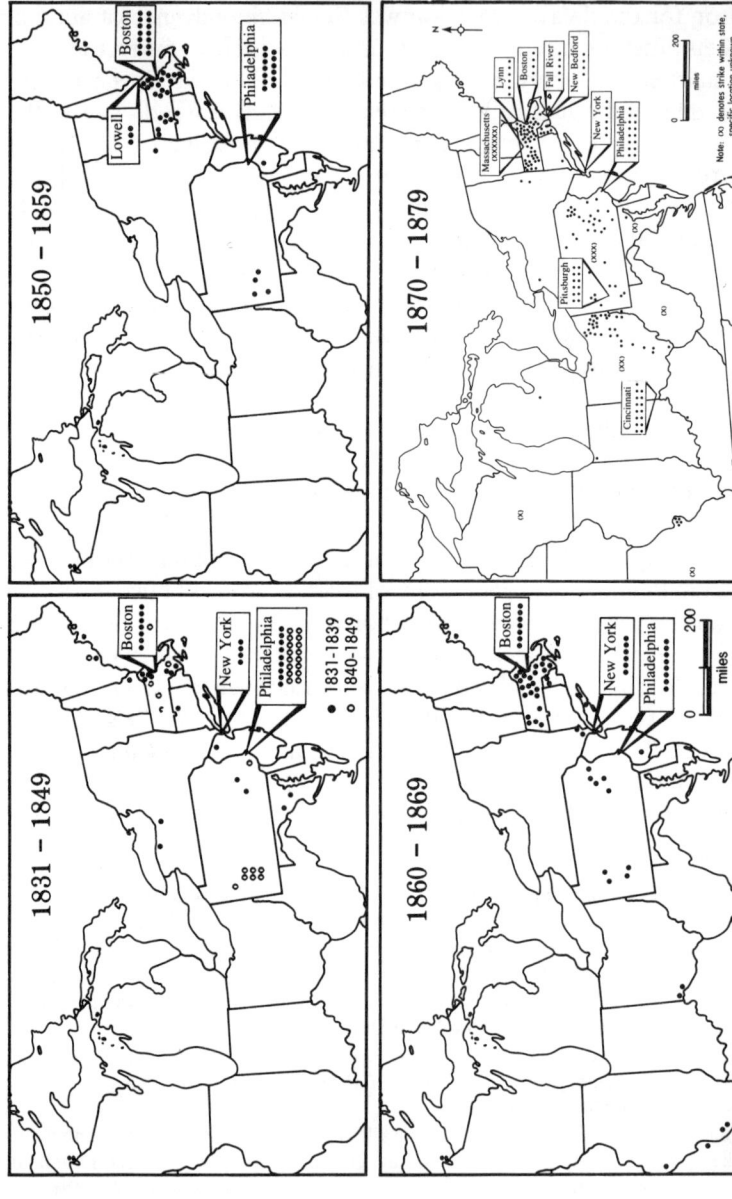

Figure 1. The location of strikes, 1831–1879. Each dot or circle represents one strike. Source: *Third Annual Report of the Commissioner of Labor, 1887: Strikes and Lockouts* (Washington, 1888), pp. 1029–1108.

intensified pressures for a new round of wage reductions, but in this case, labor resisted strenuously. Workers simultaneously stepped up the level of protest, founded or expanded some thirty or so labor unions, and attracted some 300,000 members by 1873. But labor's united front proved ephemeral; and by 1878 a great retreat reduced unions to eight or nine and membership to just 50,000.[32]

The irony of this flurry of worker protest and union activity, 1850–1875, is that it may have been too successful. Workers had jarred industrial entrepreneurs out of habitual wage-setting practices, rudely awakened them to the realities of autonomous urban labor markets, and schooled them in the new principles of wage determination in markets which were more or less competitive. And with the ascent of competitive markets in the 1870s and 1880s, unskilled workers withdrew from "combinations" and protest; skilled trade unionists, henceforth, assumed the lead in labor's uprising in the 1880s.[33]

If the quarter-century or so after 1850 defines a profound transformation in American labor markets and movements – a time when urban entrepreneurs broke "the cake of custom" (the transfer wage) and accepted the realities of autonomous and more or less competitive labor markets and when unskilled workers disengaged from labor's united front – why then did worker protest run at flood-tide in the decade and a half after 1880? The explanation has to do, I think, with a triadic division in labor markets – of segmented labor markets (skilled/unskilled) in industrial cities and of enduring labor-market asymmetry elsewhere – all of which is recorded in the geography of worker protest between 1880 and 1894.

[32] On strikes, see Earle, *Geographical Inquiry*, pp. 417–423; on unions and Gompers' remarks, Commons, *History of Labour*, 2, pp. 175–181.

[33] The elimination of seasonal wage differentials and the convergence of skilled and unskilled wages in the 1870s are suggestive of labor-market transition from rural hegemony to urban autonomy and subsidiary markets more (unskilled) or less (skilled) competitive. Robert Ozanne, *Wages in Practice and Theory: McCormick and Internal Harvester, 1860–1960* (Madison, Wisc., 1968), pp. 3–21; Earle, *Geographical Inquiry*, pp. 414–416, 440–441. On the advance and retreat of labor's united front between 1860 and 1878, see Norman J. Ware, *The Labor Movement in the United States, 1860–1895: A Study in Democracy* (Gloucester, Mass., 1959), pp. 1–21. One source of the front's fragility was the exotic mixture of ideologies which included, among others, a healthy dose of nineteenth-century market "liberalism" – a view not unappealing for unskilled workers in increasingly competitive labor markets. Daniel T. Rogers, *The Work Ethic in Industrial America, 1850–1920* (Chicago, 1974), pp. 40–46, 156–157. Martin Sheftner nibbles at the edge of these issues in "Trade Unions and Political Machines: The Organization and Disorganization of the American Working Class in the Late Nineteenth Century", in Ira Katznelson and Aristide R. Zolberg (eds.), *Working-Class Formation: Nineteenth-Century Patterns in Western Europe and the United States* (Princeton, 1986), pp. 197–276; and Erik Olssen, "The Case of the Socialist Party that Failed, or Further Reflections on an American Dream", *Labor History* 29 (1988), pp. 416–449. The quiescence of the unskilled after 1873 has more to do with rising wages and market power than with the "peasant-like" impotence ascribed to them by Andrea Graziosi, "Common Laborers, Unskilled Workers, 1880–1915", *Labor History* 22 (1981), pp. 512–544, esp. 519, 525–527.

A wave of protest broke over the nation in the 1880s, or so it seemed. With strikes increasing exponentially from forty to fifty per year in the 1870s to over 400 in the early 1880s and over 900 after 1885 (Figure 2), observers had little time for finer geographical distinctions. They were aware, however, of the obvious – that the overwhelming majority of strikes (some 85 percent) occurred in the northeastern quadrant of the nation and that most were directed toward manufacturing establishments. A closer look at the region between 1881 and 1894 reveals that half of its counties reported at least one strike, that urban counties almost invariably reported strikes, and that six large urban centers – New York, Chicago, Boston, Philadelphia, Pittsburgh, and Baltimore – were responsible for nearly half of the region's 14,455 strikes (Figure 3).[34]

The wave of protest thus ran wide and, in places, deep. And it is in these deeper spots where we can discern perhaps the sharpest division in the geography of worker protest – a division between preindustrial and industrial worlds, between smaller communities and larger industrial cities. That division is most evident in the scale reversal of labor power; in the declension of labor power in preindustrial communities and its reconstitution in the larger cities of industrializing American – cities sufficiently large to sustain autonomous labor markets (Figure 4).

But the differences in worker protest in these two worlds extend beyond sheer scale and market autonomy. Consider, for example, the supplemental causes of strikes in the industrial world. In the region's fifty or so largest counties (population of 85,000 persons or more) labor power (the strike rate per 1,000 persons) is largely a function of labor-market autonomy and segmentation. Four market-related variables – population, wage ratios, industrial concentration, and manufacturing wages – account for 65 percent of the variance in strike rates between 1881 and 1894. Population or city size is, of course, a proxy for autonomous labor markets; the convergence of skilled and unskilled wages reflects segmentation into competitive (unskilled) and imperfectly competitive (skilled) markets; rising manufacturing wages are self-explanatory; and industrial concentration implies less imperfection in skilled labor markets and, hence, somewhat more leverage for these workers. These determinants in tandem tell a story of autonomous and segmented labor markets wherein skilled workers, with modest assistance from formal labor organizations or the unskilled, protested against market imperfections and for higher wages and shorter hours. In these protests, neither labor unions nor the Knights of Labor played significant roles. Nor again did factors such as ethnicity or government.

The analysis also underlines the process of market segmentation in urban-industrial America. Skilled workers stood at the forefront of protest and resistance. They conducted the overwhelming number of strikes, and

---

[34] This section on Gilded Age worker protest is based on Earle, *Geographical Inquiry*, pp. 346–377.

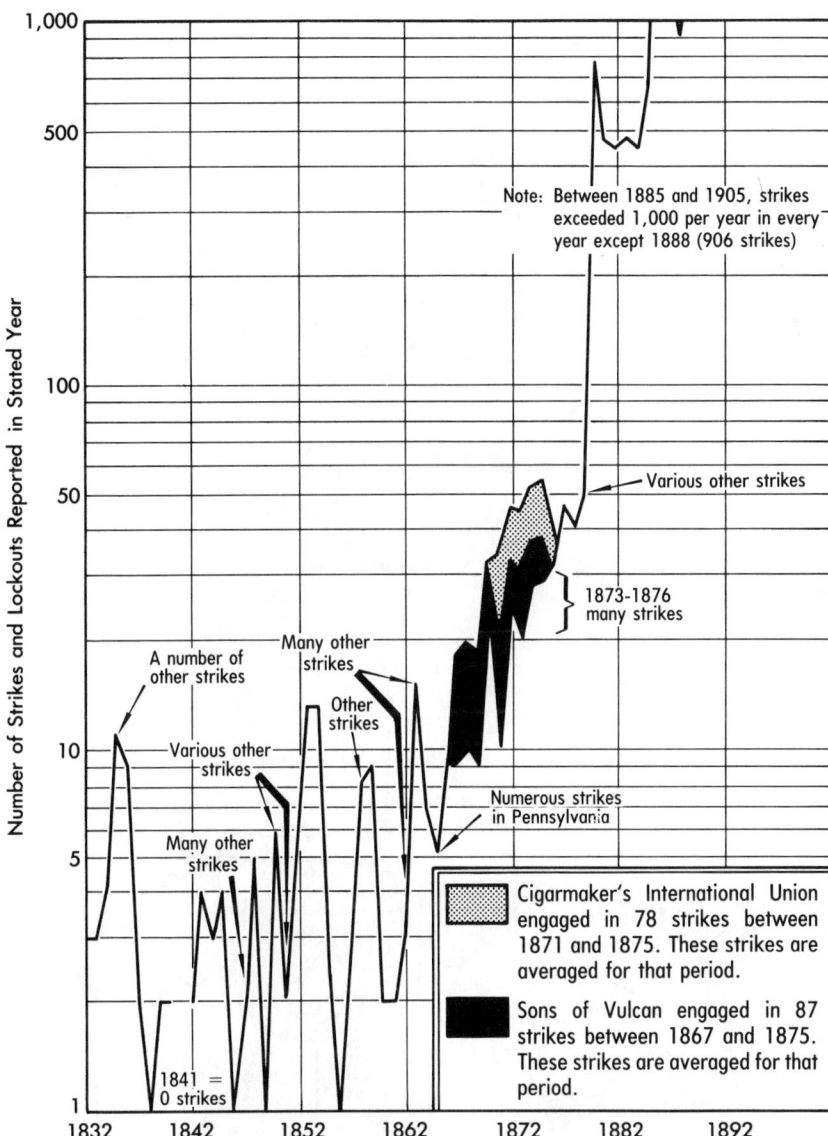

Figure 2. Strikes and lockouts in the United States, 1832–1885. Although the strike count before 1880 is incomplete, the numbers reported here are probably of the right orders of magnitude. Sources: *Third Annual Report of the Commissioner of Labor, 1887; Tenth Annual Report of the Commissioner of Labor, 1894; Strikes and Lockouts* (2 vols.; Washington, 1896).

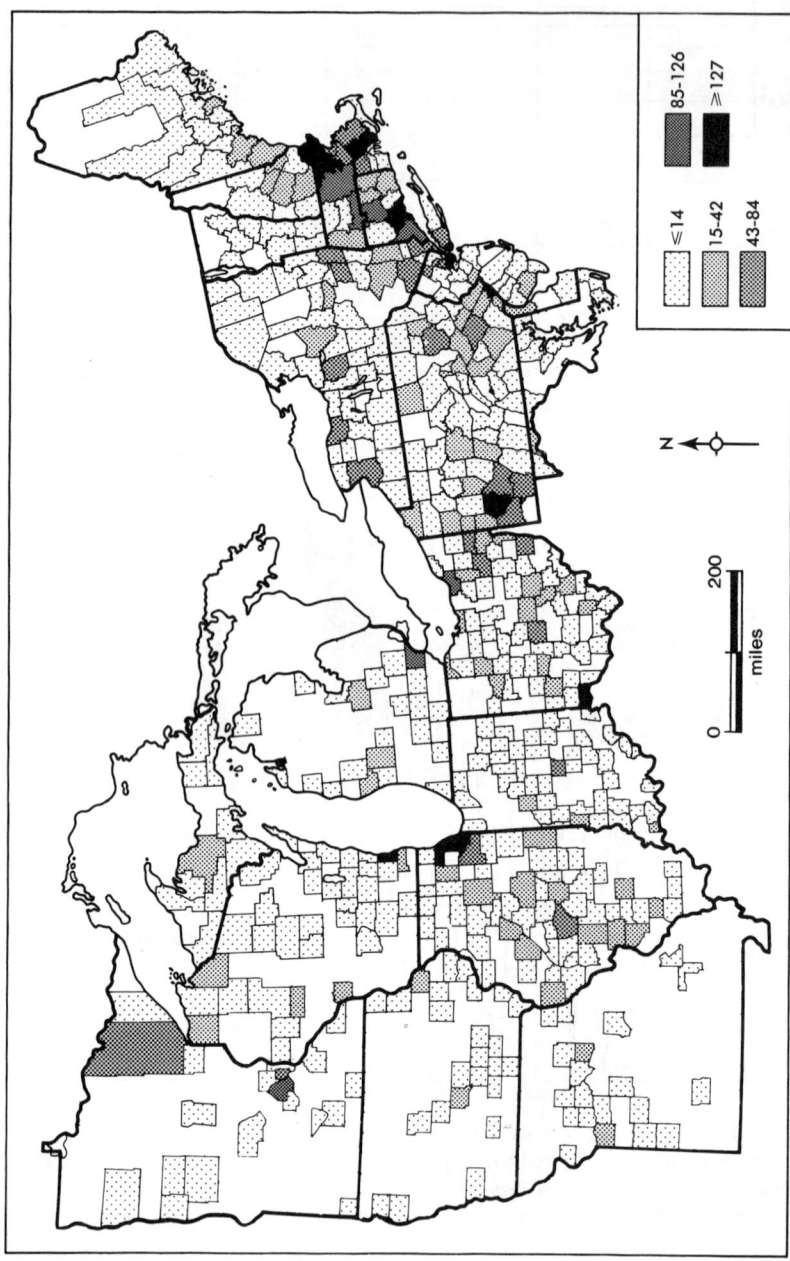

Figure 3. Strike frequency in the northeastern United States, by County, 1881–1894. Sources: *Third Annual Report of the Commissioner of Labor, 1887; Tenth Annual Report of the Commissioner of Labor, 1894.*

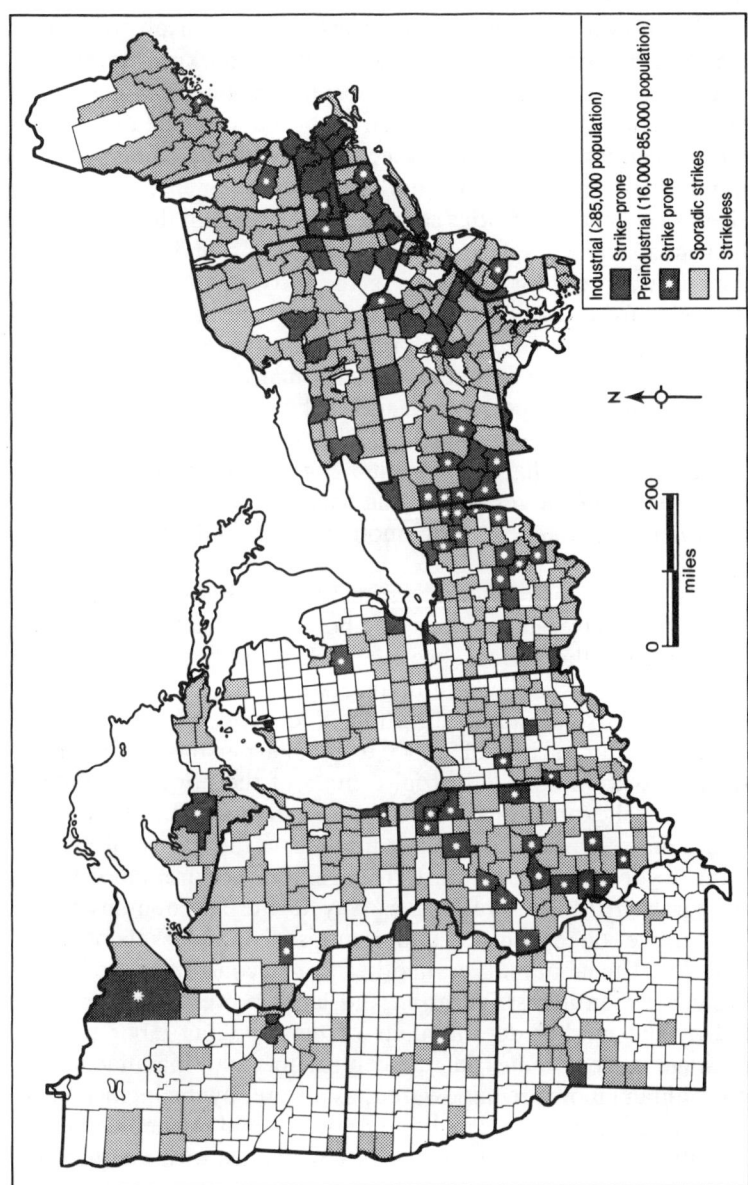

Figure 4. The Geography of Preindustrial and Industrial Worlds, 1881–1894. Shaded counties report one or more strikes in the period. The darkest shadings represent strike-prone counties which report strikes in nine or more of the 15 years. The latter divide, in turn, into industrial and preindustrial worlds at the threshold of 85,000 population. *Third Annual Report of the Commissioner of Labor, 1887; Tenth Annual Report of the Commissioner of Labor, 1894.*

they targeted them in cities where particular industries were concentrated – thus reducing the oligopsonistic power of firms – and where unskilled and skilled wages were convergent – thus underlining the ease of exercising labor power in competitive markets and the difficulty of doing so in markets rent by imperfection. Operating in loosely knit "combinations" or in localized trade unions, skilled workers organized protest as a means of "perfecting" imperfections in their labor markets; the unskilled, meanwhile, disengaged from protest and complied with the benign forces of supply and demand in competitive markets.

Beyond these fifty or so large cities stood a world apart. In the preindustrial world of small cities, towns, and mining camps, industrialization steadily chipped away at labor's power. In the sixty or so counties with populations ranging from 16,000 to 85,000, strike rates declined as communities made the transition from preindustrial to industrial worlds or, more precisely, from asymmetric to autonomous labor markets. Yet within this context of declension, labor power was fueled by organizations such as the Knights of Labor and the Knights" insistence that workers receive larger and more equitable shares of profits. Formal labor organizations accordingly assumed a far larger role in the asymmetric labor markets of preindustrial America than in the autonomous markets in the larger industrial cities.

This geographical analysis of worker protest in the Gilded Age affords a glimpse of the multi-layered relations in labor power, scale, and labor-market transitions. On the surface, we see a cleavage between the two worlds of American labor, a cleavage delineated by the scale reversal of labor power in the course of industrialization. The power of preindustrial labor declines to its nadir in cities of 75,000 to 100,000 persons, after which it is reconstituted in the larger industrial centers of the northern United States. These surfacial expressions of labor power are underlain, however, by a more profound restructuring of labor markets in the course of industrialization. At this level, the preindustrial hegemony of rural labor markets and the agrarian transfer wage gives way to the autonomous (and variously competitive, oligopsonistic, and monopsonistic) markets of metropolitan America. The labor market, in other words, constitutes the intervening variable between industrialization and labor power. All of which is underlined by the market determinants of metropolitan labor power (i.e., scale, wage ratios, industrial concentration, and manufacturing wages). Metropolitan labor is reempowered, as it were, by the ineluctables of scalar shift, the concomitant ascent of autonomous and segmented labor markets, and labor's strategic responses – of compliance with marginalist wage determination in competitive unskilled labor markets and resistance to wages less than marginal product in the imperfect markets for skilled craftsmen.[35]

---

[35] Gutman's thesis of the declension of labor power is inverted in the large cities of industrializing America, Gutman, "The Workers' Search for Power", pp. 38–68. The simultaneous

The dynamics of labor-market transition thus offers a series of insights on the geographical foundations of worker protest and the deepening schisms within the ranks of labor in the Gilded Age. They also resolve one of labor history's great paradoxes – namely that the least powerful and least educated American workers made the greatest advances in the Gilded Age and that these advances into unskilled labor's "golden age" were accomplished, even more paradoxically, with a modicum of protest and "combination".

The unusual economic success of unskilled workers in the half-century between 1870 and 1920 has been often noted, though less often explained. Much of their success can be traced to the restructuring of labor markets. Had the unskilled continued to earn the transfer wage prevailing in asymmetric labor markets, their wages in 1890 would have hovered around a dollar a day instead of the $1.45 which they in fact earned.[36] This dividend of over 40 percent and the curiously privileged status of unskilled workers has perplexed many scholars, including the author of a pioneering study of workers and wages in the McCormick Reaper Company of Chicago. In the company's round of wage reductions after 1886, Robert Ozanne observes that "common labor" [. . .] was exempted completely from the cuts of 1886–1896". Ozanne attributes this situation to benevolence rather than labor markets. "Common labor," he notes:

received favored treatment in 1886 because of the lessons President McCormick had learned in the strikes of 1885 and 1886. Much of the public's antagonism to the company in the 1885 strike, he believed, came from his across-the-board wage cut of December, 1884, which aroused public sympathy for the low-paid workmen. In the negotiations preceding the strike of 1886 he had raised common labor rates handsomely. When the 1893–1898 recession began, the McCormick Company, to avoid a repetition of the 1885 debacle, cut only the skilled workers and those on piece rates.[37]

Perhaps McCormick's preferential treatment of the unskilled represents an irrational "corporate departure from economic motivation', but the benevolence alleged by Ozanne is just as easily interpreted as calculative rationality. McCormick had sound economic reasons for his actions if we acknowledge the emergence in Chicago of a competitive unskilled labor market. That market provided a wide variety of jobs in hundreds of firms engaged in everything from commodity handling to manufacturing and construction. Firms which failed to pay the market rate in this competitive market swiftly experienced labor flight to neighboring firms. From this vantage point, McCormick's irrational benevolence dissolves into a

ascension of marginalist economics and autonomous, if variably competitive, labor markets seems not altogether fortuitous. Daniel Bell, "Models and Reality in Economic Discourse", in Daniel Bell and Irving Kristol (eds.), *The Crisis in Economic Theory* (New York, 1981), pp. 46–80, esp. 47–52.

[36] Douglas, *Real Wages in the United States*, pp. 174–184.

[37] Ozanne, *Wages in Theory and Practice*, pp. 26–33, esp. 32.

rational response to competitive labor markets characterized by many buyers and sellers, ease of mobility, and efficient communication of job opportunities. Note, moreover, that McCormick's benevolence stopped short in negotiations with skilled workers upon whom he imposed repeated wage reductions – responses one would expect from a rational actor acutely aware of the oligopsonistic market for skilled labor in the 1880s and 1890s.[38]

If the realities of labor-market segmentation eluded McCormick until the "debacle of 1885', they also confused skilled trade unionists who, in that very year, set about the task of healing the divisions in the ranks of American labor. Under the banner of the Federation of Organized Trades and Labor Unions, trade unionists formulated plans for a general strike on 1 May 1886 and issued a call for a united front for the eight-hour day. In short order, they would learn a great deal about: (1) the peculiar geography of their parochial constituency and (2) following the eruption of violence in Chicago's Haymarket Square on the evening of 4 May, the spatial insularity of American sociogeography. A rehearsal of these events brings us up to speed on a strike which constituted labor's last great chance for uniting the American working class.[39]

FOTLU strategists sought a united front on 1 May, and toward that end they made several overtures to Terrence Powderly and the Knights of Labor. When the Knights reneged, FOTLU decided to proceed alone. On 1 May, some 100,000 workers responded with strike actions of varying size, length, and effect. As the largest strike in American history to that date, organizers were pleased, but it was the spatial lessons of the strike which proved most instructive to them. The first of these indelibly defined the trade unionists'' constituency. Most of their support came from large industrial cities and skilled workers therein. *Meanwhile, unskilled workers in these cities as well as virtually all workers in preindustrial America remained on the sidelines.* These defections notwithstanding, the general strike on Saturday, 1 May mobilized over 100,000 workers in some 200 separate strike actions conducted in over thirty communities. Even after sympathy strikers returned to work on Monday, some 76,000 remained off the job.

The violence on Tuesday evening changed everything, however. Attention, public and historiographic, shifted abruptly from the strike to the independent events of Haymarket and the ensuing trial of anarchists and radicals. In these weeks and months, trade unions learned a second spatial lesson about the remarkable insularity of American sociogeography. Much to their surprise, perhaps, the general strike did not collapse after Hay-

---

[38] On oligopsonistic conditions in Chicago's farm implements industry, see Ozanne, *Wages in Theory and Practice*, p. 32. On the adoption of McCormick's wage strategies in other industries, *ibid.*, pp. 26–33.

[39] For more details and sources of the general strike, see Earle, *Geographical Inquiry*, pp. 378–399.

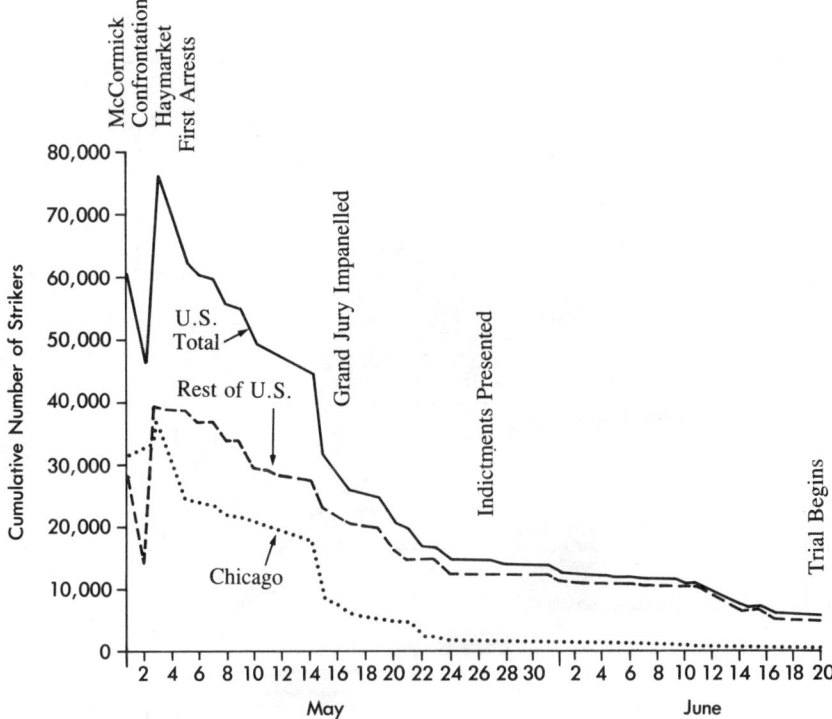

Figure 5. The trajectory of the general strike, 1 May–20 June, 1886. The daily totals of general strikers involve subtraction of general strikers who had concluded their strike from the total number of general strikers who began their protest between 1 May and 3 May, 1886. Source: *Third Annual Report of the Commissioner of Labor, 1887.*

market. To be sure, these events crippled the strike in Chicago, the locus of violence, where by 11 May strike actions and participants had fallen by 60 and 77 percent, respectively. Elsewhere, however, the rate of dissipation was considerably less – some 40 percent of strike actions and 42 percent of strikers (Figure 5).

These crude spatial divisions are embroidered into a more complex series of ellipses in the accompanying map of the general strike's duration (Figure 6). At the center of the series is Chicago, where the average strike lasted just over two weeks. Just beyond is an inner ellipse arching from Detroit to Pittsburgh to Cincinnati and Minneapolis, where the typical strike lasted two to three weeks; and last is an outer ellipse, where workers stayed off the job for three weeks or more. For trade unions, this elliptical geography taught a straightforward spatial lesson: the impact of violence (or of any other injurious action) on the labor movement diminished rapidly with distance from the center of that action. This lesson – that the United States in the Gilded Age was an insular and distended society in which impulses from one place were weakly transmitted to others – had

Carville Earle

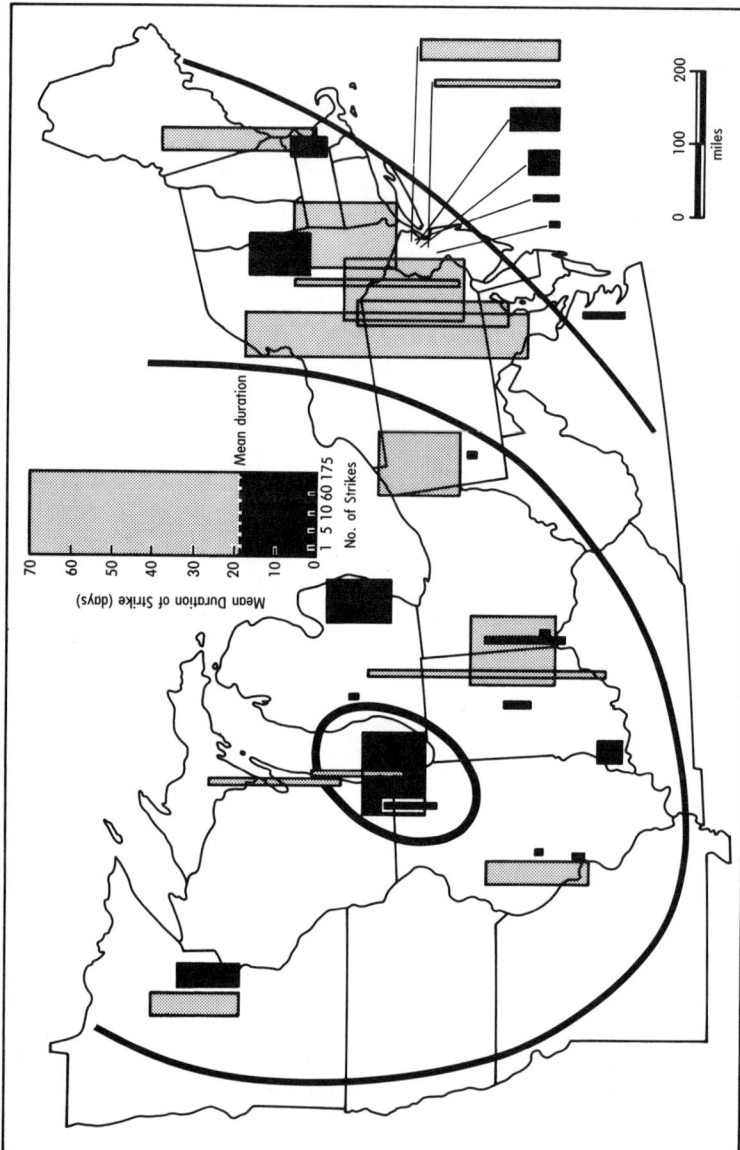

Figure 6. The elliptical geography of the general strike of 1886: duration and frequency. Among cities with five or more strikes, the duration of protest tended to increase with distance from Chicago. The ellipses approximate the divisions between weekly durations of less than two, two to three, and three or more. Source: *Third Annual Report of the Commissioner of Labor, 1887.*

been hammered home to trade unionists long before the historian Robert Weibe made the point.[40] In such a society, Americans had no reason to believe that Haymarket violence constituted a systemic problem. What happened in Chicago was Chicago's problem, not the nation's at large.

Trade unionists swiftly translated these spatial lessons into policy. In the months ahead, they focused their energies on loyal constituencies in northern urban-industrial centers and on a decentralized mode or organization appropriate to a distended, insular, and weakly articulated socio-spatial system. Within the year, trade unionists met in Columbus, Ohio, founded the American Federation of Labor, and embarked on a strategy of "pure and simple" trade unionism. Few now recall that just eight months earlier, these same trade unionists had pursued an alliance of all workers, skilled and unskilled, in large cities and small. At that moment, and despite the deepening structural divisions occasioned by labor markets, wages, and political interests, labor had a unique opportunity for joining ranks, for subordinating interests to solidarity. Failure to do so ensured that the various factions of the labor movement would go their own way. Trade unions, henceforth, decamped in the cities of industrial America and left the rest to the Knights of Labor and their socialist successors in the small towns of preindustrial America.

But industrial America was contested terrain and trade unionists knew that their adversaries had not been idle. McCormick and few industrialists had also learned a great deal about the geography of strikes and labor markets during the 1880s, and putting their erudition into practice, they ushered in unskilled labor's golden age and skilled labor's time of trial.

Preindustrial and industrial worlds: radical labor politics, scientific management, and the imperfecting of labor markets

The founding of the AFL marked a critical turning point in the history of American labor. Visions of a unified working class henceforth gave way to a triadic division in labor's ranks, a division between skilled and unskilled in industrial America and between them and the workers of preindustrial America. In the half-century that followed, these divisions were accentuated. Skilled trade unionists rapidly expanded their ranks in large cities where they contested the wages and working conditions imposed by imperfect labor markets. Unskilled workers in these industrial centers meanwhile eschewed unionization in favor of compliance with competitive markets. They continued to enjoy the market's benefits until the turn of the century when these were undermined (imperfected) by industry's adoption of Scientific Management practices. And lastly, workers in preindustrial America, bereft of unions or competitive markets, turned toward the radicalism of socialist politics. In summarizing the his-

[40] Robert H. Weibe, *The Search for Order, 1877–1920* (New York, 1967), pp. 11–43.

toriographies of these several labor movements, keep in mind that my intent is less a rehearsal of their literatures than a revision in our angle of vision on their geographies and the role of labor markets therein.

Perhaps the best-known of these labor movements is the storied rise and fall of socialism between 1890 and 1920. What has not been so fully appreciated in these recountings, however, is socialism's intimate association with preindustrial America and the antecedent radicalism of the Knights of Labor. Although the Knights eschewed a political agenda, their radical commitment to organizing all workers within a community had widespread appeal. Founded in 1869, the Knights" membership expanded exponentially and peaked at 700,000 in 1886. While the Knights operated in the full range of Gilded Age communities, their power seems to have been concentrated primarily in preindustrial America – in cities and towns of less than 85,000. Conversely, they were impotent in big cities and that fact, in tandem with a series of strategic blunders in the mid-1880s – rejecting FOTLU's call for a general strike, refusal to condemn the sentences of Haymarket radicals and anarchists, and the loss of several key strikes – contributed to a devolution equally exponential.[41]

The collapse of the Knights by 1890 created a vacuum filled by socialist party politics in the ensuing two decades. Although the urban-based Socialist Labor Party made little headway in preindustrial America, it nonetheless paved the way for the more inclusive politics of the Socialist Party of America founded in 1901. That party's perennial presidential candidate, Eugene Debs – a resident of the preindustrial Terre Haute, Indiana – scored a number of successes. Debs garnered six percent of the presidential vote in 1912; more significantly, socialist candidates won election to over 1,200 offices and seventy-nine mayorships – virtually of all of which were in the smaller cities and towns of preindustrial America.[42]

The geography of these socialist victories underscores the divisions in the ranks of American labor. Few of them occurred in the large cities of industrial America. Socialist candidates did best in communities in transition between preindustrial and industrial worlds, that is in cities of 50,000 to 100,000, and between asymmetric and autonomous labor markets. In these places, socialists attempted to get out the vote by uniting all workers in industrial unions. An analysis of Debs' 1912 presidential vote in New York state reveals the extent of their successes. In these transitional communities, proxies for industrial unionism account for 90 percent of the variance in the Debs' vote. When larger industrial cities are incorporated

[41] Ware, *The Labor Movement in the United States*; Jonathan E. Garloch, "A Structural Analysis of the Knights of Labor: A Prolegomenon to the History of the Producing Classes" (Ph.D. diss., Univ. of Rochester, 1974); Earle, *Geographical Inquiry*, pp. 428–432.
[42] *Ibid.*, pp. 432–445; James Weinstein, *The Decline of Socialism in America, 1912–1925* (New York, 1967).

into the analysis, however, the level of explanation drops to just 56 percent.[43]

Socialist politics thus flourished among cities in transition from one world to another. They failed utterly, however, in industrial America where trade unionists had consolidated their power in the quarter-century after Haymarket and where unskilled workers enjoyed the protection of competitive labor markets. Radical labor politics thus experienced a brief but useful life in those cities on the hinge between past and future. In this ephemeral stage in the advance of industrialism, defections from socialist ranks were, perhaps, inevitable as the forces of industrialization swept over these cities. To be sure, government repression exacerbated socialism's devolution, but one suspects that these measures were redundant – and thus all the more unsavory.[44]

The second and third labor movements of the Progressive Era evolved independently of socialism in the industrial worlds of metropolitan America. Labor markets there had achieved autonomy in the preceding half-century of economic involution. Autonomy was accompanied by segmentation into more or less competitive markets for the unskilled and the skilled, respectively, and wages behaved accordingly. By the 1890s, unskilled wages tended to rise as firms competed fiercely for common labor; skilled wages, meanwhile, advanced more slowly and gains were contingent on the efficacy of trade-unionist strategies of combination and protest. And, judging from an analysis of industries in 1890, the results were mixed. Unions yielded positive earnings premia for skilled workers in pig and bar iron, steel, and glass; modest premia in cotton and wool; and negative premia in coal and coke. And given the geography of these industries, unions seem to have been more effective in the Midwest than in the Northeast. Equally significant, unions exerted spillover effects for less skilled, non-union workers. Unskilled and semiskilled workers earned sizable premia in bar iron, steel, wool, and glass. Indeed, semiskilled workers in these industries earned higher premia than the skilled or unskilled.[45]

Yet even as less skilled workers enjoyed the dual benefits of competitive markets and the free rider, their "golden age" was coming to an end.

---

[43] Sari Bennett, "Continuity and Change in the Geography of American Socialism, 1900–1912", *Social Science History* 7 (1983), pp. 267–288.

[44] Weinstein, *The Decline of Socialism*; Gabriel Kolko, "The Decline of Radicalism in the Twentieth Century", in James Weinstein and David W. Eakins (eds.), *For a New America: Essays in History and Politics from Studies on the Left, 1959–1967* (New York, 1970), pp. 197–220.

[45] Patricia Dillon and Ira Gang, "Earnings Effects of Labor Organizations in 1890", *Industrial and Labor Relations Review* 40 (1987), pp. 516–527; Eichengreen, "The Impact of Late Nineteenth-Century Unions", pp. 501–515. These essays suggest that wage leveling across classes of skill is indicative of union impact on unskilled free-riders, but leveling could just as easily have resulted from competitive markets for unskilled labor.

Two factors contributed to the post-1900 deterioration in their bargaining power. On the supply side, the market for unskilled and semiskilled labor was occasionally glutted by the vast number of immigrants arriving in the United States. On the demand side, and more critically, the market for their labor was redefined by revolutionary changes in industrial management and the production process. Scientific Management, as it was known, consisted of an array of corporate strategies and concerns – time-and-motion studies, worker efficiency, task simplification, turnover reduction, and worker welfare. Of these, the analytic reduction of industrial production into a series of discrete tasks and correspondingly discrete labor markets may have been the most decisive for unskilled workers. Although the unskilled were still required for hauling and lifting, the new system of hyper-differentiated, firm-specific tasks accented their roles as semiskilled machine tenders. In scientifically managed factories, these operatives expanded as rapidly as the firms' tool and die shops could turn out the templates, jigs, and patterns required for task simplification.[46]

All of this is well known, thanks to David Montgomery and his students; less well understood, however, are the implications of the hyper-differentiation of tasks on labor markets and their imperfection. The key in this case turns on the spatial instantiation of labor markets, on the fact that the new semiskilled jobs (and their labor markets) were firm-and task-specific. These jobs required training, and hence workers could not easily port their skills from firm to firm. Immobility in turn had two appealing consequences for industrial managers: first, it reduced turnover among semiskilled workers; and second, it imperfected their labor markets which now consisted of few buyers and many sellers. With this new and more elaborate division of labor, scientific managers immobilized semiskilled workers and facilitated their exploitation via monopsonistic and oligopsonistic labor markets. All of which is hardly surprising given management's commitment to differentiation in product markets; was it not logical for managers to extend this venerable principle to labor markets – which they in fact did after 1910?[47]

The numerous applications of Scientific Management at the turn of the century provide important clues on the diffusion of hyper-differentiated or balkanized labor markets. These geographic reconstructions are hardly straightforward, however, owing to the various versions of Scientific Management propounded and applied by Frederick Taylor and his disciples. C. Bertrand Thompson's 1917 survey may be the most authoritative. He reports adoption of one or another version of these new management

[46] Among others, Daniel Nelson, *Managers and Workers: Origins of the New Factory System in the United States, 1880–1920* (Madison, Wisc., 1975); Noble, *America by Design*; and David Montgomery, *Workers' Control in America*.

[47] Ton Korver, *The Fictitious Commodity: A Study of the U.S. Labor Market, 1880–1940* (Westport, Conn., 1990), pp. 23–42, 107–122, esp. 38. Edwards, *Contested Terrain*; and Graziosi, "Common Laborers, Unskilled Workers", pp. 1–21.

principles in fifty-two separate industries and in 169 plants. Of the latter, 117 were located in New England and the Middle Atlantic states. In the case of Taylor's principles, Daniel Nelson notes full application of his system in twenty-nine firms between 1903 and 1918 – and of these, thirteen were in New England, ten in the Middle States, and only two in the Midwest. Scientific Management practices thus seem to have advanced most rapidly in the Northeast and for good reason. There, labor markets were imperfected by the flood of immigration as well as the balkanization of industrial tasks. Unionization, meanwhile, had failed to eliminate these imperfections (recall that unionization of regional industries was associated with lower, even negative, wage premia for all classes of workers).[48]

These East-Coast applications of Scientific Management constituted the first tentative phase in labor-market transition. In the nation as a whole, however, semiskilled workers in manufactures actually declined relative to the number of unskilled workers in the first two decades of the century. Their twofold advantage in the manufacturing workforce of 1900 fell to just 40 percent by 1920 – a shrinkage that was probably attributable to wartime labor scarcity. Thereafter, however, the ranks of the semiskilled expanded rapidly, rising over two-and-a-half-fold by 1940, as unskilled workers were "upgraded" to machine tenders. In this second, post-1920 phase, the balkanization of labor markets proceeded most rapidly in a series of new and more widely distributed industries – electrical machinery, petroleum refining, canning, drugs and medicines, rubber, and automobiles – as well as a few familiar ones – sawmills, furniture, knitting mills, apparel, yarn-thread-fabric, pulp and paper, and printing and publishing. Labor-market instantiation had spread from the east to the American manufacturing belt as a whole.[49]

The two-step diffusion of Scientific Management practices can be regarded, in retrospect, as industry's response to growth – to the rapid expansion of manufacturing after 1900 and to a concomitant shrinkage in the supply of semiskilled operatives. Taylor's system provided a measure of order and discipline in unruly factories where unskilled workers (often immigrants) had been thrown into the breech, and where they came and went in rapid succession. By reducing tasks to their simplest terms and by training unskilled workers to do them, Taylor's system at once combated turnover, converted common laborers into semiskilled machine tenders, deskilled artisans and craftsmen, and, above all, balkanized the division of labor and labor markets. In place of generalized markets for skilled and unskilled labor, the new system of management created a myriad of

[48] C. Bertrand Thompson, *The Theory and Practice of Scientific Management* (Boston, 1917), pp. 37–40; Nelson, *Managers and Workers*, pp. 68–78.
[49] *Historical Statistics*, Part 1, pp. 143–145; Graziosi, "Common Laborers, Unskilled Workers", pp. 533–534.

small labor markets each associated with a routinized and firm-specific task.[50] And incidental to the progressive search for order, competitive labor markets were eliminated, wages were leveled, and routinized workers were alienated from their products. All of this came to pass in the 1920s and 1930s, a half-century or so after McCormick's wage policies had heralded the unskilled workers' "golden age". Managers heralded, by contrast, a new age of labor relations. Having discerned the complexities of industrial processes, they installed a commensurately complex hierarchy of routine tasks for semiskilled machine tenders and operatives in particular firms.

In this fashion, Scientific Managers undermined the golden age of unskilled labor. The competitive markets and marginalist pricing which had prevailed in unskilled labor markets since 1870 were largely eliminated after 1920 by a splintered division of semiskilled labor and attendant market imperfections. Semiskilled workers, of course, resisted their maneuvers and closed ranks in an ironic struggle for competitive markets and a just share of their marginal products. That they came up short has been repeatedly confirmed. By the 1950s – when balkanization of the manufacturing workforce was largely a *fait accompli* – laborers and service workers were paid only half of their marginal revenue products; craftsmen and operatives even less. Exploitation arising from labor-market imperfections, in other words, hit hardest at the skilled and the semiskilled – a pattern which traces its origins to the half-century between 1880 and 1930, and its climax to the 1950s.[51] Unskilled workers fared better owing to the presence of more competitive markets; but the key point is that there were far fewer of them (16 percent) in manufacturing jobs in 1950 as compared either to their contemporaries in skilled (34.4 percent) and semiskilled jobs (50.0 percent) or to their unskilled predecessors (nearly a third) before 1930.[52]

The geography of hyper-differentiation in industrial labor markets after 1900 began in the northeastern states (1900–1920) and spread slowly thereafter into the industries of the Midwest. The imperfections which accompanied these splintered divisions of labor invited a new round of industrial conflict as skilled and semiskilled workers sought their marginal products. The spatial patterning of worker protest reflects this diffusion process (Figure 7). Between 1890 and 1920, strike rates were highest in New England and the Middle States where the principles of Scientific Management and the new division of labor were most refined. A half-century hence, as these methods and markets diffused throughout the American manufactur-

[50] Noble, *America by Design*, esp. p. 300; Korver, *The Fictitious Commodity*, p. 74.
[51] On manufacturing wages and market imperfections in the 1950s, see Peter Gottschalk, "A Comparison of Marginal Productivity and Earnings by Occupation". *Industrial and Labor Relations Review* 31 (1978), pp. 368–378.
[52] *Historical Statistics*, Part 1, pp. 143–145.

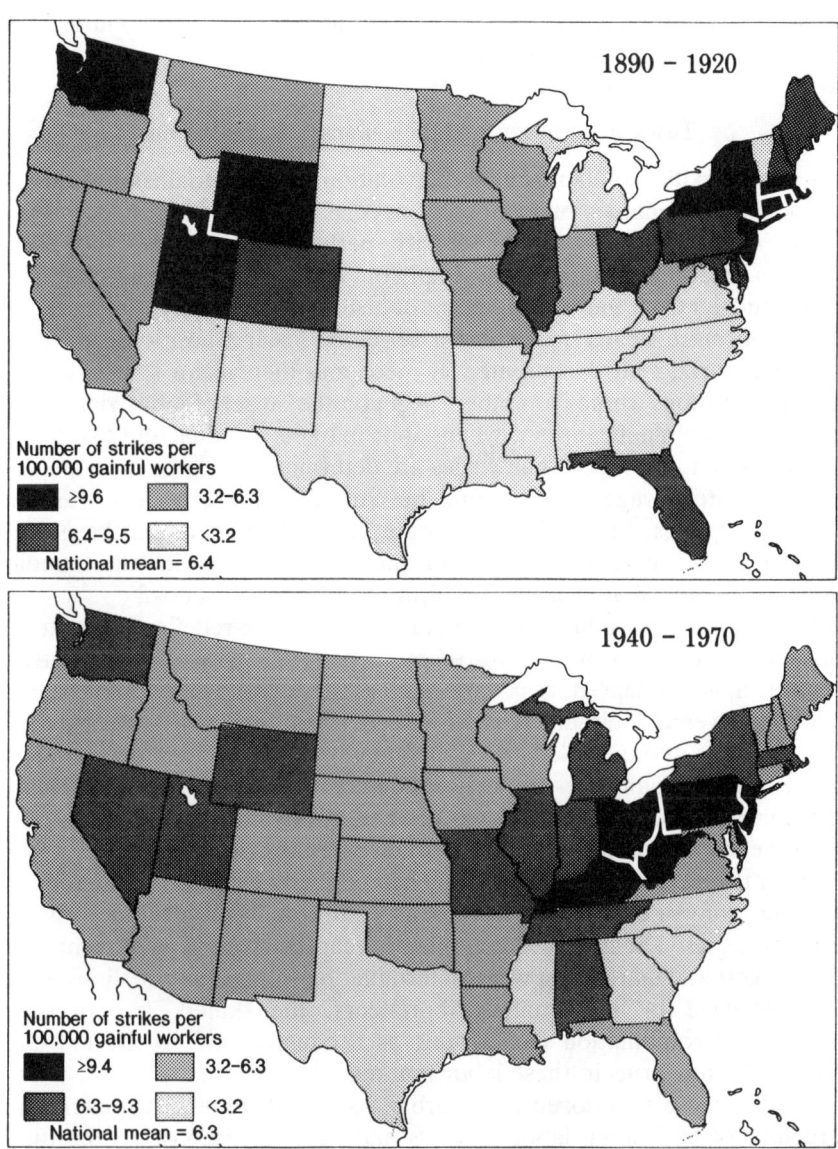

Figure 7. The geography of strike rates 1890–1920 and 1940–1970. The strike rate equals the number of strikes in the period divided by the labor force at the period's end. Source: Earle and Bennett, "The Geography of Worker Protest", pp. 15–22.

ing belt, similarly high rates of worker protest spread into the Midwest and spilled southward into Kentucky, Tennessee, and Alabama. Semiskilled workers, confronted by market imperfections, recapitulated the response of skilled workers in the 1880s. Through "combination" and protest, they sought little more than the wages to which, in accordance with marginalist economic theory, they were entitled.[53]

Toward a theory of labor market instantiation

The complexities of labor-market evolution in industrializing America mock the doctrinal simplifications of neoclassical economic theory. That theory's presumptions of labor scarcity, perfectly competitive labor markets, and marginalist pricing are simply out of touch with market realities. When judged from the vantage point of historical geography, the market's evolution more nearly resembles a series of scalar transitions in which abstract markets are instantiated at meso and then micro spatial scales. These transitions, three in number, begin on the outset of industrialization when rural dominates urban, when labor markets are dual and asymmetric, and when unskilled urban wages are determined, in large measure, by the alternative wages which could be earned in more or less seasonal agrarian regimes. In the American case, or more precisely in the northeastern states, cheap unskilled labor and machines provided the foundations for industrial advance and schism in the ranks of labor.[54]

Once underway, industrialization and urbanization redefined the extent of labor markets by narrowing them to particular cities and industrial centers. Space collapsed, as it were. And as these newly autonomous labor markets severed their linkages with region-wide agrarian systems, they also fissioned into unskilled and skilled markets which varied dramatically in their spatial boundaries and hence their competitiveness. Unskilled markets functioned citywide; they embraced many buyers and sellers and were more nearly competitive. Skilled markets were restricted to one or a few firms in the city. They operated under imperfectly competitive conditions of monopsony or oligopsony. In response, workers deployed equally divergent strategies. The unskilled compliantly reaped the benefits of competitive markets and marginalist wage determination – once these realities were acknowledged by industrial entrepreneurs; the skilled, by contrast, resorted to combination and protest as a counterpoise to the unusual power of a few firms in these labor markets.

Beyond these two dozen or so urban-industrial centers, however, the structure of traditional labor markets endured. In response to the dual

---

[53] Carville Earle and Sari Bennett, "The Geography of Worker Protest in the United States", *Journal of Geography* 82 (1983), pp. 15–21. On the intraurban geography of segmented labor markets, see Allen J. Scott, *Metropolis*.

[54] The scalar instantiation of labor markets might also be regarded as a version of transactional behavior in which firms internalize transactions until their marginal costs equal the transaction costs on the open market – or, in unvarnished prose, until the savings from labor exploitation are exhausted. See Ronald Coase, "The Nature of the Firm", *Economica* 4 (1937), pp. 386–405; Scott, *Metropolis*, pp. 27–35. Transactional-cost models tell us very little, however, about the historical preconditions for the internalization of transaction costs within firms (after 1900) or within cities (after 1840) – that is, about scalar transition.

and asymmetric labor markets of preindustrial America, workers there adopted a strategy of inclusivist radicalism. In their attempts to unite the entire working class of particular localities, the Knights of Labor, and later the Socialist Party of America, provided a temporary salve for a world in transition.

As industry achieved dominance over the American economy after 1880, labor markets entered their third stage. In the large industrial centers in New England and the Middle States, scientific managers further collapsed labor's space. They reduced the complexities of industrial production to its simplest tasks, narrowed each of these tasks to the particular firm, and then enskilled common laborers with the semiskilled capacity for machine tending. In so doing, they collapsed labor-market space from the city as a whole to a particular job in a particular firm, that is, via a process of scalar instantiation. Market imperfections, of course, ensued; workers earned less than their marginal products; and they responded in kind. In the wake of the diffusion of Scientific Management, semiskilled workers dusted off the repertoires of protest which skilled labor had earlier honed to a fine point. Worker protest, accordingly, spread first throughout New England and the Middle States and, after 1940, into the Midwest and the central South.

Labor-market evolution continues, but the evidence suggests that the process of spatial instantiation has reached its limits. In two centuries, the spatial extent of these markets has been progressively, if unevenly, narrowed – from the agrarian region to the autonomous urban market to the particular job in a particular space in a particular firm. What is left? At the moment, industrial relations seems to pose one of three distinct spatial choices: stay in, move from, or obliterate space. Many firms do all three simultaneously. Staying means an in-place search for alternatives to adversarial relations through schemes such as worker participation, horizontal management, shareholding, and the like. Leaving means a search for new sites and new (and usually unorganized) workers at home or abroad. Obliterating means eliminating labor markets altogether by installing "intelligent" machines in their space. None of these alternatives, of course, is particularly attractive for workers in a technically complex, global society.

In any event, from this historical geography of American labor emerges an enduring axiom for workers, and it is this: the wages of labor are limited only by the spatial restraints on the market which – owing to agrarian seasonality and the several imperfections of monopsony, oligopsony, and splintered divisions of labor – are (and have been) more typical than not.

Polymorphous Synchrony: German Industrial Workers and the Politics of Everyday Life

ALF LÜDTKE

Class formation: clear-cut distinctions or "fuzzy" multiple layering

In West Germany during the 1950s, the social history of modernity was initiated by raising a series of questions probing the "internal structure" (*inneres Gefüge*) of industrial society.[1] The predominant conception was of a self-contained era, shaped by a small number of structural elements. In such a perspective centered on static formations, little attention was given to internal ruptures and dynamic processes. This structuralist approach was in fact the linear continuation of a view of the social order which had been developed in the 1930s and '40s by Otto Brunner, one of its chief proponents, in his studies exploring the way "land and power" were constituted during the early modern period.

Since the late 1960s, there has been a substantial shift in emphases in historiography. Social and political conflict has become a key topic which is often addressed under the impact of a heightened openness vis-à-vis social-scientific questions and approaches, especially those transported from across the Atlantic. Critical confrontation with diverse brands of Marxism and the challenges presented by new tendencies in "cultural studies" have sparked further modulations, indeed expansions in angle and perspective: increasingly, scholars feel a need to include the category of secular dynamism termed "class formation".

Jürgen Kocka, one of the principal representatives of "historical social science" in Germany, has pointed to the dissolution of older macrogroupings in society, their internal "bonds [and] identities", their external defining "boundaries".[2] In his view, "the same class position" – such as that of wage labor, where raw materials, the means of production and the product

---

[1] See the programmatic statement by W. Conze, *Die Strukturgeschichte des technisch-industriellen Zeitalters* (Cologne, 1957); for the background of this view see the writings of the eminent historian of societal structures and *Verfassung* in late medieval times, Otto Brunner; cf. idem, *Sozialgeschichte Europas im Mittelalter* (Göttingen, 1978), p. 5.

[2] J. Kocka, *Arbeitsverhältnisse und Arbeiterexistenzen. Grundlagen der Klassenbildung im 19. Jahrhundert* (Bonn, 1990), pp. 4, 521; cf. idem, *Lohnarbeit und Klassenbildung. Arbeiter und Arbeiterbewegung in Deutschland 1800–1875* (Berlin and Bonn, 1983), pp. 24ff.; on the approach of "historical social science", cf. idem, *Sozialgeschichte*, 2nd ed. (Göttingen, 1986), chap. IV. Such a structural-analytical view is the predominant tendency (save for contributions on France) in the comparative volume on West Germany, France and the United States edited by I. Katznelson and A. R. Zolberg, *Working-Class Formation. Nineteenth-Century Patterns in Western Europe and the United States* (Princeton, 1986).

International Review of Social History 38 (1993), Supplement, pp. 39–84

are used and processed (but not appropriated) by the wage laborer –
provides the basis for *shared common interests*. Such interests are aimed
at bringing about improvements in one's situation, or at least forestalling
any deterioration. A person's "class position" also creates opportunities
for accumulating and exchanging "common experiences and shared attitudes, hopes and fears".[3] Emphatically rejecting all notions predicated on
the *inevitability* of particular structures and behavior, Kocka stresses that
there can be joint action or shared organization – albeit only "under certain specific conditions".[4] He conceives of the multiplicity of active factors
which either promote or impede such a "community of interests"
(*Gemeinsamkeit*) as a synchrony of "competing structures".[5] As Kocka
theorizes, ethnic and religious "affiliations" and gender distinctions "cut
like furrows" through and across socioeconomic class positions.

The historiography of everyday life helps to take us a basic step further,
facilitating a perspective not dominated by the weight of the assumed
"grand overall picture" – i.e., class reified as a social "object" or "entity".
In *Alltagsgeschichte*, attention centers on the simultaneous character, the
essential synchrony of different practices, which may in part even be contradictory. What is salient here is the dynamic process unfolding *within*,
below or even *at odds with* the framework of "common shared" interests.[6]
To formulate it more concretely: there is no doubt that wage laborers
were dependent in a myriad of respects; yet in those very relations of
dependency, they managed to stake out or win over bits of time and chinks
of space *in which they were able to create and develop their "own sense"
of things – for themselves (and with others)*. Of course, the resultant array
of exclusions, of laying down lines and boundaries, was always directed
against their "class brothers and sisters". Indeed, such boundaries may
have even been predominantly aimed at them. The markers of respectability ran deep and were highly resilient: factors such as pride in the
product and seniority of the jobholder, or the sociogeographical divide
separating locals (and commuters from nearby localities) and relocated
workers who had moved in from other areas. In any event, the classic

---

[3] Kocka, *Lohnarbeit*, pp. 26f.

[4] It is an open question whether justice is really done to the richness of various brands of
Marxism – many by no means so "doctrinaire and certain" or rigidly one-dimensional – by
assuming that only after the "Weberian" shift in perspective is there any possibility for
Marxist approaches grounded in undogmatic analysis. After all, the rich range of Marxist
ideas includes observations on the "unequal development" of "material and artistic production" (cf. *Grundrisse der Kritik der politischen Ökonomie* [1857/58], Frankfurt/M and Vienna,
n.d. [1973], pp. 30f.) as well as the empirically dense look at French society around 1850
contained in the "Eighteenth Brumaire of Louis Bonaparte".

[5] Kocka, *Sozialgeschichte*, pp. 29f.

[6] For greater detail, see my introduction, "Was ist und wer treibt Alltagsgeschichte?", in
A. Lüdtke (ed.), *Alltagsgeschichte. Zur Rekonstruktion historischer Erfahrungen und Lebens-
weisen* (Frankfurt/M, 1989), esp. pp. 11–26, in English translation: Lüdtke (ed.), *The History
of Everyday Life*, trans. W. Templer (Princeton, forthcoming).

"determination" of labor by the owners of capital, managers and master craftsmen or other middlemen, constituted only *one* element in a multiply layered, complexly structured field of social forces.[7] Workers' concrete practice and experience cannot simply be reduced to a zero-sum game. Labor was far more than mere instrumental action. That is evident from the way in which laborers experienced their practice: namely as a process geared to making a product for third parties, while *simultaneously* assuring their own survival and making creative use of opportunities for autonomous activity and self-affirmation, as well as affection – or even animosity. The term "labor" denoted a practice that was multiple and diverse in structure – a *polymorphous complex* in which economic, social and cultural factors all had a significant role to play.[8]

Historical reconstructions of women's work have provided a major impetus for broadening this view, pointing to fresh ways of looking at the meaning of "labor". Moreover, such gender-specific research has served to put the other half of historical reality – excluded from view or suppressed by male historiography – back on the stage of scrutiny.[9] At long last, it has finally become academically respectable to pose questions about gender relations.[10] These studies indicate that the basic meaning of women's wage-labor in settings such as department stores, the service industries and in private households were essentially reducible to one basic occupational reality: "profession: female".[11] Even in factories, the low wages paid to female workers and the formal designation of "jobs for women" in mechanized spinning and weaving mills were the expression of a gender-based class-internal boundary – one that in many cases tended to intensify the inequalities and discriminations suffered by the laboring class as a whole.[12]

[7] But cf. Kocka, *Lohnarbeit*, p. 24.

[8] On this linkage, cf. esp. G. Sider, *Culture and Class in Anthropology and History: A Newfoundland Illustration* (Cambridge, 1986), pp. 6f., 120f., 192f.

[9] See H. Docekal, "Feministische Geschichtswissenschaft – ein unverzichtbares Projekt", *L'Homme: Zeitschrift für Feministische Geschichtswissenschaft*, 1 (1990), pp. 7–18; G. Pomata, "Partikulargeschichte und Universalgeschichte – Bemerkungen zu einigen Handbüchern der Frauengeschichte", *L'Homme*, 2 (1991), pp. 5–44.

[10] As much as women's history predominates (probably initially with good reason), more recent publications indicate that it is principally female scholars who are now taking a serious look at the theme of gender relations and masculine life, cf. J. W. Scott, *Gender and the Politics of History* (New York, 1988), and for relevant literature in German, see K. Hausen and H. Wunder (eds.), *Frauengeschichte – Geschlechtergeschichte* (Frankfurt/M and New York, 1992); conceptually stimulating, since it stresses the self-interpretations of historical subjects, is A. Kessler-Harris, "Gender Ideology in Historical Reconstruction", *Gender & History*, 1 (1991), pp. 31–49.

[11] U. Nienhaus, *Berufsstand weiblich: Die ersten weiblichen Angestellten* (Berlin, 1982); cf. D. Wierling, *Mädchen für alles: Arbeitsalltag und Lebensgeschichte städtischer Dienstmädchen um die Jahrhundertwende* (Berlin and Bonn, 1987).

[12] Exemplary is K. Canning, "Class, Gender and Working-Class Politics: The Case of the German Textile Industry, 1890–1933" (Ph.D., Johns Hopkins University, 1988); cf. K. Canning, "Gender and the Politics of Class Formation: Rethinking German Labor History", *American Historical Review*, 97 (1992), pp. 736–68.

Even more important is the insistence from this perspective of recogniz-
ing the salient fact that wage-labor in bourgeois society has always been
reinforced by the institution of housework.[13] In this domestic sphere,
women were exposed to multiple pressures, often in addition to their gainful employment outside, or contract work at home. The mundane everyday reality of women was shaped by the wearying contours of domestic
labor: housework as the effort to maintain familial relations,[14] to ensure
the daily reproduction of the labor of the male (so-called) "breadwinners",
to bring up children and secure the biological reproduction of the species.
    The painstaking reconstruction of women's work also reveals the pres-
ence of certain possibilities for a mode of female counterpower. Women
invested their energies, time and ambition in cooking up a "hearty" stew,
especially one containing meat or fat; or they made an effort to prepare
a nice, tasty dessert (perhaps because desserts had a special power to
evoke certain childhood memories). Such culinary creativity was particularly important in working-class kitchens, under the constrained conditions
in which the majority of workers' families or those of "junior" civil servants eked out a modest existence. These cooks derived inner satisfaction
from the savory meals they prepared. At the same time, the obvious con-
tentment of those who ate their homemade dishes provided clear recognition from meaningful others, especially the family "breadwinners".[15] Even

[13] U. Knapp, *Frauenarbeit in Deutschland*, vol. 2: *Hausarbeit und geschlechtsspezifischer Arbeitsmarkt im deutschen Industrialisierungsprozeß – Frauenpolitik und proletarischer Alltag zwischen 1800 und 1933* (Munich, 1984); see also the case study on the "segment" of women organized in a Social Democratic framework by K. Hagemann, *Frauenalltag und Männerpolitik. Alltagsleben und gesellschaftliches Handeln von Arbeiterfrauen in der Weimarer Republik* (Bonn, 1990).
[14] The following remain highly thought-providing: G. Bock, B. Duden, "Arbeit aus Liebe – Liebe als Arbeit", *Frauen und Wissenschaft* (Berlin, 1976); L. Tilly and J. W. Scott, *Women, Work and Family* (New York, 1978); T. Hareven, *Family Time and Industrial Time: The Relationship between Family and Work in a New England Industrial Community* (Cambridge, 1982); K. Hausen, "Große Wäsche. Technischer Fortschritt und sozialer Wandel in Deutschland vom 18. bis ins 20. Jahrhundert", *Geschichte und Gesellschaft*, 13 (1987), pp. 273–303; H. Rapin (ed.), *Frauenforschung und Hausarbeit* (Frankfurt/M and New York, 1988); and more generally, H. Medick and D. Sabean (eds.), *Interest and Emotion: Essays on the Study of Family and Kinship* (Cambridge, 1984); cf. also the mixture of personal recollections and careful reconstruction in C. Steedman, *Landscape for a Good Woman: A Story of Two Lives* (New Brunswick, 1986).
[15] Cf. my "Hunger, Essens-'Genuß' und Politik bei Fabrikarbeitern und Arbeiterfrauen. Beispiele aus dem rheinisch-westfälischen Industriegebiet, 1910–1940", in A. Lüdtke, *Eigen-Sinn. Fabrikalltag, Arbeitererfahrungen und Politik vom Kaiserreich bis in den Faschismus* (Hamburg, 1993); for a similar perspective with examples drawn from industrial towns in northwest Lancashire, see E. Roberts, *A Woman's Place: An Oral History of Working-Class Women 1890–1940* (Oxford and New York, 1984), esp. pp. 110ff. regarding a sharp separa-tion of roles from spaces for action; on working-class fathers, see H. Rosenbaum, *Proletari-sche Familien. Arbeiterfamilien und Arbeiterväter im frühen 20. Jahrhundert zwischen tradi-tioneller, sozialdemokratischer und kleinbürgerlicher Orientierung* (Frankfurt/M, 1992), chap. 4; in her study on Social Democratic women in Hamburg, Hagemann found that comparat-ively little value was placed on domestic duties, cf. *Frauenalltag*, p. 644.

during the crisis winter 1916/17, married and single women tried to produce some kind of casserole or sweet pie for their loved ones from the meager makeshift ingredients of turnips – a dinner that was more than just a mundane meal, despite the modesty of available ingredients.

Buoyed by the experience gained in caring and cooking for their families, women gained the confidence to venture into a new species of autonomous action – not limited to the sphere, but extending into the streets. The intensified struggle for survival triggered by the war spurred public action, and it is particularly noteworthy that the street protests over hunger beginning in 1915 were organized largely by young people and women. Consequently, it is not simply coincidental that studies on working-class women have tended to focus on the war years.[16] By contrast, research on the lives of working-class men, has almost always tended to focus on peacetime conditions. Critical debate over "historical social science" in Germany has been fuelled by deepening skepticism vis-à-vis its structural-historical penchant, its tendency to simplify and reduce a multiply layered practice in order to separate sharply differentiated profiles.[17]

Various factors have shaped the debate, of which the influence West German scholarship has been only one. I would like to single out three key sources for the altered perspectives in working-class history. Edward P. Thompson's magisterial class biography, *The Making of the English Working Class*,[18] presented a vivid, complex panorama of the experiences of the "unpropertied classes", male and female pre-industrial wage-laborers. Thompson also generated a variety of stimulating new ideas on how to examine forms of cultural and self-interpretation. His emphasis is not on wages and prices, but on how they relate to the criteria of a just economic order. Barrington Moore also underscored this dimension: in his analysis, the struggle against "injustice" was the decisive cultural and material motivating force for working-class action in a number of countries.[19]

Highly influential, though less often cited in the relevant literature, is the work of the late Herbert Gutman. In a study of the silk industry in Paterson, New Jersey, he scrutinized an area of industrialization generally neglected by German historiography, namely small-scale factories. In particular, Gutman's investigation of the sweat and toil of black slaves and

---

[16] U. Daniel, *Arbeiterfrauen in der Kriegsgesellschaft. Beruf, Familie und Politik im Ersten Weltkrieg* (Göttingen, 1989), on the "counter-public sphere", p. 241; aspects of this topic are also dealt with in S. Meyer and E. Schulz, *"Wie wir das alles geschafft haben". Alleinstehende Frauen berichten über ihr Leben nach 1945* (Munich, 1984).

[17] A stimulating summary of such critique can be found in Th. Lindenberger and M. Wildt, "Radikale Pluralität. Geschichtswerkstätten als praktische Wissenschaftskritik", *Archiv für Sozialgeschichte*, 29 (1989), pp. 393–411, esp. pp. 401ff.

[18] (London, 1963). The 1987 German edition has the somewhat misleading title *Die Entstehung* [i.e., genesis] *der englischen Arbeiterklasse*.

[19] B. Moore, *Injustice. The Social Bases of Obedience and Revolt* (Boston, 1978).

black industrial workers has shed welcome light on the multiplicity of expressive cultural forms with which workers create and promulgate their *own* interpretations of their *own* history. An array of practices as diverse as the naming of babies or the everyday care of children reflect a clear effort to achieve some modicum of dignity, to strive for a sphere and substance of "their own".[20]

A third impressive study along these lines is Michelle Perrot's monograph on strikes in France during the 1870s and '80s.[21] From Perrot's perspective, the proper way to locate patterns of collective refusal by workers lies outside the variations of wages and prices. She contends, rather, that struggles for pay and improved working conditions only become comprehensible against a broader backdrop: the networks and rhythms of social communication. In her view, strikes are inseparable from the web of possibilities and necessities for "*s'endimancher*" – for "putting on one's Sunday best" and celebrating, the realm of restday festivity.

In the light of such research, our historical interest in the realities of everyday life, the hopes and anxieties of people at grass roots level, appears to be a kind of "compensatory modernization" – a way of amending for historiographic oversights in the past. Despite the productive thrust of *Alltagsgeschichte*, I believe the genuinely new vistas opened up by this approach have so far been only partially recognized. Let me point out three key shortcomings.

First, the industrial labor processes themselves are often reduced to little more than statistical descriptions. Typical emphasis centers on reconstructions of the ideal contours of labor – how it *ought to be*, as seen from the angle of economists, engineers and even shop-floor functionaries. A distorting prism is created, making it difficult to discern the extensive array of actual situations and their contradictions; lines of fracture – and thus the very dynamism of historical processes – fail to catch the attention. In this approach, "experience" denotes what is apparently recurrent and "always the same". It becomes a synonym for "routine" – suggesting a parallel to Fernand Braudel's often cited notion of "*vie materielle*": humankind is submerged "up to its neck" in this flux of material life, for the most part "totally unaware of its existence".[22]

Second, this view goes hand-in-hand with a corresponding conception of "politics" guided by a notion of the "big picture", the "grand connec-

---

[20] H. Gutman, *Work, Culture and Society in Industrializing America* (New York, 1977); H. Gutman, *The Black Family in Slavery and Freedom, 1750–1925* (New York and London, 1976); a revised version of key arguments is contained in idem, "Family Ties among Afro-Americans before and after the Emancipation of the Slaves in North America", in Medick and Sabean, *Interest and Emotion*.

[21] M. Perrot, *Les ouvriers en grève. France 1871–1890*, 2 vols. (Paris and The Hague, 1974); for the following, ibid., vol. 2, pt. III, esp. pp. 548ff., quote p. 550.

[22] F. Braudel, "Materielles Leben und wirtschaftliches Leben", in F. Braudel, *Die Dynamik des Kapitalismus* (Stuttgart, 1986), pp. 11–37, here p. 16.

tions" in world history – a view which first evolved within the dual histor-ical process that first began in the late eighteenth century, characterized by capitalization and the formation of the state. Politics in this framework, refers to phenomena at *state* level, to national communication; any separ-ate and independent practice developed at local grass-roots level is then conceived to be merely a kind of prefatory stage, a prelude to this "higher" form of politics.

Third, the multiplication of ways of life and experience, the presence of *multiple* voices commenting on their own history, gives rise to another question: what is the connection between such multiplicity and other forms of action aimed at achieving a sphere and substance "of one's own making" – both in the heartland of industrial development and at the so-called periphery? What simultaneities – or better, dyssynchronisms – can be identified? I.e., what might it mean to develop a *comparative* approach to labor experiences and working-class politics?

Labor processes and experience in the workplace

For both male and female factory employees, "work" was steeped in a fluid mixture of ambivalent experiences. Yet what was incompatible did not necessarily have to be contradictory. These diverse "varieties" of workplace experience did not corroborate the extreme positions: they were not isomorphic with pessimistic images of a (dys)utopian "brave new world", nor did they confirm technocratic phantasies about the end of human toil and tribulation in a scientific millennium where there was a "rational solution" to all problems.

Alfred Schütz defined the distinction between the two German terms for "experience" – *Erfahrung* and *Erlebnis* – by proposing that the former was made up of *Erlebnisse* that had been "singled out, distinguished by attention".[23] But what, one may ask, are the threshold and characteristic forms of attention? In any case, the degree and mode in which the worker's *body* was used were a key element in factory labor.[24] Within one's own group and class, physical work was both a stigma and mark of distinction. For many laborers, especially those who had recently migrated into indus-trial regions, menial jobs and work in transport were the first – and for a long time often the sole – source of gainful employment they could find. Men were expected to push and heave heavy loads of all kinds: sacks of potatoes, barrels of butter, piles of coal or earth, blocks of wood and

---

[23] A. Schütz and Th. Luckmann, *Strukturen der Lebenswelt*, vol. 2 (Frankfurt/M, 1984), p. 14. [In common speech, *Erlebnis* tends to denote "any event through which one has lived", whereas *Erfahrung* stresses "knowledge gained from experience in that event", or the "sum total of knowledge accumulated". – trans. note.]

[24] For more detail, cf. my "Wo blieb die 'rote Glut'? Arbeitererfahrungen und deutscher Faschismus", A. Lüdtke, *Alltagsgeschichte*, pp. 224–282, esp. pp. 240–248 and now in English translation in: Lüdtke, *The History of Everyday Life*.

metal. At times, females also performed such back-breaking labor, while menial shop-floor tasks such as scouring and scrubbing were set aside exclusively as "women's work".

Many of those who had to survive by irregular employment found a temporary hand-to-mouth "means of livelihood" in these physically gruelling tasks.[25] At the same time, menial laborers who hauled heavy loads, or cleaning women, were frequently looked down upon and excluded by other manual workers – especially those who had to prove their skilled "dexterity" working at machines.[26] In this regard, there was no difference in the assessments made over the span of several decades by the first and second generation of factory employees.

A second significant kind of experience was not group-specific, but depended on different levels of physical exertion. In the eyes of many workers – of women even more than men – both the hard physical difficulty and attraction of manual labor were linked with the perception of the so-called "collar line" – how blue, how white, how soiled. The divide between the social classes was at play here, charged with powerful feelings of resentment and envy: how could any activity still be called "work" if it did not entail dirt, sweat and pain, and only rarely led to accidental injury?[27] Moreover, how could men who had little or no personal everyday knowledge of hard physical labor climb the managerial ladder in factories and reach the height of power in government and society?

This sort of experience was little influenced by the degree of mechanization on the shop floor: mechanical aids provided virtually no relief from manual labor. For example, the charging of blast furnaces and brick ovens was not made any easier in physical terms by the introduction of new machine-systems and faster motors – on the contrary, it became even more strenuous.[28] The results of a survey conducted in 1910 by Adolf Levenstein among some 6,000 unionized mine workers, metal workers (lathe oper-

---

[25] For regions on the periphery and outside of urban industrial conglomerations, cf. K. M. Barfuss, *"Gastarbeiter" in Nordwestdeutschland 1884–1918* (Bremen, 1986); for the mid-nineteenth century, see also H. Gerstenberger (ed.), *Wanderarbeit. Armut und Zwang zum Reisen* (Bremen, 1984).

[26] On this distinction between menial and more skilled labor, highlighting the example of dockworkers and emphasizing the refractory behavior of "casual laborers", cf. M. Grüttner, *Arbeitswelt an der Wasserkante. Sozialgeschichte der Hamburger Hafenarbeiter, 1886–1914* (Göttingen, 1984), esp. pp. 85ff., 92ff.

[27] This particular aspect of the delimitation "from below" remains marginal in the detailed case study by J. Kocka, *Unternehmensverwaltung und Angestelltenschaft am Beispiel Siemens 1847–1914. Zum Verhältnis von Kapitalismus und Bürokratie in der deutschen Industrialisierung* (Stuttgart, 1969), chap. IV; for an international comparison, see O. Zunz, *Making America Corporate 1870–1920* (Chicago, 1990).

[28] N. Osterroth, *Vom Beter zum Kämpfer*, 2nd pr. (Berlin and Bonn, 1980; 1st ed.: 1920), pp. 42ff.; B. Parisius, *Lebenswege im Revier. Erlebnisse und Erfahrungen zwischen Jahrhundertwende und Kohlenkrise* (Essen, 1984), pp. 32ff., 80ff., 98, 104ff.; N. R. Nissen (ed.), *Menschen – Monarchen – Maschinen. Landarbeiter in Dithmarschen* (Heide, 1988), pp. 31ff., cf. p. 95.

ators, drillers and fitters) and textile plant workers pointed in the same direction. The predominant feeling in all three groups was a pervasive sense of dissatisfaction.[29]

They shared a fundamental mood of discontent, but differences could be discerned. Levenstein asked his interviewees whether work at a machine was "pleasurable" – or "is it devoid of any interest for you personally?"[30] While three-quarters of the textile workers who responded gave answers which Levenstein interpreted as reflecting a basic "dissatisfaction", the miners and metal workers who expressed dissatisfaction were fewer (60 percent and 56 percent respectively). The written responses ranged from an unqualified "hate" mentioned by one worker to the "pleasure" voiced by a carpet weaver when his product turned out "nice and beautiful". The decisive factor was not just the specific industry, the mode for calculating wages (mainly piecework) or the final amount in the pay-packet. A toolmaker summed up what many felt when he said that "work that was constantly monotonous" suffocated any and every "joy" on the job.

The attitudes expressed by mining and metal workers were a mixed bag – reflecting more than simply disinterest in or even a dislike of machinery. On the contrary: their tasks necessitated a high degree of attention both to the piece being worked on and also to the operation of machinery (or to the immediate natural environment, such as the "pit"). Moreover, pleasure could be derived (and with it certain material advantages) on exploring and learning to control the leeway for action present "at" the machines,[31] and to preserve such personal space for autonomous activity.[32]

Despite the sporadic nature of statements by workers on their everyday factory experience, these remarks raised doubts about any thesis postulating an all-pervasive sense of "monotony" on the factory floor. Even when a machine was operated on a regular, clockwork basis, it might look different when seen from "inside", from the perspective of the worker actually at the controls. Levenstein cited a lathe operator:

Your eyes are transfixed, staring at the slowly revolving piece in the lathe. You hold your hand casual, cool, yet ready to respond. But your thoughts are free to

[29] A. Levenstein, *Die Arbeiterfrage – mit besonderer Berücksichtigung der sozialpsychologischen Seite des modernen Großbetriebes und der psychophysischen Einwirkungen auf die Arbeiter* (Munich, 1912), pp. 47ff., 53–75; cf. pp. 123ff., 187ff., 199ff.

[30] Ibid., pp. 44, esp. 53ff.

[31] On the distinction between working "at" and "with" (the aid of) machines, such as operating a crane, cf. H. Popitz *et al.*, *Technik und Industriearbeit*, 3rd ed. (Tübingen, 1976), pp. 112ff., 128ff.; such distinctions on the basis of activity are far more appropriate to work experience than designations that refer to various but abstract degrees of "skill".

[32] On this orientation, as well as intra-class distinctions, see the penetrating reconstruction of work processes and more general interpretations of the way of life of coal miners, slate quarry laborers and saltworkers in R. Samuel (ed.), *Miners, Quarrymen and Saltworkers* (London, 1977).

roam, they drift out through and beyond the red factory walls; and only your ear, ever attentive, records any change in the pace of the machine, the wearing down of the cutter. [. . .] You stop thinking of anything but the beat of the rhythm [. . .][33]

The response of a weaver indicated that such "rhythms" could also mark a kind of *synchrony* between what was near and further afield: "I hope I'll always have enough to fill my belly", he confided, speaking at the same time of his wish "to awaken in my children the spark of divinity".[34]

Work signified many different things in the worker's experience. It was not reducible to a simple contrast between "joy on payday" and the miseries of monotony. "Slaving away" at one's job and "time pressures" did not preclude a certain satisfaction. Among both male and female workers, furtive glances alternated with cheerful smiles.[35] Nonetheless, the contours of everyday synchronisms and "patchwork" mixtures often differed depending on the branch of industry involved, firm size and type of activity – though physiognomy of workplace experience in factories was formed by the typical features.

The reconstruction of everyday practice, which explores such hints, discloses a second code, repeatedly masked, in the rhetoric of working-class movements. At least in the case of *male* workers, one can discern a so-called "long wave" in the assessment of work with machinery in factory settings – one which demanded (and facilitated) both physical effort *and manual dexterity*. This was based on the experience that daily wage-labor in factories, even in carefully supervised or physically gruelling production environment, involved far more than just passive endurance of unreasonable demands and enervating toil. Again and again, autonomous action proved indispensable. Handling the materials and machines required a diversified, hands-on approach – an activity which each individual had to learn to handle on his/her own. In exchanges with fellow workers and superiors, whether cooperating or in disagreement, those involved utilized traditional signs and forms – but did so *in their own way*.

Autonomous activity also encompassed phenomena such as unauthorized rest periods and fooling around on the job, that risky horseplay and shopfloor "tomfoolery" combatted vigorously by supervisors – i.e., a kind

[33] Levenstein, *Die Arbeiterfrage*, p. 107.
[34] Ibid., p. 227.
[35] On female factory workers, see T. Hareven, *Family Time* and esp. K. Canning, "Gender and the Politics of Class Formation", pp. 744ff.; starting about 1908/10, an attempt was made in the German Textile Workers' Association (DTAV) either to justify more extensive protective regulations for women – or to exclude them from the functions of union leadership singling out their "special characteristics" as females, cf. ibid., pp. 762ff.; on the range of experience in factory work and the synchronisms of factory employment and housework, see A. Lüdtke (ed.), *"Mein Arbeitstag – mein Wochenende". Arbeiterinnen berichten von ihrem Alltag 1928* (Hamburg, 1991); on the array of such "glances", ibid., p. 29.

of *Eigensinn*[36] with and at machines (especially during cleaning operations performed on running machinery). The aim was to get even for all the stress and strain, staking out niches for one's own time, free temporal space for oneself. Moreover, expectations, incentives and unreasonable demands on time and energy – set down in orders, forms of wages, factory regulations and duties toward fellow workers – were not merely ignored or passively accepted, but were repeatedly transformed in everyday practice. These forms of *appropriation* of industrial labor were not based on neglect of the actual work process. On the contrary: intimate familiarity with the various required operations and a precise knowledge of the field of social forces in the factory were the essential prerequisites for being able to satisfy one's own needs and *simultaneously* carry out work orders. Work offered a dual opportunity: to prove one's competence to oneself and others, and then to be able – if only for a few short seconds – to ignore everything and everybody in order to be alone, "with and by oneself".

Traces of the multiplicity of forms of appropriation are reflected in the participant observations made by outsiders. The Protestant minister Paul Göhre and Minna Wettstein-Adelt (who expressly tried to imitate Göhre's initiative three years later) noted that factory and machine work comprised more than just operating hand-wheels or adjustment of screws, cleaning equipment or transporting unfinished and final products.[37] In Göhre's case in particular, his efforts to describe every detail attest to the fact that he was no superficial observer on the factory floor. Indeed, his report provides the reader with an "echo" of those "now silent voices" which Walter Benjamin termed a "secret index" of the past.[38] This outside observer did not see labor solely as some sort of "metabolism with nature" (Marx). His report reflects the insight that one element was quite indispensable for the workers he observed: namely their own autonomous action and activity.

Both observers recorded the expressive forms manifest in the workplace in extensive detail. Wettstein-Adelt described the way female weavers adorned "their" looms with tiny pictures and ribbons, marking them out

[36] *Eigensinn* is a central term in the author's analysis of workers' everyday life, denoting willfulness, spontaneous self-will, a kind of self-affirmation, an act of (re)appropriating alienated social relations on and off the shop floor by self-assertive prankishness, demarcating a space of one's own. There is a disjunction between formalized politics and the prankish, stylized misanthropic distancing from all constraints or incentives present in the everyday politics of "*Eigensinn*". In standard parlance, the word has pejorative overtones, referring to "obstreperous, obstinate" behaviour, usually of children. The "dis-compounding" or writing it as "Eigen-Sinn" stresses its root signification of "one's own sense, own meaning". – Trans. note.

[37] P. Göhre, *Drei Monate Fabrikarbeiter und Handwerksbursche. Eine praktische Studie* (Leipzig, 1891); M. Wettstein-Adelt, *Dreieinhalb Monate als Fabrik-Arbeiterin* (Berlin, 1893).

[38] W. Benjamin, "Über den Begriff der Geschichte", in idem, *Gesammelte Schriften*, vol. 1, pt. 2 (Frankfurt/M, 1974), pp. 691–704, here 693.

as their own turf. Göhre sketched a varied panorama of verbal and non-verbal languages: the laborers utilized these idioms in order to communicate with their fellows on the job, or to gain some distance and latitude from them. He depicted in detail the varieties of teasing – probably both painful and embarrassing to an academic outsider like himself, and the practice of *Bartwichsen* ("beard-polishing") in that decidedly "male" shop environment.[39]

Eigensinn

"Living together" on the job was marked by forms of cooperation dictated by necessity.[40] But sandwiched in between these were elements of recalcitrant, bloody-minded *Eigensinn*.

Cooperation dictated by necessity

This category included forms of cooperation and self-monitoring among workers which helped them "survive and get by" on the job. Two aims were important: to reduce the risks of accident[41] and to secure the expected or desired wage level. However, such a mode of cooperation was also useful in "appropriating" the various managerial attempts to discipline the workers,

[39] Göhre, *Drei Monate Fabrikarbeiter*, p. 78; treated in greater detail in my "Cash, Coffee-Breaks, Horseplay: *Eigensinn* and Politics among Factory Workers in Germany circa 1900", in M. Hanagan and Ch. Stephenson (eds.), *Confrontation, Class Consciousness, and the Labor Process* (New York, 1986), pp. 65–95.

[40] For the following, I have drawn on my article "Die Ordnung der Fabrik. 'Sozialdisziplinierung' und Eigensinn bei Fabrikarbeitern im späten 19. Jahrhundert", in R. Vierhaus *et al.* (eds.), *Frühe Neuzeit – frühe Moderne?* (Göttingen, 1992), pp. 206–231, esp. 217–244. On the practice and experience of manual labor "at" and "with" (the aid of) tool machines, see my "Wo blieb die 'rote Glut'?", esp. pp. 240ff., 253ff.; on the so-called "internal life" of German factories, see the well-documented analysis by L. Machtan, "Zum Innenleben deutscher Fabriken im 19. Jahrhundert. Die formelle und informelle Verfassung von Industriebetrieben, anhand von Beispielen aus dem Bereich der Textil-und Maschinenbauproduktion (1869–1891)", *Archiv für Sozialgeschichte*, 21 (1981), pp. 179–236. In individual studies, the ever-recurrent "icons of industry" tend to be reproduced, i.e., heavy industry and mining – by comparison, other spheres of production and branches of industry have attracted little research to date; on the mining industry, however, note the superb studies by F.-J. Brüggemeier, *Leben vor Ort. Ruhrbergleute und Ruhrbergbau, 1898–1919* (Munich, 1983) and H. Steffens, *Autorität und Revolte. Alltagsleben und Streikverhalten der Bergarbeiter an der Saar im 19. Jahrhundert* (Weingarten, 1987), pp. 109–164; cf. also K.-P. Mallmann and H. Steffens, *Lohn der Mühen. Geschichte der Bergarbeiter an der Saar* (Munich, 1989); and for an international comparison, see K. Tenfelde (ed.), *Sozialgeschichte des Bergbaus im 19. und 20. Jahrhundert* (Munich, 1992).

[41] Cf. A. Andersen and R. Ott, "Risikoperzeption im Industrialisierungszeitalter am Beispiel des Hüttenwesens", *Archiv für Sozialgeschichte*, 28 (1988), pp. 75–109; H. Trischler, "Arbeitsunfälle und Berufskrankheiten im Bergbau 1851 bis 1945. Bergbehördliche Sozialpolitik im Spannungsfeld von Sicherheit und Produktionsinteressen", *Archiv für Sozialgeschichte*, 28 (1988), pp. 111–151.

making such incursions easier to handle. This was a daily necessity – especially under the system of team piecework, an increasingly common wage mode after 1900. This form of wage-earning was dominant in work processes involving the shaping of materials,[42] e.g., in the metal industry and in all branches of machine manufacture.[43] Productivity quotas, quality standards and time-periods were coupled with a constant self-discipline to toe the line, accommodate and conform. Work to be performed was not assigned to individual workers, but to an entire work team. The team – and that usually meant the foreman – handled the matter of how the wages were divided up, but was supervised by a master craftsman. It was necessary to maintain open communication with your fellow workers, and to agree on procedures, both within and between teams.

In such team piecework, an individual's wages depended on whether the group fulfilled its assigned quota or even managed to exceed it. It was essential for "newcomers" to learn the proper pace. It was also important to "restrain" overenthusiastic novices: they had to be forewarned that assigned quotas should not be overfulfilled by too wide a margin. If performance went beyond 130 percent of the quota, the quota would be increased in the future with a consequent worsening of the wage rate. The figure of 130 percent mentioned in autobiographical reports and interviews is a standard that remained fresh in workers' memories even decades later. Apparently, that magic figure allowed employees some breathing space for recuperation and some elbowroom to create their "own" work pace. The product of the manufacturing process, wages and invested effort remained calibrated in a way that was generally felt to be "fair and just". But gentle hints, warnings and friendly persuasion did not always have the desired result. It then became imperative to give a worker's readiness to cooperate a "gentle little shove" in the right direction by resorting to more physical means of persuasion.

Eigensinn

The workers did not simply work in the same area, cooperating as the occasion arose – they virtually lived together in intense contact hour after hour. Göhre's participant-observer reports and the autobiographical inter-

[42] H. Kern, M. Schumann, *Industriearbeit und Arbeiterbewußtsein*, vol. 1 (Frankfurt/M, 1974), pp. 147ff.; cf. L. Lappe, "Technologie, Qualifikation und Kontrolle", *Soziale Welt*, 37 (1986), pp. 310–330, esp. 316ff.

[43] L. Bernhard, *Die Akkordarbeit in Deutschland* (Leipzig, 1903); M. Bernays, *Auslese und Anpassung der Arbeiterschaft der geschlossenen Großindustrie, dargestellt an den Verhältnissen der "Gladbacher Spinnerei und Weberei" AG zu Mönchen-Gladbach im Rheinland* (Leipzig, 1910), p. 189; D. Landé, "Arbeits-und Lohnverhältnisse in der Berliner Maschinenindustrie zu Beginn des 20. Jahrhunderts", in Verein für Sozialpolitik (ed.), *Auslese und Anpassung der Arbeiterschaft in der Elektroindustrie, Buchdruckerei, Feinmechanik und Maschinenindustrie* (Leipzig, 1910), pp. 302–498, here 356. Team piecework is mentioned only in passing in Th. v. Freyberg, *Industrielle Rationalisierung in der Weimarer Republik, unter-*

views of the 1920s and '30s,[44] refer to a multitude of forms of mutual
contact among the men, as well as practices aimed at creating a modicum
of distance. These included both ritualized playfulness and "serious" conversations. In addition, everyone apparently also took part in non-verbal
exchanges, and body contact was often sought quite naturally – in any
case, it was hard to avoid.[45] There was a broad spectrum of interaction,
including rough physical teasing, the practice of "beard-polishing" so
graphically described by Göhre, getting into short playful scraps, and just
"horsing around" on the job. Often, this involved badgering fellow
workers when "no one was looking". Machine operators, who had been
briefly inducted, as well as highly experienced repairmen would repeatedly
stake out physical and social space in the workplace for themselves, demonstrating a developed sense of *Eigensinn*.

Such body contact, often quite painful, demonstrated the existence of
a fund of shared experience among both, the "players" and their victims:
to be stuck in one place, soiled and made dirty, constantly subject to
intrusions and manipulations engineered by persons largely or totally
beyond the control of those manipulated. For the space of a few moments
at least this rough teasing created or established the presence of a double-
edged distance: vis-à-vis hierarchies within one's own class, as well as those
beyond. Such boisterous horseplay carved out a spatial and temporal niche
in which the foremen and bosses – and indeed any and all demands from
outside and above – were held at temporary arm's length.

Eigensinn was the attempt to gain some welcome respite, at least for a
few brief minutes, from unreasonable external (and shop floor) demands
and pressures. In the eyes of fellow workers, this behavior was often interpreted as genuine "hostility": thus, the lathe operator Moritz Bromme
expressed his disgust for the "jackass talk" of most of his fellow workers.
He was not alone in feeling that fellow workers could be "absolute
devils".[46] Brusquely creating a space of demonstrative distance vis-à-vis

sucht an Beispielen aus dem Maschinenbau und der Elektroindustrie (Frankfurt/M and New
York, 1989); "group fabrication" is dealt with on pp. 152ff., but team piecework is touched
on solely in connection with Siemens, where it was lauded in 1926 as highly especially useful
for inducing self-control and monitoring among workers – and thus for procedures geared
to maintaining a "tight production schedule", ibid., p. 237.

[44] See my "Deutsche Qualitätsarbeit", "Spielereien" am Arbeitsplatz und "Fliehen aus der
Fabrik", in F. Boll (ed.), *Arbeiterkulturen zwischen Alltag und Politik* (Vienna, 1986), pp.
155–197, esp. 163, 165, 178ff.

[45] See Göhre, *Drei Monate Fabrikarbeiter*, pp. 76ff. In other industrial branches of industry,
such as mining, the "physicality" of factory work and life in the workplace has likewise
received little attention – or has even been regarded as a quasi-taboo topic; but cf. F.-J.
Brüggemeier, *Leben vor Ort*, pp. 138ff.; and for a more fundamental treatment of related
questions, W. Kaschuba, "Volkskultur und Arbeiterkultur als symbolische Ordnungen", in
Lüdtke, *Alltagsgeschichte*, pp. 191–223, esp. 205ff., and in English translation: Lüdtke, *The
History of Everyday Life.*

[46] M. Th. W. Bromme, *Lebensgeschichte eines modernen Fabrikarbeiters* (1905, repr.
Frankfurt/M, 1971), p. 282; cf. Levenstein, *Arbeiterfrage*, pp. 97, 129.

others could go to extremes, even involving the stealing of tools.[47] Among other things, such theft reflected the severe competition between the men.[48] But it is also evident that pilfering on the job opened up a space for maneuver where more was at stake than just making sure you had a slight advantage when it came to pay. It was also a source of simple fun to "put one over" on a fellow worker by roughing him up or ripping him off. *Eigensinn* – in the sense of "having it one's own way" – could refuse *any* mode of compliance or participation, even in the face of all expectations raised by (political) alternatives for a new or "better" social order.[49]

Eigensinn's physicality created brief respites, spaces of at least a few moments when a worker could be *bei sich* – "by and for himself" – brusquely turning his back(side), so to speak, on the others. Isolated individual distancing was not uncommon, manifested in daydreaming or taking an unauthorized break. Yet here too, distinctions remained fuzzy: "turning off" or "tuning out", withdrawal could lead to a breach of regulations, for the most part unspectacular, such as during the risky cleaning of operating machinery with its potential for accidents. More ostentatious "nonsense" was also possible, like trying one's hand at a gymnastic feat, clowning around perched on a transmission belt up near the ceiling. *Eigensinn* was always ambiguous, not just divisive: it also opened up options for togetherness. Obstinate physical acts reproduced and reconfirmed the social hierarchy between older and younger men – for example, between the semi-skilled and apprentices or those assigned to do the donkey work. It was a demonstration of "masculinity". At the same time, they created situations of mutual perception and recognition: the next time round a

---

[47] Regarding the stealing of tools by fellow workers, see reports contained in biographical accounts put together by the Gutehoffnungshütte mill in Oberhausen in the 1930s using interviews with retired workers, cf. Haniel Archive, GHH 40016/9 and my "Cash, Coffee-Breaks, Horseplay", p. 82. By contrast, the widespread practice of "ripping stuff off", apparently regarded by Hamburg dockworkers as a legitimate form of compensatory (re-)appropriation, was not directed against one's "own people", cf. M. Grüttner, "Unterklassenkriminalität in Hamburg. Güterberaubungen im Hamburger Hafen, 1888–1923", in H. Reif (ed.), *Räuber, Volk und Obrigkeit. Studien zur Geschichte der Kriminalität in Deutschland seit dem 18. Jahrhundert* (Frankfurt/M, 1984), pp. 153–184.

[48] The increasingly detailed formulations of factory conduct codes over the years indicate that precisely in this area, there was an effort to stiffen regulations; for a more thorough treatment, see my "Die Ordnung der Fabrik", in Vierhaus, *Frühe Neuzeit – frühe Moderne?*, pp. 206–231, esp. 223, fn. 45.

[49] This corresponds to the particular form of "self-representation" that Luisa Passerini has examined among Turin industrial workers in the 1920s and '30s as a widespread alternative to an attitude aimed at changing society as a whole and oriented toward the level of state politics, cf. Passerini, *Fascism in Popular Memory. The Cultural Experience of the Turin Working Class* (Cambridge, 1987), pp. 22 f.: "On self-representation . . . is characterised by irreverence, *thanks to the ability to be detached from the existing order of things and even from oneself, and to reflect critically on, and laugh at, the current state of the world* [emphasis mine, A. L.]. It is an approach that turns the world on its head. . . . But it is acting nonetheless . . . we have promises, symbols, and stimulus to action, not real and lasting transformation of power relations".

former victim could easily cross over and become one of the "players". Everyone knew he was a potential target for prankishness.

Eigensinn was polymorphous, had multiple manifestations: moseying around the shop floor, momentarily "tuning out" or daydreaming. But it was especially evident in mutual body contact and teasing, joshing around, ragging. In doing this, workers did not directly suspend working operations; rather, they just allowed them to "run on", "letting them go", as it were. Changes brought about by "efficiency" measures in the work place had little or no impact on these everyday practices.[50]

Scholarly (and would-be learned) observers of "folk life" in the late eighteenth century believed the great majority of farmers, craftsmen and the propertyless in rural and urban Germany evinced a dogged "obstinacy", a willful stubborness they termed *Eigensinn*. Such behavior was permissible, but only among children.[51] Adults could not give in to the "enjoyment of the brief moment", they weren't supposed to get upset if their wishes were thwarted. Such "dangerous bad habits" had to be knocked out of children. It was imperative to promote physical and mental disciplining by constant admonishment and continuous constraint. Only in that way would "human goodness" find its proper expression in daily life.[52]

From this historical perspective, *Eigensinn* involved a particular kind of physicality – gestures and gesticulations commonly associated with a tight-lipped unwillingness to communicate. It was thus akin to that mode of taciturn behavior often interpreted as "dim-wittedness".[53] Such "dullards" were socially awkward, never found the right word, and were unable to participate in social intercourse. Blushing and lowering one's glance were considered to be the unmistakable signs of thick-headedness. "Dim-wittedness" revealed a lack of social skills, an inability to function in

---

[50] Cf. Lüdtke, 'Deutsche Qualitätsarbeit''', pp. 190ff. There is likewise no parallel here to the suggestion by M. Seidman that the numerous forms of hidden and inconspicuous appropriations or evasive action, ranging from factory sabotage to refusal to work or restraint on the job, should be interpreted as proof for the existence of a *fundamental* orientation of "workers against work". Seidman overlooks the variety of concrete modes of behavior and the various forms of independent interpretation of factory work and serial production. Yet see idem, *Workers against Work: Labor in Paris and Barcelona During the Popular Fronts* (Berkeley, 1991), pp. 170, 188, 231ff., 313ff. Expressive forms of physicality underwent change *outside* the factory workplace, especially in connection with mass sports – not just for the participating athletes, but for the spectators (overwhelmingly male) as well, see R. Lindner, "Die Sportbegeisterung", in U. Jeggle *et al.* (eds.), *Volkskultur in der Moderne* (Reinbek, 1986), pp. 249–259, esp. 252.

[51] But note the references to folktale traditions in which the wish is that "refractory" children might die rather than be so "doggedly obstinate", cf. O. Negt and A. Kluge, *Geschichte und Eigensinn* (Frankfurt/M, 1981), pp. 765ff.

[52] Cf. L. Sulzer, *Versuch von der Erziehung und Unterweisung der Kinder* (Göttingen, 1748), cited in K. Rutschky, *Schwarze Pädagogik* (Frankfurt/M, 1968), pp. 25ff.

[53] G. Stanitzek, *"Blödigkeit". Beschreibungen des Individuums im 18. Jahrhundert* (Tübingen, 1989).

normal society. "Dullards" tended to be modest, and their bashful diffid-
ence could at times be interpreted as a naiveté meant to please, a first
accommodating step in the direction of willing obeisance. However, *Eigensinn* could also turn into aggressive contrariness. The refractory Silesian
peasants described by the popular philosopher Christian Garve remained
motionless and taciturn in direct confrontation with their manorial lord.
Yet hardly had he turned his back then they burst out laughing, mimicking
his actions, and apparently did not take the "master" very seriously.[54]

Two characteristics link the "manual-laboring classes" at the end of the
eighteenth century with the industrial working class in the late nineteenth
(or mid-twentieth) century. First, there is a fundamental continuity in the
importance accorded to physical exertion – strength and "muscle" remain
in high demand. Second, the forms of forced collectivity in work teams
have been retained over the centuries. Both in craft workshops of the
distant past and on the work teams in industrial factories, workers were
generally cramped together in close physical proximity. Fellow workers
were literally unavoidable, their proximity occasionally becoming downright insufferable.

Joshing and highly physical "ragging" interpreted, reflected (and indeed
"processed') the various work operations on the shop floor. Boisterousness
also had a verbal component; abuse and brutally "affectionate" forms of
address were all "part of the game". But most important were the tactile
dimensions: physicality and direct bodily contact. These were a constant
element in agricultural work, small workshops,[55] small-scale and larger
factories. In this regard, one can postulate a singular species of Braudelian
"longue durée". The experience of manual labor in workshops and factories was given special expression in the *Eigensinn* of the workers
themselves.

Eigensinn and Resistance?

Eigensinn is generally conceived to be a subcategory of resistance or lack
of cooperation. In the predominant perspective, historical modes of
behavior swing between two poles: obedience and submission on the one
hand, uncooperativeness and open resistance on the other.[56] By contrast,

[54] Chr. Garve, "Über den Charakter der schlesischen Bauern und ihre Haltung gegen die
Regierung (1786/96)", in K. Wölfel (ed.), Chr. Garve, *Popularphilosophische Schriften*, vol.
2 (Stuttgart, 1974), pp. 799–1026, here p. 859f.
[55] On manual trades, see R. Wissell, *Des Alten Handwerks Recht und Gewohnheit*, 2nd. rev.
ed., 6 vols (Berlin, 1971–1988); A. Grießinger, *Das symbolische Kapital der Ehre*
(Frankfurt/M, 1982); cf. R. Darnton, "Workers' Revolt: The Great Cat Massacre of the Rue
Saint Severin", in R. Darnton, *The Great Cat Massacre and Other Episodes of French Cultural History* (London, 1984), pp. 75–104.
[56] J. Peters generally agrees to this framework, see his "Eigensinn und Widerstand im Alltag.
Abwehrverhalten ostelbischer Bauern unter Refeudalisierungsdruck", *Jahrbuch für Wirt-*

an analysis centered on *Eigensinn* explores a complex realm of behavior
beyond such black-and-white, "either–or" juxtapositions. Workers tended
to ignore broader practical calculations in their efforts to be "by themselves" or "together with their buddies". The implementation of
cooperation, the inculcation of respect for older workers or those who
"set the tone" took priority over strategies aimed at some personal advantage, such as recognition by more distant superiors or an improvement in
individual earnings.

Yet there were limits to the applicability of team logic. An individual
worker might try to be completely "by himself": through a variety of
means: by "tuning out" or attempts to "escape" from the confining presence of the others, by "fooling around" at his bench or concealing information about the degree of material hardness during shearing operations or
changes in transmission ratios on the lathe. In such situations, the main
aim was not to earn the respect of other workers or get something in
return, but to generate elbowroom and distance oneself from the immediate environment. Bodily contact and physical proximity apparently motivated workers to try again and again to gain some space and to be left
alone. This form of obstinacy was not resistance.

Eigensinn was not intentionally directed against the factory code or the
obligations of work-place cameraderie. Social and power-related constraints were not attacked head-on, but sidestepped or ignored. It was not
a warding off of time as such, but rather an obstinate insistence on one's
own time and space – sometimes in unobtrusive silence, occasionally in
boisterous rowdiness – which emerges as the intrinsic expression of a personal sense of how things should be.

Yet here too, a variety of transitions remained a constant possibility.
Thus, even in a field of social forces charged with recalcitrance, individual
and group actions against the bosses "upstairs" might arise.[57] For example,

---

schaftsgeschichte, 1991/II, pp. 85–103; at the same time, however, he convincingly shows the
balanced importance of "action and devotion" in peasant behavior in reconstructing the
everyday life of estate-dependent peasants in Brandenburg in the eighteenth century. In the
light of this description, the existence side-by-side – and the often smooth interchange – of
careful calculation on the one hand, and lack of planning, on the other, becomes quite
plausible.

[57] In this connection, see the characterization of individually "unobtrusive", frequently sub-
dued or even taciturn forms of confronting intrusions and attempts at control originating
"from above" in J. Scott, *Domination and the Arts of Resistance: Hidden Transcripts* (New
Haven and London, 1990), esp. pp. 183ff. Scott views symbolic actions as being closely
intertwined with practices of refusal or appropriation. Explosive outbursts – at celebrations,
for example – do not impede individual actions, but rather serve to pave the road for them.
Such activity includes the avoidance of tax demands, the forbidden planting of a small plot
of rubber trees, ignoring various rules and regulations, and illegal consumption, ranging from
the theft of food for one's own personal needs to the stealing of small amounts of the harvest.
In his analysis, a decisive aspect is that these "hidden-unobtrusive" interpretations and practices do not function as a "safety valve" for releasing pent-up pressure against economic or
authority-related constraints and compulsion (though I think the practices are seen here too

when master craftsmen or foremen resorted to the familiar "intimate" form of address instead of the formal pronoun of respect (i.e., "*Du*" rather than "*Sie*"), workers would respond loudly in kind, replying to their superiors with that same disrespectful "*Du*" – if they were in fact paying any attention at all. Joint action was also an option in the machine-manufacturing shop, as Bromme reported. Workers there were normally on an "each man for himself" basis. However when pay cuts were instituted, joint action could be organized in suprisingly short time – for example, a demand by workers to have the time spent cleaning up the lathes calculated as part of formal working hours.[58]

Eigensinn and Self-Discipline

Open clashes with direct or indirect attempts to control people on the shop floor, or obstinate efforts by workers to establish some distance between themselves, both had one basic aim: to resist the encroachments of superiors. Self-discipline was unavoidable in this context.[59] The constant efforts to deal with (and rework) disciplinary demands "in one's own way" had certain consequences. Individual attempts to "escape" from the restricting ambience of the other men or "tuning out" was one mode; trying on occasion to act in unison with fellow workers was the other. If quotas in team piecework were to be maintained or reduced, then workers had to discuss the issue and arrive at some concrete agreement. But even the emphatic act of "going the limit and beyond", "no holds barred", i.e., of excess, "*dépense*" or "breaking out" of the confined togetherness were bound up with the rules of the work team or the factory environment.

much as a product of the contraints!). Rather, he postulates the operation of a kind of "infrapolitics". In Scott's view, it does not supplant resistance or resistiveness, but functions rather as a necessary precondition for it. Scott's analysis is largely based on ethnological research in rural Malaysia. On English farm workers in the twentieth century and their brand of *Eigensinn*, recognizable in modes of "deference", cf. H. Newby, *The Deferential Worker. A Study of Farm Workers in East Anglia* (Harmondsworth, 1977). Strategies of popular resistance, evasions, ruses and "*ways of using* imposed systems" in popular culture, an "ethics of *tenacity* (countless ways of refusing to accord the established order the status of a law, a meaning or a fatality)" are intriguingly explored in M. de Certeau, *The Practice of Everyday Life* (Berkeley, 1984, quotes pp. 18, 26.). See also J. Fiske, *Understanding Popular Culture* (London, 1989), pp. 32ff. On the synchronicity of evasion, participation and an inconspicuous process of repeated withdrawal, manifested in the case of a "middle-class child" growing up in the era of German fascism, see P. Brückner, *Das Abseits als sicherer Ort. Kindheit und Jugend zwischen 1933 und 1945* (Berlin, 1980). On the multiply layered dimensions of fields of force and power strategies, see the very thought-provoking study by W. Sofsky and R. Paris, *Figurationen sozialer Macht* (Opladen, 1991).

[58] Bromme, *Lebensgeschichte*, pp. 259f.

[59] On self-control, self-constraint, the psychological instruments of self-compulsion and their formation within a kind of "counter-move" against the monopolization of violence by the state, see N. Elias, *Über den Prozeß der Zivilisation* (1937), vol. 2, 2nd ed. (Munich and Zurich, 1969), pp. 316ff.

And such rules had to be respected. At the very least, it was not possible or appropriate simply to ignore them in every instance. If recognition was to be achieved, staking out a more permanent space of one's own, the proper degree of "teasing" and "ripping off" had to be maintained, not going too far. There were limits. Excesses alternated with self-discipline.

This was especially true of all attempts to implement alternative modes of behavior through formal organizations. The "mass turnout" called for by Social Democracy around 1910 during its campaign for universal suffrage in Prussia propagated the "step of the masses" (*"Massentritt"*). This solemn and well-ordered way of marching along should differ from the "lockstep" of the military, because participants of Social Democratic demonstrations would avoid any machine-like presentation. However, the "step of the masses" was not predicated solely on an expected mutual agreement arrived at among left-wing workers.[60] More was required. This potentially revolutionary mode of discipline necessitated a strict regime of subordination. Such subordination was no longer justified by reference to the will of a monarch or the "state", but was nonetheless regarded as an indispensable sacrifice for achieving a "better" future. Moreover, future utopias were expressly defined in terms of a discipline that may resemble a normal standard: namely the measured beat of a clock. Watches given as gifts by Social Democrats bore an engraved demand: "8 hours work – 8 hours sleep – 8 hours education". Even a more fun-oriented variant, which replaced education by "recreation", still stuck to that strict tripartite division: 8 full hours for recreation.[61]

Multiple layers and limits to linkage:
comparisons "From the Bottom Up"

The historical reconstruction of the ways of life prevailing among industrial workers discloses a variety of modes of perceptions, experience and actual practice. In particular, it highlights the presence of multiple layering. What one discovers is not a single and unified experience, but rather a synchrony of diverse and even contradictory elements. This attempt at reconstruction is context-specific. The spatial field is comprised of individual firms and factories, localities or neighborhoods, even entire regions. Monographic or case studies are assembled, often sketching painstakingly accurate pictures of particular situations or circumstances. But how can these individual images be linked together? Or is this often voiced demand for interconnectedness inappropriate?

---

[60] See the detailed discussion of this, with numerous examples culled from speeches and the Social Democratic press, in B. J. Warneken, "'Die friedliche Gewalt des Volkswillens'. Muster und Deutungsmuster von Demonstrationen im Deutschen Kaiserreich", in B. J. Warneken (ed.), *Massenmedium Straße. Zur Kulturgeschichte der Demonstrationen* (Frankfurt/M and New York, 1991), pp. 97-119.

[61] P. Schirmbeck, comp., *Vom Beginn der Industrialisierung bis 1945*, 2nd pr. (Rüsselsheim, 1981), p. 36; on the variant of "recreation", see the 1894 example in: D. Mühlberg (ed.), *Proletariat. Kultur und Lebensweise im 19. Jahrhundert* (Leipzig, 1986), p. 262.

Since the late eighteenth century, the course of European social history has been dominated by a "double revolution" (E. Hobsbawm): sociopolitical movements for emancipation on the one hand, and processes of capitalization on the other. Seen from this macro-perspective, studies of individual localities can seem rather parochial: the focus is too low, too close to the ground. After all, the historical process appears to be identical with the formation of supralocal overarching structures and entities, especially those of class and bureaucracy. In this connection, it is by no means surprising that Jürgen Kocka has repeatedly stressed the need for a *synthetic* view.[62] The guiding question in such a synthesis concerns the nature of class formation in what Kocka terms "nationally constituted societies".[63]

Yet it may be argued that the dominant notions of "class" fail to do empirical justice to the dynamic character of industrial labor. A veritable patchwork of mixed modes of behavior, based on both cool calculation and obstinate *Eigensinn*, are reduced to a dichotomous "either–or": the inclusion or exclusion of generally large-scale social groups. A similar problem arises when the formation of the nation-state is identified as centrally influencing the history of the nineteenth and twentieth centuries. In his comparative microstudy of two industrial localities in western Germany in the nineteenth century, Erhard Lucas has convincingly shown that numerous differentiating factors were at play. Wage labor in Duisburg-Hamborn differed from that in Remscheid not only in terms of the dominant industry: large iron and steel mills and mines vs. small-scale iron manufacture. Other key differences stemmed from worker origin (locally born or immigrant), differences in dialect, residential style and neighborhood type (company settlements in Hamborn, small individual homes in Remscheid), church affiliation and religious denomination. In contrast, the dimension of nation-state did not play any pervasively significant role. Both towns were, after all, part of the German Reich, Prussia (more specifically its Rhine Province), and municipal authority for both rested in the same administrative center in Düsseldorf.[64]

---

[62] Kocka, *Lohnarbeit*, pp. 15f.; Kocka, "Sozialgeschichte zwischen Struktur und Erfahrung. Die Herausforderung der Alltagsgeschichte", in J. Kocka, *Geschichte und Aufklärung* (Göttingen, 1989), pp. 29–44, here 42ff.

[63] Kocka, *Sozialgeschichte*, pp., 135ff., 171; Kocka, "Probleme einer europäischen *Geschichte* in komparativer Sicht", in Kocka, *Geschichte und Aufklärung*, pp. 21–28, here 25; Kocka, "Sozialgeschichte zwischen Struktur und Erfahrung", ibid., here pp. 42ff. For an international comparison of societal configurations, see B. Moore, *The Social Origins of Dictatorship and Democracy* (Boston, 1966). The usual type of comparative investigation is characterized by questions regarding similarities and differences between individual features or specific social segments and/or forms of perception and action, cf. the penetrating studies by I. Steinisch, *Arbeitszeitverkürzung und sozialer Wandel. Der Kampf um die Achtstundenschicht in der deutschen und amerikanischen Eisen-und Stahlindustrie 1880–1929* (Berlin and New York, 1986) and F. Boll, *Arbeitskämpfe und Gewerkschaften in Deutschland, England und Frankreich. Ihre Entwicklung vom 19. zum 20. Jahrhundert* (Bonn, 1992).

[64] Cf. also the example of Düsseldorf: local and immigrant industrial workers supported the Catholic workers' organizations, but many of those with upgraded skills joined the ranks of

Even two generations later, under German fascism, regional features were far more salient than mere ideological/propagandistic window dressing.[65] At the same time, the influence of (party-)political "camps" and "social–moral milieus" apparently affected only political activists.[66] The orientation of the overwhelming majority of the population was in terms of region, locality and especially immediate family. The microgeographical levels of residential street and neighborhood (albeit with certain reservations) also played a role. In this respect the experiences of most individuals were ambivalent and mixed. They oscillated between much-welcome support during emergencies and often near-total obtrusive control of daily behavior in the public sphere (e.g., on streets and in bars).[67] Thus, the respective degree of penetration and salience of national, regional and local institutions, orientation patterns, zones and forms of conflict must be examined empirically in the context of wage labor, its fields of force and spaces for action – such salience cannot be postulated a priori.

The painstaking historical reconstruction of wage labor indicates that autonomous control and control by others were not mutually exclusive phenomena. But if wage labor was in fact not clearly and conclusively "determined" in its content, as presumed by the customary assumptions and "grand" theories on industrialization, then a central feature of all such macroscopic conceptions appears open to question: namely the notion that *conditions* for action were the decisive factor. If constraints on action and temptations to act are viewed not as fixed "givens" but as fluent moments in a spiral which moves from perceiving and interpreting reality to acting

Social Democracy, cf. M. Nolan, *Social Democracy and Society: Working-Class Radicalism in Düsseldorf 1890–1920* (Cambridge, 1981), pp. 42ff., 113ff.

[65] In this connection, see the large-scale project "Lebensgeschichte und Sozialkultur im Ruhrgebiet 1930–1960", including various published studies: L. Niethammer (ed.), *"Die Jahre weiß man nicht, wo man die heute hinsetzen soll". Faschismuserfahrungen im Ruhrgebiet 1930–1960* (Berlin and Bonn, 1983); L. Niethammer (ed.)., *"Hinterher merkt man, daß es richtig war, daß es schiefgegangen ist"* (Berlin and Bonn, 1983); L. Niethammer and A. v. Plato (eds.), *"Wir kriegen jetzt andere Zeiten"* (Berlin and Bonn, 1985); see also F. J. Henne, "A German Path to Fordism: The Socio-Economic Transformation of a Region: The Bergische Land and the Sauerland, 1930–1960" (Ph.D., University of Chicago, in progress).

[66] M. R. Lepsius, "Parteiensystem und Sozialstruktur: zum Problem der Demokratisierung der Gesellschaft", in W. Abel *et al.* (eds.), *Wirtschaft, Geschichte und Wirtschaftsgeschichte, Festschrift für F. Lütge* (Stuttgart, 1966), pp. 371–393, here 383f.; on "fuzziness" in respect to "camps" and "milieus" and/or their synchronism, see A. v. Plato, "'Ich bin mit allen gut ausgekommen'. Oder: war die Ruhrarbeiterschaft vor 1933 in politische Lager gespalten?", in Niethammer, *'Die Jahre weiß man nicht . . . '*, pp. 31–65, esp. 60ff.

[67] Cf. B. Parisius, *Lebenswege im Revier, Erlebnisse und Erfahrungen zwischen Jahrhundertwende und Kohlenkrise – erzählt von Frauen und Männern aus Borbeck* (Essen, 1984); E. Roberts' work remains highly provocative regarding neighborhood, since his approach rejects romanticization, see Roberts, *A Woman's Place*, pp. 189ff. There have been few attempts to date to examine the public spheres of "free" or commercial amusement (in contrast to conviviality in voluntary associations), but note the bulk of contributions in D. Kift (ed.), *Kirmes – Kneipe – Kino. Arbeiterkultur im Ruhrgebiet zwischen Kommerz und Kontrolle (1850–1904)* (Paderborn, 1992).

upon it and – in turn – to perceiving the changed state of things, the ruptures and "holes" in the "web" of historical processes emerge in a new light. Social reality is multiply layered. Consequently, I believe it is imperative that we recognize just how narrowly one-dimensional the supposedly "big questions" in historical analysis, such as the formation of social classes and the state, really are. That is, they alone are an insufficient basis for historical reconstruction.[68]

The alternatives are still rather fragmentary. For the time being, we are traversing uncharted territory, nothing is certain. Yet it is wise to avoid falling prey to the type of "anxiety reaction"[69] prevalent in such situations, the reassuring regression to what is tried, tested and familiar. One option is to focus our attention on the historical *subjects* themselves, exploring them in the context of their *immediate* modes of action and expression (so that what may appear incompatible does not have to be categorized as "contradictory"!). It may be that there is a kind of fundamental flaw inherent in perspectives where social institutions, levels and actors are viewed in terms of presumed functional relations and symbolic resonances. The assumption that all phenomena are interconnected, inter-mediating with each other, seems to be a distinctively European legacy of German philosophical idealism.[70] In my view, an approach that leaves open the question of the mediation between or the mutual interconnectedness of social phenomena (and thus likewise their presumed continuity) is more serviceable for research.[71] Such a position is doubtlessly contestable, and fraught with

---

[68] Note the references by H. Boll, "Verlust vergleichender Deutungsfähigkeit? Bemerkungen zu einigen Neuerscheinungen komparativer Sozial- und Arbeiterbewegungsgeschichte", *Archiv für Sozialgeschichte*, 28 (1988), pp. 426–459. F. Lenger, "Beyond Exceptionalism: Notes on the Artisanal Phase of the Labour Movement in France, England, Germany and the United States", *International Review of Social History*, 36 (1992), pp. 1–23 provides an example of a comprehensive panorama, including both sociostructural and cultural elements, though with reference to the level of societal comparisons of "class formation" (moreover, there is no intention to discuss the conceptual or theoretical nature of comparison as a method).

[69] Georges Devereux, *Angst und Methode in den Verhaltenswissenschaften* (Munich, 1973).

[70] This also applies to Pierre Bourdieu's suggestion (which has enjoyed a considerable support echo) that specific "forms of habitus" – i.e., a "subjective, though not individual system of internalized structures, shared schemata of perception, thinking and action" be assumed as a "precondition for every . . . perception" – based on the assumption that "everything has already been mediated", cf. P. Bourdieu, *Sozialer Sinn. Kritik der theoretischen Vernunft* (Frankfurt/M, 1987 [French 1980]), p. 112. See likewise Bourdieu's emphatic (though systematically unelaborated) comment that habitus is "caught up in a process of incessant transformation", idem, "Antworten auf einige Einwände", in K. Eder (ed.), *Klassenlage, Lebensstil und kulturelle Praxis. Theoretische und empirische Beiträge zur Auseinandersetzung mit Pierre Bourdieus Klassentheorie* (Frankfurt/M, 1989), pp. 395–410, esp. 406 f.

[71] Cf. relevant suggestions by Michel Foucault, for example in his *Sexualität und Wahrheit*, vol. 1 (Frankfurt/M, 1977 [Paris, 1976]), esp. pp. 113ff.; references to the "ubiquitous presence of power" do not presuppose a general context embracing all social levels, strategies and tactics; rather, in the discourse of sexuality, power and knowledge are considered "discontinuous segments", ibid., p. 122. On ruptures in the continuities, see also Foucault's

inconsistency. But perhaps that very inconsistency can help to disclose something of the past's irreverent discontinuities, open structures which we tend only too often to homogenize and accommodate to our own needs and views in historical reconstruction.

The reconstruction of historical practice reveals life-lines containing many breaks. Upon analysis, what you discover are fragments, i.e., synchronisms of participation (such as in the "national revolution" of the Nazis) and *simultaneous* attempts to maintain individual distance, e.g., in attitudes toward Nazi fund-raising drives or in the (admittedly rarer) decision to oppose the wishes of a party functionary. Profiles emerge of individuals who were quite unheroic.[72] The lines they move in are not straight; they twist and convolute, pausing, reversing – jumping not only forward, but unpredictably moving off at angles sideways or backwards unpredictably.

What this meant in the industrial work place was that dissimilar experiences did not result in competing behavioral orientations necessarily at odds with each other. Resistance to attempts by foremen to increase speed could go hand-in-hand with concurrence in their demands for a "respectable" level of output or affirmation of their esteem for "high-quality workmanship".[73] It was by no means inevitable for such differences to generate tensions or conflict situations. Analysis shows that mutual aid among fellow workers or helping out a buddy who felt momentarily indisposed could be succeeded fairly rapidly by massive reciprocal animosity; sometimes the very same persons were involved. This multilayered patchwork of *unconnected* preferences and dislikes even underlay what workers "shared in common". Distance and cooperation, animosity and solidarity were never far apart, and certainly were not mutually exclusive, even vis-à-vis the same individuals.

Unsuspected breaks and discontinuities in behavior, a factor of incalculability in their interaction – is that then the upshot? Behind increased levels of factory discipline, for example, there was always another layer that called everything into question once again – such as *Eigensinn*. Did

fulminating sketch *Vom Licht des Krieges zur Geburt der Geschichte* (Berlin, 1976 [recorded Paris, 1976, no French or English edition]).

[72] On the philosophical debate, cf. H. Hrachovec, *Vermessen. Studien über Subjektivität* (Frankfurt/M, 1989); K. Meyer-Drawe, *Illusionen von Autonomie. Diesseits von Ohnmacht und Allmacht des Ich* (Munich, 1990); the volume by M. Carrithers, S. Collins and S. Lukes (eds.), *The Category of the Person: Anthropology, Philosophy, History* (Cambridge, 1985) revolves around the notion that there are universal connections to a "self" in all socially and culturally specific refractions, and that "individualistic" formulations appear to regulate all "Western" critique of the subject; cf. also C. A. Lutz and L. Abu-Lughod (eds.), *Language and the Politics of Emotion* (Cambridge, 1990).

[73] In this connection, cf. the broad longitudinal investigation of literary, natural-scientific and engineering conceptions and ideas of industrial labor and their gradual elaboration into the notion of "German work" by J. Campbell, *Joy in Work, German Work: The National Debate, 1800–1945* (Princeton, 1989).

historical subjects always have some open options, "not yet realized" possibilities for self-expression, for demonstrating where they really stood? If so, then any attempt to derive a type from a set of regularities would be faulty deduction. Wouldn't it be more sensible to follow an approach that does not try to ignore multiple layers and ambiguities, but seeks instead to put them to specific historiographic use?

Modes of behavior in the work place, such as the degree and type of force present in behavior vis-à-vis fellow workers, superiors or subordinates, indicate more than just the complex of constraints and attractions of wage-labor and factory work. Rather, there is always a more extensive sociocultural force field involved, encompassing the times, rhythms and sites of work and non-work. Analysis should thus here focus on examining the identifying marks, establishing the "signatures" of various force fields – and not on interrelating the individual facets. One can determine where contours overlap and differ. The density of networks, as well as the blank spots, could be utilized as a yardstick for establishing similarity and difference. Such a tack would facilitate "comparisons from the bottom up".[74] Moreover, it would permit new angles in approaching the pivotal question of how subjectivity is actually constituted. And that is undoubtedly as much a part of the complex of the so-called "big questions" in historiography as is the formation of the "modern state" or the industrial world.

Religion and the military: order and orderliness as fulfillment?

Attempts to create distance and pursue *Eigensinn* did not fundamentally rule out the possibility of brief or longer-term participation in a political party or trade union, engagement in forms of supralocal organizing. And even inside organizations, many members behaved in refractory ways reflecting their basic hard-nosed *Eigensinn*. The same individuals exploited

---

[74] The prerequisite for this are studies on spatially and socially delimited configurations of work and non-work, population, family and relatives, public spheres and realms of privacy, cf., for example, L. R. Berlanstein, *The Working People of Paris, 1871–1914* (Baltimore and London, 1984) or W. H. Sewell Jr., "Uneven Development, the Autonomy of Politics, and the Dockworkers of Nineteenth-Century Marseille", *American Historical Review*, 93 (1988), pp. 604–637. Another special comparative perspective focusing on secular processes (in particular within a global context) is richly suggestive, namely Michael Mann's magisterial studies of power. Mann argues that societies consist of numerous overlapping social and spatial power networks that lay siege, so to speak, one to one another. Consequently, society cannot be conceptualized as a monolayered entity clearly and unambiguously fixed and defined by external boundaries. There are no sharply separable subsystems or dimensions. It is likewise impossible to proceed from clearly defined ascriptions or defining and justifying relations (in the sense of a source of "final authority'). If the claim of totality is empty and hollow, it is also incorrect to postulate that social structures are antecedent to action by persons or groups. Mann's main stress is directed against the supposition of any homogeneity of "intra-social" relations; such a homogeneity is conjured up, however, in speaking about "society" as such. Cf. M. Mann, *The Sources of Social Power*, vol. 1 (Cambridge, 1986), esp. chap. 1, "Societies as organized power networks", pp. 1–33.

different modalities for self-expression, depending on the situation or moment. The ensembles of expressive means crystallized into multilayered "force fields". These included patterns of orientation that were regulated "outside" group-specific or regional frameworks, and which were designed to "refract" such identifications: i.e., religious, church-related and military dimensions.

Religious dimensions: The pronounced "disdain for preachers and parsons" that the young pastor Göhre encountered in Chemnitz in 1890 did not reflect religious abstinence. He found there was appreciable sensitivity for religious rites and ritual, especially "proper" funerals, and he heard expressions of "respect and reverence for Jesus Christ".[75] Although socialist and church institutions struggled against each other, locked in a battle for hearts and minds, the call by church groups and individual clerics for secular justice held a fascination even for the most dedicated opponents of organized religion. And the component of salvation in the Social Democratic "utopian state of the future" apparently appealed to certain "religious" or "spiritual" needs, even among those who despised anything associated with the church.[76]

The ethos of secular fulfillment of duty characteristic of Protestant clergy (and by no means alien to the Roman Catholic church) was echoed in Social-Democratic rhetoric about the responsibility of socialists in struggling on behalf of the downtrodden and oppressed. On the other hand, religiously charged self-definitions sometimes served to harden the lines of incompatability between workers' organizations. Social Democrats considered Catholics superstitious and, in cases of doubt, readily submissive to any authority. It made no difference whatsoever if those Catholics were workers. Vice versa, many Catholics, quite apart from their own class position, regarded the "reds" as callous materialists unfamiliar with or opposed to the "piety of works".[77] At the same time, the Bible was undoubtedly read as a programme for secular justice here on earth. However, it was not important to keep the two spheres separate: Jesus and William Tell could both be celebrated as literary paragons, as in the thinking of a miner in Essen who, since the 1920s, had been an active member of both the Union of Christian Miners and a Catholic miners' association.[78]

---

[75] Göhre, *Drei Monate*, pp. 157ff., esp. 176, 180, 190.

[76] On the concepts, though not their scope and range in social and everyday practical contexts, cf. L. Hölscher, *Weltgericht oder Revolution. Protestantische und sozialistische Zukunftsvorstellungen im deutschen Kaiserreich* (Stuttgart, 1989); on the distribution and intensity of magical practices specifically in working-class circles, cf. the first-hand report by a Protestant minister who ministered to a parish in Magdeburg, *Huschenbett: Volksaberglaube. Ein Bericht aus der Gegenwart nebst Beurteilung* (Magdeburg, 1925).

[77] W. Spohn, "Religion and Working-Class Formation in Imperial Germany 1871–1914", *Politics and Society*, 19 (1991), pp. 109–32, esp. 111ff.

[78] R. Noltenius (ed.), *Alltag, Traum und Utopie. Lesegeschichten – Lebensgeschichten* (Essen, 1988), pp. 34–43; cf. Parisius, *Lebenswege*, pp. 92ff.

Military dimensions: Until 1918, all males, even those given a deferment or released from service, had to confront and deal with the anxieties and sense of fulfilment associated with military service, at least prophylactically. Military service meant an abrupt break with accustomed routines of everyday life, one's neighborhood and locality. That rupture was rendered especially painful by the practices of bullying and harassment experienced as a recruit. However, certain previous modes of orientation were not completely extinguished in the barracks; some were given a new "energy charge" – especially obedience, physical discipline and an "immaculate external appearance". Moreover, uniforms and the men who worn them enjoyed widespread popularity beyond barracks walls. A "veteran" non-com was considered a "darn good catch" for female wage-laborers, such as maids or cooks. In the words of the poet, not only "when the music sounds" did "Gertrude and Kathy and Gretchen . . . glance out from gable, gate and garden".[79]

For males, the military was the only phase in their lives when, in exemplary fashion, they could directly link their own physical efforts and accomplishments with the lofty aim of the preservation of the Reich and the Kaiser's condescension.[80] After one's stint in the military, if not before, "service" and its "discipline" often became a veritable measuring-rod for assessing personal everyday existence – even when one's own social class afforded little formal recognition to such national service. In any event, the pointed critique of militarism voiced by Social Democracy – and its constant attacks on maltreatment of soldiers by their superiors – should not mislead us into falsely concluding that every wage-laborer who had

[79] D. v. Liliencron's poem "Die Musik kommt" does not express jubilation, but is rather the consciously ironic description of a familiar street scene with youthful marching soldiers and pretty girls looking on curiously; cf. D. v. Liliencron, "Die Musik kommt", in L. Reiners (ed.), *Der ewige Brunnen. Ein Hausbuch deutscher Dichtung* (Munich, 1955), pp. 474f., freely trans. here by W. Templer.

[80] Differences between regional "workers' cultures" and associated differential compliance with authority are underlined by M. Cattaruzza, "Das Kaiserbild in der Arbeiterschaft am Beispiel der Werftarbeiter in Hamburg und Stettin", in J. C. G. Röhl (ed.), *Der Ort Kaiser Wilhelms II in der deutschen Geschichte* (Munich, 1991), pp. 131–144; on the one hand, she stresses the more pronounced corporative conceptions prevalent among workers in Stettin, but on the other points to a fundamental acceptance of the monarchy and the emperor among Hamburg workers as well (the latter staged far more strikes). Over the years, their "attitude toward the state remained reserved, but was not hostile", ibid., p. 140; cf. also R. J. Evans (ed.), *Kneipengespräche im Kaiserreich. Stimmungsberichte der Hamburger Politischen Polizei, 1892–1914* (Reinbek, 1989), pp. 322ff. In contrast, A. v. Saldern stresses the mixed attitude present at the grass-roots level in Göttingen, consisting of a strong rejection of and disinterest in the (national) "state". It is significant, however, that the topics dealt with in the local party association always concerned matters "at a far remove" from the locality itself, and thus had no direct connection with local concrete realities, idem, *Auf dem Wege zum Arbeiter-Reformismus. Parteialltag in sozialdemokratischer Provinz, Göttingen 1870–1920* (Frankfurt/M, 1984), pp. 63ff.

ever donned a uniform was filled with nothing but rage and anger when
he looked back on his days down in barracks and out on the drilling
ground.

In his memoirs, Franz Rehbein, an agricultural laborer from eastern
Pomerania and later an active Social Democrat who had been in uniform
from 1887–1890, commented that "half the drills" had been a waste, superfluous; in his fond memory, apparently the other half had not been. August
Winnig, a construction worker and SPD member, writing some thirty years
after his experience in uniform (and ten years after his abandonment of
the ranks of Social Democracy), recalled: "The part I liked best was the
drilling, a regimen we were subject to very directly. I was astonished
to discover it wasn't so disagreeable after all. The more I mastered the
movements and rifle positions, the more I loved to drill. Not only did I
derive pleasure from doing a drill well myself – I also got just as great a
satisfaction out of it when others performed a nice snappy drill with their
rifles, or some other adroitly executed exercise".[81] Perhaps that same
"quality of workmanship" which Winnig and his fellow workers strived for
or valued in the industrial work place was also manifest in the analogous
"perfect" execution of a crack rifle drill.

The military's aim was to transform the formless multitude into a disciplined "mass man" – an organ capable of carrying out orders, deployable
at will. Public presentations of military units were characterized by demonstrating perfect order and subordination. Moreover, this form of public
self-presentation also increasingly started to have an impact on a variety
of social groups appearing in the public arena from the late nineteenth
century on, quite aside from what their specific interests or goals were.
Both the churches and the efforts by Social Democrats to organize an
"alternative culture" (Vernon Lidtke) adopted similar forms when temporarily occupying public space. At church fairs as well as on May Day,
workers' festive parades were patterned along the lines of the military: a
tightly disciplined marching column. Before 1914 and during the 1920s,
the close-order column appeared to be manifest proof attesting to the
seriousness of members and their organizational aims – evidence of the
concrete power of the church or party.[82] Taking part in the rites of a public

---

[81] August Winnig, *Der weite Weg* (Hamburg, 1932), pp. 70f.

[82] For varieties of Catholic organizing, cf. J. Mooser, "Volk, Arbeiter und Bürger in der
katholischen Öffentlichkeit des Kaiserreichs. Zur Sozial-und Funktionsgeschichte der
deutschen Katholikentage, 1871–1913", in H.-J. Puhle (ed.), *Bürger in der Gesellschaft der
Neuzeit* (Göttingen, 1991), pp. 259–273, here pp. 266ff.; see also the apparently self-
explanatory adoption of the pose and conduct of the soldier from the World War in the
"Red Ruhr Army"; on self-representation, cf. H. Marchwitza, *Sturm auf Essen* (Berlin,
1930). On Social Democracy in the 1920s, see G. Hauk, "'Armeekorps auf dem Wege zur
Sonne'. Einige Bemerkungen zur kulturellen Selbstdarstellung der Arbeiterbewegung", in
D. Petzina (ed.), *Fahnen, Fäuste, Körper* (Essen, 1986), pp. 69–89. Details indicate the
extent to which the military habitus provided the yardstick: note, for example, the (printed)
"Kommando-Kunde, für den Gau Oberbayern-Schwaben des Reichsbanners Schwarz-Rot-

demonstration of strength apparently also contained its own attractions for the participants, producing a sense of "pleasure" in the rigors of the close-order "drill" – laboriously practiced and finally perfected.

Politics

In a surprising formulation, Alexander Kluge termed politics the "enhanced intensity of every everyday feeling, every practice".[83] Seen from that perspective, *Politik* is not limited to a specific concrete area. Neither the regulation of "public affairs" nor the binding distribution of scarce resources is a defining characteristic. On the other hand, politics is not rooted in the dichotomous distinction between "friend" and "foe" (in the sense of Carl Schmitt). Nor is it definable in terms of action based on the division of labor – "politics as a profession" (Max Weber) – or institutions. Likewise, its core is not "interests associated with the distribution, maintenance or transfer of power" (Weber).[84] If politics – conceived as a constantly realizable "compression" or "intensification" of feeling – can

Gold" (Munich, 1931), p. 1: "The leadership must be in a position to direct the organization as if it were an individual man . . . "; at the same time, the "exercises [should not be allowed] to degenerate into dull and dreary military drills" (p. 2) – a warning that only makes sense viewed in connection with the fact that such "drills" often were precisely that: a kind of military exercise; Bundesarchiv Koblenz, NS 26/800. Usually ignored are, however, the ways in which women reacted to this, and how they often dealt with "military airs and graces" privately and in public, ranging from love affairs between soldiers and servant girls to the sending of small gifts, "tokens of love", to men at the front.

[83] A. Kluge, "Das Politische als Intensitätsgrad alltäglicher Gefühle", *Freibeuter*, 1 (1979), pp. 56–62, here 61; cf. A. Kluge and O. Negt, *Maßverhältnisse des Politischen* (Frankfurt/M, 1992), pp. 91ff.; what is involved here is *not* a "fixation on any individual experiencing of pleasure and individual death" – a view which Thanos Lipowatz criticizes in his thought-provoking analysis of subjectivity focusing on Lacan (and Freud), see T. Lipowatz, *Die Verleugnung des Politischen. Die Ethik des Symbolischen bei Jacques Lacan* (Weinheim and Berlin, 1986), above quote, p. 240. To be sure, Carl Schmitt has employed the notion of the "ultimate intensity of connectedness or separateness" in his writings about "the Political"; see C. Schmitt, *Der Begriff des Politischen* (Munich and Leipzig, 1932), p. 14. In contrast to the point made here, however, he argues that this "connectedness or separateness" is totally distinct from moral or aesthetical (or other) domains and judgements.

[84] M. Weber, "Politik als Beruf" (1919), in M. Weber, *Gesammelte Politische Schriften* (Tübingen, 1958), pp. 493–548, here 494; on the spectrum of diverse conceptions of what is politics, cf. for example, D. Berg-Schlosser and Th. Stammen, *Einführung in die Politikwissenschaft*, 5th ed. (Munich, 1992), pp. 22ff. Th. Lipowatz develops an especially intriguing analysis in *Die Verleugnung des Politischen*, arguing passionately for a distinction between "public" and "private" spheres. In classical political theory, this opposition was developed on the basis of the "law" (p. 196, see also pp. 172ff.) and facilitates that postulation of the subject not being identical with itself that the author supports (p. 18). However, he proceeds on the assumption that in attempts to overcome the separation between those spheres, the dimension of "the social" was hypothesized to be all-encompassing or all-penetrating. As I see it, that does not affect Negt/Kluge or this attempt either, because the basic supposition here is that there is an insoluble difference between what is individual and what is "social" (despite all the tensely charged relations, including gaps and ruptures).

be localized at all, then it is not at the level of groups or organizations. No: it is *individuals* who "make" politics. They are the ones who experience emotion; at the same time, they are the actors who relate to feelings in their daily practice, creating or suppressing them. Even though Kluge does not make specific mention of *Eigensinn*, it can be regarded as politics par excellence when viewed in his emotion-centered terms of analysis, a kind of "enhanced intensity of every everyday feeling, every practice".

In the investigation of everyday reality, the forms in which feeling and action are "intensified" appear to be highly diverse and complex. They do not exclude association with other forms of longer-term strategy or even dramatic action. Nonetheless, it is possible to distinguish among different "arenas" of politics.[85]

In their specific practices of appropriating "given" conditions for life and survival, individuals experience pleasure or suffering. "Intensifications" are often related to the more narrow socio-spatial confines of workshops or neighborhoods. In this sense, an *arena of everyday politics* is indeed a meaningful concept. This should be distinguished from a separate arena involving supralocal control mechanisms and networking, one in which the state becomes a central reference point as a symbol and institutional focus of "sociality". The unfolding of this *arena of formalized and state-oriented politics* is what is generally regarded as the realization and implementation of the "modern state".

The activities of (state) officials and administrations have altered the shape of the arena in which everyday politics is made and experienced. Notwithstanding all the fluctuations and ruptures, such activities have increased markedly since the late seventeenth century, at least in central and western Europe. Nonetheless, micrological investigations indicate that everyday politics was not pared down or "absorbed" by the actions of these regulating authorities or the measures imposed by policing agents. On the contrary: it was everyday politics that expanded, increasingly codetermining the scope and contours of formalized politics. Both arenas can be conceptualized as aspects of a single field of force and action.[86]

"Intensified" feelings and practice are not bound to the level of quotidian life and struggle. Rather, they are often related *simultaneously* to

---

[85] The term used here has been stimulated by ideas elaborated by Theodore J. Lowi; in a seminal article, he distinguished several types of constellations of interest and political activity, postulating three political "arenas": "distributive", "regulatory" and "redistributive", cf. idem, "Decision-Making vs. Policy-Making", *Public Administration Review*, 30 (1970), pp. 314–25.

[86] Note in this regard the substantial contribution of Foucault's theses, persistently ignored in previous historical analyses, on the "ubiquitousness of power" qua relation, not as a thing or "possession" (though these latter are utilized by individuals or groups in interactions and situations – a point which Foucault fails adequately to acknowledge), cf. idem, *Sexualität und Wahrheit*, vol. 1, pp. 113ff.; also useful to examine in this connection is Foucault's thinking about the forms of "self-affirmation" mediated via perception or respect for the body, ibid., pp. 147ff.

both the far and the near, the insignificant and the "big time". Of course, a certain asymmetry persists. The power of emotion and physical practice is manifested in innumerable refractions in every arena. But feelings do not constitute some sort of formless "raw material". The ability to get by in everyday life is undoubtedly also even a part of a total concentration on formalized and state-oriented politics: even state officials, parliamentarians, or party functionaries have their private lives. Nonetheless, the everyday world of functionaries and professional politicians of the late nineteenth and twentieth centuries is especially marked by the constant reference to formalized and state-oriented politics.

In a study of the work experiences of linen weavers in northern France around 1900, William Reddy has shed helpful light on the forms in which interlinkages can occur. That linkage was directly realized within the matrix of the work process. Insistence on maintaining the difference between fathers and sons (which simultaneously marked the divide between skilled and menial workers) was in keeping with the interest of those same skilled workers (and fathers) in preserving their power on the shop floor and protecting their wages vis-à-vis the owners and entrepreneurs.[87] Yet this example is not reducible to a zero-sum game. Collective action to maintain and shield a "wage scale" structured in terms of age and qualification was not based on ignoring the actual differences between the men. On the contrary: it was precisely the intensity of support for maintaining the vertical inequality among the workers, perceived to be fair and justifiable, which ultimately spurred on action against third parties – those who wished to siphon off profits and tighten their controlling grip. The "intensification" of emotion did not peak in manifestations of class antagonism. Rather, it remained something equivocal, ambiguous. The arena of everyday politics was preserved, and even bolstered, alongside that of public and formalized action.

Power blocs of the political regime as well as supralocally organized opposition movements all followed their own rhythms of alteration, radical change or continuity. This applies to socialist and Christian trade unions as well as the Christian (in particular Roman Catholic) workers' associations and the "party of the proletariat" – the SPD (until 1917/18), and the later Social Democratic, socialist and communist parties spawned in the wake of its break-up.[88] Specific boundaries and horizons of attention

[87] W. M. Reddy, "Entschlüsseln von Lohnforderungen: Der Tarif und der Lebenszyklus in den Leinenfabriken von Armentières (1889–1904)", in R. Berdahl *et al.*, *Klassen und Kultur* (Frankfurt/M, 1982), pp. 77–107.

[88] On the SPD and the associated Free Unions up to 1914, cf. G. A. Ritter, "Die Sozialdemokratie im Deutschen Kaiserreich in sozialgeschichtlicher Perspektive", *Historische Zeitschrift*, 249 (1989), pp. 295–362; idem (ed.), *Der Aufstieg der deutschen Arbeiterbewegung. Sozialdemokratie und Freie Gewerkschaften im Parteiensystem und Sozialmilieu des Kaiserreichs* (Munich, 1990); on a Bavarian case deviating from the customary type of large northern German urban conglomeration, see K. H. Pohl, *Die Münchner Arbeiterbewegung. Sozialdemokratische Partei, Freie Gewerkschaften, Staat und Gesellschaft in München 1890–1915*

Alf Lüdtke

emerged in the various organizations; activists cultivated their own fields of engagement, often differing from locality to locality.[89] The step-by-step nationalization of social insurance programs and the enactment of legislation for the maintenance of industrial health and safety standards starting in the 1880s and 1890s created a new interface of contact between the working masses and the representatives of state authority. At the same time, these state programmes entailed heightened interaction with functionaries of workers' organizations: both in formal arbitration proceedings as well as in their own independent workers' bureaus, they acted as the trustees and champions of the interests of their "class comrades".[90]

(Munich, 1992); in his *The Alternative Culture: Socialist Labor in Imperial Germany* (Oxford and New York, 1985), V. Lidtke examines "alternative" orientations in the cultural practices of the Social Democratic workers' movement; a highly convincing combination of reconstruction of ways of living and political organizing is presented in W. Maderthaner (ed.), *Sozialdemokratie und Habsburgstaat* (Vienna, 1988). Two instructive local monographs that consider work with persons seeking assistance (in the offices of the workers' organizations and trade unions) and relations *between* the organizations, exploring the local limits to "revolutionary" programmes (in Frankfurt and Cologne): R. Roth, *Gewerkschaftskartell und Sozialpolitik in Frankfurt am Main* (Frankfurt/M, 1991) and M. Faust, *Sozialer Burgfrieden im Ersten Weltkrieg. Sozialistische und christliche Arbeiterbewegung in Köln* (Essen, 1992). The literature on developments after 1918 is disparate and uneven; some brief references to studies containing further bibliography should suffice, though it must be mentioned that the various oppositional groupings and splinter factions are given only marginal consideration. For the SPD, see H. A. Winkler, *Von der Revolution zur Stabilisierung. Arbeiter und Arbeiterbewegung in der Weimarer Republik 1918–1924* (Berlin and Bonn, 1984); idem, *Der Schein der Normalität. Arbeiter und Arbeiterbewegung in der Weimarer Republik 1924–1930* (Berlin and Bonn, 1985); H. A. Winkler, *Der Weg in die Katastrophe. Arbeiter und Arbeiterbewegung in der Weimarer Republik 1930–1933* (Berlin and Bonn, 1987); for the KPD, S. Koch-Baumgarten, *Aufstand der Avantgarde. Die Märzaktion der KPD 1921* (Frankfurt/M and New York, 1986); H. Weber, *Die Wandlung des deutschen Kommunismus* (Frankfurt/M, 1969); for the Christian organizations, see M. Schneider, *Die Christlichen Gewerkschaften, 1894–1933* (Bonn, 1982); D.-M. Krenn, *Die Christliche Arbeiterbewegung in Bayern vom Ersten Weltkrieg bis 1933* (Mainz, 1991); on the Catholic Zentrum party, cf. E. L. Evans, *The German Center Party 1870–1933* (Carbondale, 1981); for the "Yellows" to 1914, see K. Mattheier, *Die Gelben* (Düsseldorf, 1973).

[89] In this connection, there is a highly illuminating comparison between the local SPD organizations in Braunschweig and Hannover and their "political styles" during the World War and down to about 1920 in F. Boll, *Massenbewegungen in Niedersachsen 1906–1920* (Bonn, 1981), esp. pp. 196ff., 251ff, 313ff.

[90] Reports from the social arbitration courts before 1914 are informative, though limited to individual cases, see R. Wissell, *Aus meinen Lebensjahren* (Berlin, 1983); see also U. Borsdorf, *Hans Böckler. Arbeit und Leben eines Gewerkschafters von 1875 bis 1945* (Cologne, 1982); for a more general conspectus, see G. A. Ritter, *Sozialversicherung in Deutschland und England. Entstehung und Grundzüge im Vergleich* (Munich, 1983), pp. 62–75 and U. Frevert, *Krankheit als politisches Problem, 1780–1880. Soziale Unterschichten in Preußen zwischen medizinischer Polizei und staatlicher Sozialversicherung* (Göttingen, 1984). On the official position and the struggle of interests at the level of the central government regarding the further development of protective measures in social policy, cf. H.-J. von Berlepsch, *"Neuer Kurs" im Kaiserreich? Die Arbeiterpolitik des Freiherrn von Berlepsch 1890 bis 1896* (Bonn, 1987); on state strategies for control, the best source is still Klaus Saul, *Staat, Indus-*

After 1918, the structures and duties of the social-welfare state spelled out in the Weimar constitution had a major impact in various spheres, including the administrative and judicial regulation of work relations. The forerunners here were trade union functionaries who rapidly transformed themselves into experts on wage law (motivated in part by their own interest in preserving a permanent job).[91] In their eyes, wage agreements were the only effective instrument, and functioned as a symbol for the implementation of workers' rights. In this perspective, efforts by individuals (and their families) to get by and survive coincided with class and party interests in areas such as wage agreements and agreed working hours as well as insurance against risks on the job.

Experiences and the various forms of action in the industrial work place exhibited a characteristic "long wave" of their own. That wave was only partially linked with the fluctuations in state policy; on the other hand, it was certainly not isomorphic with movements in the economy or among social groups. From the 1870s, in almost all industrial branches work with machine tools focussed time and again on the "fit" of the specific products.[92] Inseparable from this was the ongoing struggle over the type of wages and their mode of calculation, especially the practice (and division) of team piecework rates.

These conflicts were, however, largely separate from those revolving around legal conditions, wages and wage agreements. Only fundamental issues such as these latter directly impinged on the arena of formalized state-level politics.[93] And only when it came to conflicts in the sphere of wage policy did the degree of coalition freedom restricted by – or conceded by – the representatives of the respective political regime become an important factor.

The nearer ordinances and functionaries came to affecting the actual praxis of work itself, the more circumscribed was the degree of penetration of *this* mode of political regulation. Even fascism changed nothing in that

trie, *Arbeiterbewegung im Kaiserreich. Zur Innen- und Sozialpolitik des Wilhelminischen Deutschland 1903–1914* (Düsseldorf, 1974).

[91] On such union bureaucrats viewed from the perspective of a contemporary observer, see R. Michels, *Zur Soziologie des modernen Parteiwesens in der modernen Demokratie. Untersuchungen über die oligarchischen Tendenzen des Gruppenlebens* ([1911/1925], Stuttgart, 1958); cf. now esp. D. Brunner, *Bürokratie und Politik des Allgemeinen Deutschen Gewerkschaftsbundes 1918/19 bis 1933* (Cologne, 1992).

[92] Cf. the measures on "Improving Efficiency in Industrial Production" which the Reich Minister for Armaments and Munition, Albert Speer, tried to impose in February 1942, particularly in the area of machine manufacture, see Historisches Archiv Krupp WA 41/5–56 and the "empirical reports" later published as a "confidential memo": Hauptausschuß Maschinen (ed.), *Fließende Fertigung in deutschen Maschinenfabriken* (Essen, 1943).

[93] In connection with the quite different English context, see the debate in recent years on "rank and fileism" – i.e., whether conflicts between union functionaries and "simple" members should be seen as the crucial issue in labor and working-class history, or whether it is more productive to view these conflicts in the context of "industrial relations", increasingly influenced and regulated by the state; cf. the debate between R. Price, "'What's in a Name?'

regard. The continuity of this distance maintenance may also have been bound up with the fact that some labor functionaries entertained their own notions about their specific organizational "base". In his diary, an anonymous shop steward in a large spinning mill, for example, complained bitterly about the "foolishness of the masses". After all, the main job as he saw it was to "deal with the dozens of demands and desires of the workers in daily interaction with factory management". The individual cases he described were actually a corroboration for him of just "how much valuable time" had been wasted "by the Sisyphean task that had to be performed". It was, he contended, irksome and repulsive to be drawn into all these mundane little quarrels and conflicts – for example, disputes regarding locker space or suspicions about "pilfering by fellow workers". The job was a thankless one, involving nothing but more and more claims by workers, ever more outrageous. In this functionary's view, workers seemed driven by pure selfishness. Yet it is noteworthy that one of the free trade unions found his diary interesting enough to publish; the volume appeared in 1925.[94]

Such opportunities for friction provided an impetus for new strategies stemming from the "other side". In the wake of restructuring on the national level and in the armaments industry after 1914, entrepreneurs and managers spearheaded new forms of paternalistic co-opting of workers. The concept and the ideology of the so-called "plant community" (*Werksgemeinschaft*) were specifically designed to encourage personal loyalty to the firm, especially in large enterprises.[95] This was also an approach that after 1933 perfectly accorded with Nazi notions of the "plant work force" (*Betriebsgefolgschaft* – and not only when it came to the question of who had the power of ultimate decision on the shop floor and beyond! [96] In the close bond forged between performance for cash renumeration

Workplace History and 'Rank and Filism'", *International Review of Social History*, 34 (1989), pp. 62–77; J. Cronin, "The 'Rank and File' and the Social History of the Working Class", ibid., pp. 78–88 and J. Zeitlin, "'Rank and Filism' and Labor History: A Rejoinder to Price and Cronin", ibid., pp. 89–102.

[94] Deutscher Textilarbeiter-Verband (ed.), *Aus dem Tagebuch eines Betriebsrates* (Berlin, 1925); quotes ibid., pp. 3, 6, 8 f. I am grateful to Volker Jäger, Leipzig, for this reference.

[95] See my "Deutsche Qualitätsarbeit", "Spielereien", pp. 188ff.; on the following, also cf. my "'Ehre der Arbeit': Industriearbeiter und Macht der Symbole. Zur Reichweite symbolischer Orientierungen im Nationalsozialismus", in A. Lüdtke, *Eigensinn. Fabrikalltag, Arbeitererfahrungen und Politik* (Hamburg, 1993) (a shorter version in English translation as "The 'Dignity of Labour'. Industrial Workers and the Power of Symbols under National Socialism", in D. Crew (ed.), *Recent Developments in German Social History* (forthcoming). Re the "long wave" of industrial paternalism, see also the material in K.-H. Gorges, *Der christlich geführte Industriebetrieb im 19. Jahrhundert und das Modell Villeroy & Boch* (Stuttgart, 1989); on the problematic more generally and for a French "case", cf. G. Noiriel, "Du 'patronage' au 'paternalisme': la restructuration des formes de domination de la main-d'oeuvre ouvrière dans l'industrie metallurgique française", *Mouvement social*, No. 144 (1988), pp. 17–35.

[96] In greater detail in M. Frese, *Betriebspolitik im "Dritten Reich". Deutsche Arbeitsfront, Unternehmer und Staatsbürokratie in der westdeutschen Großindustrie 1933–1939* (Paderborn, 1991).

and symbolic awards for "plant loyalty", even immediate family members were offered a chance to reap direct material benefits: summer camp for a worker's son, sewing courses for his or her daughter.

"Generational linkages" and "shifting involvements"

In historical studies of societies in the modern era, the term "movement" almost inevitably connotes an underlying image of oscillating rise and fall. Arrows of varying length serve to illustrate the moving dynamics. Only comparatively recently has the recurrence of arc-shaped movements been observed in biographical trajectories: i.e., for generations now income among industrial workers during the final years of their employment careers has been seen gradually to decline.[97] This dynamic process is associated with the sense of belonging to a group claiming reciprocally that all members share a certain set of experiences. It also entails an exclusion: anyone lacking (and who could not have had) this fund of biographical experience is automatically discounted out, distanced. One striking example of this concretely experienced (and nonetheless mythical) *"generational linkage"* (K. Mannheim) is participation in the (First) World War.

The constant rise in the numbers of voters or sporadic increases in the membership of the SPD and other working-class organizations provided the generation born before 1880 with good reason for solid hope for a better life in the future. In the context of everyday life, there were phases marked by rising levels of real wages – signaling a definite "advancement", despite constant substantial fluctuations in the amount of disposable income. In the two decades preceding 1914, the synchrony of these growth cycles could be interpreted as a guarantee heralding a "long wave" of further improvements. Yet after 1919/1920 – and the failure of the mass strike movements particularly in the Ruhr and in central Germany – such longer-term expectations were dashed, leading to a mood of massive disappointment. In the case of the generation born after 1900, the picture was different. Their "rite of passage" was experienced in the midst of industrialized, destructive chaos, namely the war (if indeed they had managed to survive).[98] Thus, there were two totally different generational experiences among adults in the 1920s. Nonetheless, these very diverse experiential

[97] See especially. H. Schäfer, "Arbeitsverdienst im Lebenszyklus. Zur Einkommensmobilität von Arbeitern", *Archiv für Sozialgeschichte*, 21 (1981), pp. 237–267.
[98] On the patterns of interpretation of the war generation, see E. Jünger, *In Stahlgewittern* ([1920], 32nd pr. Stuttgart, 1990) and K. Theweleit, *Männerphantasien* (Frankfurt/M, 1977); an alternative view is presented in E. Toller, *Eine Jugend in Deutschland* ([1933], Munich, 1978), (= *Gesammelte Werke*, vol. IV). For a psychoanalytic approach to the generational experience of those born in 1906–1910, see P. Loewenberg, "The Psychohistorical Origins of the Nazi Youth Cohort", *American Historical Review*, 76 (1971), pp. 1457–1502; an examination of prewar, wartime and postwar generations in the context of World War II can be found in W. Deppe, *Drei Generationen Arbeiterleben. Eine sozio-biographische Darstellung* (Frankfurt/M and New York, 1982). The narrative construction of "family" in family narrat-

patterns in the older and younger generations were closely interconnected. The loss of a predictable and "normal" intact world – either experienced personally in moments of mortal danger or vicariously in tales told by a father, brother, fiancé or husband – delineated the presence of a chilling common denominator mediated by the Great War.[99]

From the mid-1920s (and in another guise in the 1950s), points of tension shifted once again. Millions of children had to learn to cope with the loss of their father killed during the war. On the other hand (or perhaps precisely for this reason), after 1924/25 (and in the later 1950s) this new generation was eager to seize the opportunities for increased consumption offered by the expanding urban centers. It would appear that in the eyes of the generation born roughly after 1910, the binding power of the older notion of workers' respectability had been drastically attenuated. For them, the guiding principle was no longer a "secure", "orderly" and respected life in the bosom of relatives, neighbors and fellow workers, but "getting ahead on one's own", "making it".[100] This *cultural divide* between the generations was particularly evident in leisure patterns, such as the virtually "addictive" passion among the younger generation for motion pictures, a preference for American pop music or fast motorcycles. The older generation was dismayed, especially the "veteran" industrial workers and experienced SPD and communist party activists.[101]

Following hyperinflation in the autumn of 1923, there was another life-pattern shift for the older generation, namely a pronounced decline in the

ives is thematized in an exploratory study by I. Vesper and A. Weber, *Familien-Geschichten. Mündliche Überlieferung von Zeitgeschichte in Familien* (Hamburg, 1991).

[99] This experience of rupture is also reflected in the notion that a new type of man – i.e., the amalgam of frontline soldier and (industrial–skilled) worker – could remedy the supposed evils of the bourgeois age, cf. E. Jünger, *Der Arbeiter* ([1932], Stuttgart, 1985); on Jünger's totalistic (and thus "metapolitically" oriented) conception of "work" as the aesthetic linking of performance and pleasure, see the penetrating study by H. Segeberg, "Krieg als Arbeit – Ernst Jünger und der Erste Weltkrieg", in H. Segeberg (ed.), *Vom Wert der Arbeit. Zur literarischen Konstitution des Wertkomplexes "Arbeit" in der deutschen Literatur (1770–1930)* (Tübingen, 1986), pp. 335–378.

[100] Cf. U. Herbert, "Zur Entwicklung der Ruhrarbeiterschaft 1930 bis 1960 aus erfahrungsgeschichtlicher Perspektive", in L. Niethammer and A. v. Plato, *'Wir kriegen jetzt andere Zeiten'*, pp. 19–52, here p. 22f.

[101] J. Wickham, "Working-Class Movement and Working-Class Life: Frankfurt am Main during the Weimar Republic", *Social History*, 8 (1983), pp. 315–343; on the popular mass culture of the 1920s, see A. v. Saldern, "Arbeiterkulturbewegung in Deutschland in der Zwischenkriegszeit", in Boll, *Arbeiterkulturen*, pp. 29–70, esp. 59ff.; on gender-specific aspects, cf. A. v. Saldern, "Cultural Conflicts, Popular Mass Culture, and the Question of Nazi Success: The Eilenriede Motorcycle Races, 1924–39", *German Studies Review*, 15 (1992), pp. 317–338. Studies of generational conflicts among workers have tended to presuppose a "previous" unanimity of outlook and sense of collectivity. In such a view, the success of the political propaganda and practice of National Socialism, which propagated "redemption" by "honor" and "(folk) community", is reductively conceptualized as nothing but a reaction to the 1920s. Such a perspective fails to grapple with the question of the extent to which longer-term ambivalent attitudes present in worker orientations were indeed significant – and lent themselves to being usefully "exploited" by the Nazis.

worker migration. There was an unmistakable geographical solidification in working-class life.[102] One feature of this immobility was the enormous rise in popularity of workers' cultural movements (rather than overtly "political" organizations). Along with the new policy of direct confrontation between communists and Social Democrats, the importance of local ties was probably contributed to a change in popular phraseology during this period: expressions gained currency that presupposed or stressed a fixed local position "in town", as well as the kindred political rhetoric of political "camps".

A readiness to engage in action, in conjunction with reluctance to engage in any form of political organization in the narrower sense, were among the consequences of the ruptures and shifts between the generations directly observed and noted by party leader and functionaries. It remains an open question whether (and to what extent) experiences with the state apparatus and society shaped in the Kaiserreich were actually shattered or simply brushed aside: e.g., experiences of class separation (such as social exclusion) or the formation of an independent "alternative culture" (Lidtke). In any event, in the early 1920s, *national orientations* had become a highly visible factor in the arena of supralocal politics, and had also begun to spread among the "proletarian masses". Before 1914, discourse within the Socialist International had hardly gone beyond the level of grandiloquent rhetoric at political meetings, even among Social Democratic activists. For the majority of workers, whether politically organized or not, reference points like the "Reich" or the "Germans" (or the "Saxons" or "Bavarians") were far more salient and palpable than appeals to any global (and thus totally abstract) bond of cameraderie, the rallying cry of "class solidarity".[103]

Moreover, the murky underside of working-class politics was involved: the presence of *ethnic* (and *racist*) intra-class tensions.[104] Poles, Masurians,

---

[102] On this, see remarks in D. Langewiesche, "Mobilität in deutschen Mittel-und Groß-städten. Aspekte der Binnenwanderung im 19. und 20. Jahrhundert", in W. Conze and U. Engelhardt (eds.), *Arbeiter im Industrialisierungsprozeß* (Stuttgart, 1979), pp. 70–93, esp. table 2, pp. 84f.; F. Lenger, D. Langewiesche, "Räumliche Mobilität in Deutschland vor und nach dem Ersten Weltkrieg", in A. Schildt and A. Sywottek (eds.), *Massenwohnung und Eigenheim* (Frankfurt/M and New York, 1988), pp. 103–126; however, such global figures on mobility do not reveal whether the various movements (and patterns of immobility), quite different depending on such factors as occupation, formal qualification, industrial branch, age and sex (see Langewiesche, "Mobilität", pp. 78ff.), were universally changed in the process.

[103] Cf. v. Saldern, *Auf dem Wege zum Arbeiter-Reformismus*, pp. 64f.; Evans, *Kneipenge-spräche im Kaiserreich*, pp. 322ff. and especially 361ff. On the question of a fundamentally national or "patriotic" orientation – i.e., appeals to "the people of England" or "the British people" and not to the priority of class – an attitude present even among the unpropertied and wage-laboring classes of industrial England, see the illuminating study by P. Joyce, *Visions of the People: Industrial England and the question of class 1848–1914* (Cambridge, 1991).

[104] Chr. Kleßmann, *Polnische Bergarbeiter im Ruhrgebiet 1870–1945. Soziale Integration und nationale Subkultur einer Minderheit in der deutschen Industriegesellschaft* (Göttingen, 1978);

Russians and Italians were not seen by German workers as fellow laborers, "class comrades" or representatives of exotic "subcultures". Rather, laborers from the "Slavic and Romance-language countries" were often rejected as unwanted competitors. What mattered was not just the fear (or belief based on past experience) that they could depress wages in the labor market; the differences in the everyday habits or behavior of these foreigners also upset their German counterparts. Factory inspectors and even union members expressed concern about "concepts of cleaniless" that were grievously "underdeveloped in comparison to our own standards" amongst alien workers temporarily hired for construction "campaigns" and longer-term jobs in mining and the steel mills. In a report on attempts to break a strike by transport workers in Berlin in 1904, the Social Democratic paper *Vorwärts* was hardly able to restrain itself in denouncing "Russian garbage cossacks".[105] "National" vocabulary was thus often loaded with a double (ethnic, racist and social) meaning: the brusque rejection of "all those aliens", along with the drawing of a clear stratificational distinction between "us" and "them": German workers vs. the foreign "underclass".[106]

After 1918, the struggles in the Ruhr in 1923 led to a crescendo of national feeling and tension, extending beyond existing class divisions.[107] In this heated confrontation with the "victorious powers", expectations were apparently raised that served as a mass rallying point long before the advent of the Great Depression in late 1929. The "national" foci of such an orientation submerging class differences were not limited to the level of formal politics. Trade unionists and representatives of management alike were quick to discover the industrial key to overcoming the economic crisis and counteracting the widely felt humiliation of the German nation-

for an enlightening parallel from Appalachia, cf. the study by J. W. Totter, *Coal, Class and Color: Blacks in Southern West Virginia, 1915–1932* (Urbana, 1990).

[105] U. Herbert, *A History of Foreign Labor in Germany, 1880–1980*, trans. W. Templer (Ann Arbor, 1990), pp. 57–72, quotes pp. 57f.; on transport workers, overlooked by Herbert, and the rigorously negative defensive attitude prevalent toward them in the Social Democratic movement, see Th. Lindenberger, "Straßenpolitik. Zur Sozialgeschichte der öffentlichen Ordnung in Berlin" (Ph.D., Technical University Berlin, 1992), pp. 289ff.

[106] The local "underclass" – which generally had only migrated into most industrial combinations one or two generations earlier especially in the Ruhr – has been little examined to date; a penetrating photographic study on such a neighborhood ('Segeroth') in Essen can be found in F. Bajohr and M. Gaigalat (eds.), *Essens wilder Norden. Segeroth – ein Viertel zwischen Mythos und Stigma*, (Hamburg 1990).

[107] Cf. M. Ruck, *Die freien Gewerkschaften im Ruhrkampf 1923* (Cologne, 1986); however, Ruck also points to the limits of this "charged emotional situation", noting "extreme right-wing sentiments" among those who had little or no experience in organizations, cf. M. Ruck, *Bollwerk gegen Hitler? Arbeiterschaft, Arbeiterbewegung und die Anfänge des Nationalsozialismus* (Cologne, 1988), pp. 56–73; but see also references to the protesting behavior of "socially declassé" young men in the '20s who had flocked to join the separatist movements in the Rhineland, cf. J. Thomassen, "Arbeiterschaft und rheinischer Separatismus im Krisenjahr 1923", *Geschichte im Westen*, 7 (1992), pp. 53–61.

state: namely a rejuvenated emphasis on the old watchword of "German quality workmanship".[108] Thus, specifically among the workers, the seeds of organized "national" agitation later sowed by the Nazis fell on fertile soil that had already been ploughed.

To characterize the withdrawal from "leftist" movements that has just been outlined as a "retreat into the private sphere" would be to narrow the aperture of historiographic vision, concentrating solely on a single isolated aspect. Such one-dimensional yardsticks fail to do justice to the practice of the multitude, especially their "shifting involvements".[109] The dynamics entailed oscillation back and forth rather than a rigorous either–or divide. In his memoirs, recorded starting in 1919, the lathe operator Paul Maik noted the following dissimilar phenomena, reporting them *seriatim*: local prices for groceries, a distant catastrophe at sea, his daughter's toothache, and the results of elections for the factory committee and the Reichstag. Maik's span of attention encompassed more than what was either public or private. As separate as was work in his garden from the plant lockout or from changes in the Reichstag majority, the interconnections between these disparate phenomena were still quite clear: party politics and government policy were not considered something "totally different" and distant from the realm of everyday concerns. On the other hand, the tenor of one's personal life was not rendered meaningful solely on the basis of the pronouncements and activities of the (professional) politicians. The "intensity of private affairs" retained its own specificity, space and priority. This gave rise to a basic and insoluble ambivalence: the individual and familial sphere formed the basis for participation in the public arena, while simultaneously providing a space for retreat, a private corner for putting some distance between yourself and the broader society, a bit of breathing space.[110]

Experience and symbolic practice: "German quality workmanship"

Human action and behavior facilitates and supports experiences, but can also destroy them. Experiences for their part, stimulate perceptions, but can also function as a filter. At the same time, experiences or *"Erlebnisse,* singled out, distinguished by attention"[111] facilitate that behavior which "realizes given conditions", accepting, appropriating and changing them.

---

[108] Lüdtke, "Deutsche Qualitätsarbeit", "Spielereien'", pp. 182 f.

[109] A. O. Hirschman, *Shifting Involvements* (Princeton, 1982).

[110] In this connection, also note H. Rosenstrauch's precise observations on the "organizational culture" and ordinary commonplace nature of common bonds of understanding – as well as isolation (in everyday life!) – among Austrian (card-carrying) communists and socialists from the 1930s on, but esp. from the 1950s until the 1980s, cf. idem, *Beim Sichten der Erbschaft: Wiener Bilder für das Museum einer untergehenden Kultur; eine Nacherzählung* (Mannheim, 1992).

[111] Schütz and Luckmann, *Strukturen der Lebenswelt*, p. 14; see also note 23.

Put in another way, action, behavior and interpretation are reciprocally interrelated. Toiling in order to cope with things and to relate to (or distance oneself from) events is based on perceptions of the world and of others that inevitably contain interpretations. Symbols provide representations for needs as well as for calculations of interests. But symbols are not reflecting "mirrors". Rather, they *illuminate* both objects and persons, highlighting some distinguishing characteristics while obscuring others. Thus, it was possible to link increased labor effort in 1938 or 1942 with the "greatness of the Reich"; such acceleration in the name of the national effort could be encouraged, even justified. Take another more personal example: back in 1900, a marital row did not have to be interpreted as clear proof of a lack of respect for one's husband, but could be seen as form of punishment for a wife's disregard for the "natural" inequality between the sexes, a supposed "given fact" in biological and ethical terms. For their part, such interpretations generated actions designed to underscore their saliency. In other words: the appropriation and production of symbols mobilizes both interpretive and intrusive action.

This understanding of the nature and function of symbols derives from suggestions by the English anthropologist Victor Turner. In his *Forest of Symbols*, he analysed practices among the Ndembu that show the universe and human history in a new light.[112] In Turner's view, symbols do not simply mirror a tertiary element – they do not point to a signified entity beneath and behind their referent, but rather they have their *own* justification and importance. Symbols always have a bi-directional effect as stimuli: they encourage cognitive meanings, and at the same time address emotive and sensory needs. Symbols generate conceptions about something "exalted", along with emotions of loving care or disgust. They make "powerful" phenomena and "grand" concepts come alive, while simultaneously stimulating personal sensations. The latter in turn contain some recollection of the reality of that "powerful and exalted" thing.

One such symbol that was salient and meaningful for the great majority of workers, facilitating a sense of understanding extending beyond any one social class, was encapsulated in the image and concept of "German quality workmanship" (though it should be borne in mind that there was no consensus among all workers as a result of this symbol). Differing experiences and their interpretations overlapped in the concept denoted by this formula. Initially, an abiding ingredient was a suggestion of manual labor – a straightforward mode of activity, but with the added special value associated with physically exhausting work performed using the simplest of equipment. One typical example was the shoveling common to road

---

[112] V. Turner, *The Forest of Symbols. Aspects of Ndembu Ritual* (Ithaca and London, 1973), pp. 27ff., esp. pp. 48ff.; V. Turner, "Symbols in African Ritual", in J. L. Dolgin, J. S. Kemnitzer and D. M. Schneider (eds.), *Symbolic Anthropology* (New York, 1977), pp. 183–194.

construction gangs, or the tapping of blast furnaces. Of course, manual labor had been elaborated and upgraded in the craft trades and industry, expanding to encompass the category of "quality workmanship". This included the notion of orderliness – a value expected to be upheld in the work place. But above all else, this concept of genuine labor was rooted in that manual "dexterity" (*Handfertigkeit*) which derived from a fundamental knowledge of the sequencing of the work process at the point of production itself – intimate familiarity with both tools and materials. Essentially, it was characterized by the sense of confidence and experience founded on skill in handling the most "modern" machine tools. It was this "skillful dexterity" – and it alone – which made it possible to create a string of high-quality products from what had been ordered and sketched out on the drawing boards.

Certain groups of workers felt a special affinity for descriptions of "work" in words or visual images. But even more than this, the formula of "quality workmanship" was reflected in patterns of industrial development that had significantly shaped the physiognomy not just of individual groups, but of entire regions and regional societies. Specialized "flexible production" had by no means ground to a halt in the heavy shadow of "mass production" based on a highly complex division of labor. In the manufacture of machine tools, the production of precision instruments (such as clocks and scales) and weapons, flexible methods had never become outmoded and been replaced.[113] Specialized production from the days of home industry continued to be practiced in the manufacture of cutting tools and small-scale iron products in and around the cities of Remscheid and Solingen, as well as in the making of jewelry in the Pforzheim area or clock manufacture in the Black Forest. This was also true when it came to the sector of machine and vehicle production in central Württemberg (and for industrial "islands" in southern Swabia, such as rifle and handgun production in Oberndorf). There was a continuous process of further industrial development and "modernizing" of specific qualifications along highly flexible lines, adapting them to particular "tastes" and consumer demands. References to "skillfulness" or "nimble-fingered ingenuity" (*Tüftlersinn*) were never simply restricted to the classes engaged in the manual arts. Thus, the attraction that comparable icons have for admirers from various social classes can be related to a body of social experience extending over a period of comparatively "long duration".

Another relatively long-term feature was the fact that a substantial proportion of production personnel in these branches were worker-peasants.

---

[113] Ch. Sabel, J. Zeitlin, "Historical Alternatives to Mass Production: Politics, Markets and Technology in Nineteenth-Century Industrialization", *Past & Present*, No. 108 (1985), pp. 133–176; for a study on change and redefinition of skills in an industry based on smaller-scale production units, see R. Whipp, *Patterns of Labour: Work and Social Change in the Pottery Industry* (New York, 1990).

Consequently, one focus of their attention was the maintenance of their position as peasants, the safeguarding of their family livelihood in the village.[114] Their experiences were stamped by the rich variety of their own initiatives and constant physical toil, as well as the knowledge of their abiding isolation as very small agriculturalists, indeed "Sunday peasants".

Yet manual (ambi-)dexterity and skill were not the monopoly of expressly "adroit" specialist and special-order production shops. That degree of skillfulness so indispensable down in the mineshaft, up on the blast furnaces and in the "fire mills" was also at a high premium in the centers of mass production, especially in regions with heavy industry. Moreover, this image of "labor" sported an additional aesthetic dimension. It was no accident that in Essen – "the city that Krupp built" – the town fathers erected a fountain in connection with festivities marking the incorporation in 1907 of the Rhineland province into Prussia: the fountain featured a half-nude male figure. That statue, patterned after the image of a steelworker, was not intended by the sculptor simply to represent the portrait of an idealized worker, but rather to allegorize "labor" per se – and thus celebrate emblematically the prime characteristic of the city and surrounding region.[115]

Beginning with mobilization the war in the autumn of 1914, quality workmanship was pointedly transformed into patriotic effort: "national labor".[116] After 1918, "national labor" and "quality workmanship" were fused in the modifier-plus-noun formula of *deutsche Qualitätsarbeit*. From union leaders to industrial bosses, technicians to shop stewards, the goal of "German quality workmanship" was intended to facilitate and encourage industrial recovery, sparking an improvement in the living standards of workers and their families. Before the inner eye of a host of authors and their diverse readers, images were conjured up of skilled and experienced machine-tool operators, cool and composed, fully in control of the situation, ready to master any challenge the future might present.

The images and formulae of *deutsche Qualitätsarbeit* carried a double load of semantic freight: on the one hand, an appeal to work experiences and attitudes; on the other, a patriotic reference to their significance for

---

[114] Cf. the thought-provoking article by J. H. Quataert, "Combining Agrarian and Industrial Livelihoods. Rural Households in the Saxon Oberlausitz in the 19th Century", *Journal of Family History*, 10 (1985), pp. 145–162; on "commuting migration" (and its genesis in the regional industrializations of the twentieth century), especially illuminating is J. Thomassen, "Pendelwanderung im Bereich der Industrie und Handelskammer Krefeld im ersten Viertel des 20. Jahrhunderts", paper presented at the conference "Städtische Bevölkerungsentwicklung in Deutschland im 19. Jhdt. im internationalen Vergleich" (University of Bremen, 27–28 January 1989); cf. also Lenger and Langewiesche, "Räumliche Mobilität in Deutschland", pp. 109ff.

[115] Cf. H. Schröter, "Der Jahrhundertbrunnen in Essen", *Beiträge zur Geschichte von Stadt und Stift Essen*, 73 (1957), pp. 152–158.

[116] See Campbell, *Joy in Work, German Work* and Trommler, *Die Nationalisierung der Arbeit*.

the "whole nation". To urge on the great masses of workers – and in particular, first-generation workers – the Weimar government and the Nazi regime both praised the values of "living labor" and the readiness to roll up one's sleeves and pitch in, as well as the utility of the manual skills of (male!) workers. This was true not only in Germany: similar pronouncements could be found in the waves of modernization and industrialization that swept over the Soviet Union from the introduction of the first Five-Year Plan, and were also echoed in the rhetoric and reality of Roosevelt's "New Deal". Yet here too, there were features in which the specific aspects of national-state ideology were unmistakable. The "Stakhanov" campaigns in the Soviet Union from 1935 on revolved around the "ideology of tonnage", i.e., the primacy of physical strength and endurance.[117] By contrast, within Roosevelt's New Deal and the Democratic Party in the USA, images predominated that associated national greatness with praise for the dexterous "working-man" and celebration of the benevolence of industrialism, while characteristically stressing the value of each individual worker as a "citizen".[118]

"German quality workmanship" had not only factory-internal and national components; its symbolism was also in keeping with the dominant *sex-role stereotypes*: the "quality worker" embodied the ideal of the male "breadwinner". This was associated with an image of the family in which the "frugal" housewife served as helpmate to her breadwinning spouse, setting aside the butter for him alone, or the only (or biggest) portion of meat.[119] The enhanced evaluation of women working at so-called men's jobs during World War I, and the rapid and apparently silent return to the old situation and familiar hierarchies in the wake of demobilization in 1919, demonstrated the enduring salience of the symbol: women accommodated themselves to the fact that many areas of gainful employment were closed to them once again, considered off-limits occupationally. "Normality" returned and women resumed their roles as "accomplices" in their own oppression, contributing to the preservation of "patriarchal structures".[120]

[117] R. Maier, *Die Stachanov-Bewegung 1935–1938* (Stuttgart, 1990), pp. 119ff.

[118] G. Gerstle, *Working-class Americanism: The Politics of Labor in a Textile City 1914–1960* (Cambridge, 1989), esp. pp. 166ff.; see likewise L. Cohen, *Making a New Deal: Industrial Workers in Chicago 1919–1939* (Cambridge, 1990), esp. pp. 283ff.

[119] On the unequal treatment of women and men in household and family settings, see C. Lipp, "Die Innenseite der Arbeiterkultur. Sexualität im Arbeitermilieu des 19. und frühen 20. Jahrhunderts", in R. van Dülmen (ed.), *Arbeit, Frömmigkeit und Eigensinn* (Frankfurt/M, 1990), pp. 214–259 and 323–328, especially pp. 254ff.; see also Bromme, *Lebensgeschichte eines modernen Fabrikarbeiters*, pp. 351ff. and W. Seccombe, "Patriarchy Stabilized: The Construction of the Male Breadwinner Wage Norm in 19th C. Britain", *Social History*, 11 (1986), pp. 53–75.

[120] Chr. Thürmer-Rohr, "Aus der Täuschung in die Ent-Täuschung. Zur Mittäterschaft von Frauen", in Chr. Thürmer-Rohr, *Vagabundinnen. Feministische Essays* (Berlin, 1987), pp. 38–56, esp. pp. 49ff.

The equating of quality workmanship and male labor was manifested with brutal consistency, particularly in times of heavy unemployment. Using the example of the impact of the Depression 1931/32 on the industrial village of Marienthal in Lower Austria, Marie Jahoda and her associates provided a vivid description of how unemployed males, after losing their jobs, gradually "wearied" and subsequently skidded off the pavement of a regulated life "into chaos and emptiness".[121] The women, by contrast, remained "active": the household and family demanded their constant attention, but also offered them a chance to evade slipping into the abyss of a "disintegration of time" – a pitfall which the men were apparently unable to avoid.

The penetrating power of the symbol of "German quality workmanship" was not linked with economic prosperity, depression or any specific political regime. Nor was it influenced by the boundaries dividing the various political camps. In any event, the complaint voiced by a German machinist who, inspired by high ideals, had ventured to the Soviet Union in 1931, is instructive. In a letter to the Moscow Comintern Central Office written on September 7, 1932, the machinist noted that he had been employed only as an "auxiliary driller" at a tractor factory in Kharkov, and not as a master lathe operator, as had been initially agreed in the contract. He had made numerous suggestions for improvements, but these had fallen on deaf ears. Nor had there been any response to his stubborn attempt "to contribute to the construction of the fatherland of the workers in accordance with the level of his qualifications". The letter, in effect a farewell cum complaint, had been sent from Berlin, which the disillusioned skilled workman had returned to in deep disappointment.[122]

During the transition phase to National Socialism, it became evident just how important the consensus regarding this class-transcending image of labor was in facilitating the process by which workers accommodated themselves to the needs and demands of National Socialism, especially in the field of armaments and defense production.[123]

---

[121] M. Jahoda, P. Lazarsfeld and H. Zeisel, *Die Arbeitslosen von Marienthal*, 3rd pr. (Frankfurt/M, 1975), esp. pp. 70ff., 83ff.

[122] Central State Archive of the October Revolution, Register 5451, inventory list 39, item 100, folios 42–42a. I am grateful to Dr. Viktoria Tyashelnikova (Institute for Russian History RAN, Moscow) for her assistance in making this text available to me.

[123] For a more detailed treatment, see my "The 'Dignity of Labour'". Regarding the various "benefits" provided by Nazi organizations, see also the illustrated volumes by J. Pöchlinger (ed.), *Front in der Heimat. Das Buch des deutschen Rüstungsarbeiters* (Berlin, Vienna and Leipzig, 1942) and H. Hoffmann (ed.), *Me 109 – der siegreiche deutsche Jäger* (Munich, 1942). The question of the range and degree of acceptance remains open in its particulars, but should be scrutinized in connection with fluctuations in the tide of success and failure on the battlefield; cf. the basic studies by G. Rosenthal, *"Als der Krieg kam, hatte ich mit Hitler nichts mehr zu tun". Zur Gegenwärtigkeit des "Dritten Reiches" in Biographien* (Opladen, 1990) and L. Niethammer, "Heimat und Front", in Neithammer, *"Die Jahre weiß man nicht . . ."*, pp. 163–232.

The consequences: *Eigensinn* and accommodation

As historians, we tend generally (and in cases of doubt) to wind up on the side of the victors, however unintentionally.[124] For that reason, it is all the more important that we do not, ex post facto, ignore the rich "intensity" of concrete lives. One positive option lies in trying to avoid a reduction of individuals to some sort of simple sum, mechanically adding up the digits of their existence. Neither the dense patchwork complexities of social relations nor their changes or continuity can be adequately encompassed by mere operations of addition. More important questions involve the multiplicity – or more precisely, the polymorphous diversity – of synchrony. This focuses attention on the spectrum and range of what is historically possible in any given conjuncture.

It is not just a question of gaining new knowledge about unrecognized and previously ignored programmes and actions of the "downtrodden and vanquished", redressing past historiographic neglect. Though such a romanticizing undertone reverberates at times through reconstructions of everyday historical reality, it cannot be sustained. The data stand at odds with such romanticist historiography: not just their vast variety, but often the sheer incompatability of disparate, mulishly obstinate appropriations of expectations and demands coming from above. *Eigensinn* does not refer solely to benevolent needs and practices by the multitude of workers – but also to actions and attitudes that are downright misanthropic, full of contempt for one's fellows. Indeed, such practices are often motivated by the desire to see others squirm and suffer.

History "after Auschwitz" cannot overlook the fact that autonomous activity and *Eigensinn* were and remain ambiguous in a quite bitter sense. Between 1933 and 1945, they opened up a space, a convenient corner for countless individual opportunities to withdraw, step aside and stand at a distance. The goal was survival. In a system that demanded, ever more emphatically, an unlimited "intensive" and ultimately "total" commitment, this amounted to an act that was eo ipso distinctly *political*. At the same time, such distancing functioned to help solidify Nazi rule in the arena of state and formal politics. Alongside popular concurrence, there was a broad area of accommodation with Nazism and its demands, a species of complaisant compliance, assuring the regime substantial space in which to maneuver. Thanks to this tactic of distancing, the occasional resistance that crystallized had no real impact. And people did not just

---

[124] Cf. W. Benjamin, "Über den Begriff der Geschichte" (ca. 1940), in idem, *Gesammelte Schriften*, vol. I/2 (Frankfurt/M, 1974), pp. 691–704; cf. likewise L. Niethammer, *Posthistoire: Has History Come to an End?* (London, 1992) ; R. Konersman, *Erstarrte Unruhe. Walter Benjamins Begriff der Geschichte* (Frankfurt/M, 1991), pp. 58ff., 97ff.; A. McRobbie, "The *Passagenwerk* and the Place of Walter Benjamin in Cultural Studies: Benjamin, Cultural Studies, Marxist Theories of Art", *Cultural Studies*, 6 (1992), pp. 147–169, esp. pp. 154 f., 160ff.

adopt a modus operandi of *participant compliance* (*hinnehmendes Mitmachen*) during the early years of military success in the war – they adhered to it even "after Stalingrad", indeed right down to May 1945.[125]

Perhaps both views contain a kernel of truth: autonomous activity in keeping with the "intensity of the private sphere" cannot provide any guarantee for a reduction in domination and oppression. Nonetheless, it remains the indispensable prerequisite for attempts to advance supralocal organizing which respect the *politics of the private and the personal.*

Translated by William Templer

---

[125] This is not actually thematized by B. Kroener and M. Steinert; rather, in their contributions to a recent volume on Stalingrad, they stress the repression "of the regime", see J. Förster (ed.), *Stalingrad. Ereignis – Wirkung – Symbol* (Munich, 1992), pp. 151–170, 171–185; cf. an illuminating chapter (V) in W. F. Werner, *'Bleib übrig!' Deutsche Arbeiter in der nationalsozialistischen Kriegswirtschaft* (Düsseldorf, 1983); see also Marc Roseman, "World War II and Social Change in Germany", in A. Marwick (ed.), *Total War and Social Change* (London, 1988), pp. 58–78.

Class Formation and the Labor Movement as the Subject of Dialectic Social History

HARTMUT ZWAHR

Introduction

As an introduction to this essay, three points need to be made. First, the European labor movements of the nineteenth and early twentieth centuries, on which we focus here, were part of bourgeois society. Secondly, they were a factor that challenged bourgeois society and thus contributed in several different ways to its change. Thirdly, as a result of this interaction, the labor movements themselves underwent changes. All of those were lasting changes. The systemic changes, imposed by revolutionary or military force, that accompanied the experiment in socialism, were not. In countries where the labor movement pursued socialist aims prior to the First World War on the crumbling foundations of a primarily pre-bourgeois society, such as in eastern and south-eastern Europe, it was the most radical force behind political democratization and modernization (Russia; Russian Poland: the Kingdom of Poland,[1] Bulgaria). But it could not compensate for the society's evident lack of basic civic development, whereas the socialist experiment in Soviet Russia led not only to the demise of democratization but also to a halt of embourgeoisement.[2]

The collapse of institutionalized (party-administrated) socialism, that is, the (state) communist branch of the labor movement in Europe, has prompted the large community of labor historians to ask how the achievements, effects, and experiences of the nineteenth-century labor movements should be evaluated both in light of these new experiences and with respect to the recent crises in civilization. What did millions of wage earners contribute to bourgeois society simply by living and working in this society, by endeavoring to give their lives direction, honor and meaning, by creating movements and placing their hopes in these? More specifically, how have labor movements contributed to the realization of demands for civil liberty and emancipation while caught in the tension between economic and social inequality, on the one hand, and the universal character of such demands, on the other? In particular, what role did the social democratic-socialist movements play in calling for social and political

[1] See Ryszard Kolodziejczyk (ed.), *Historia Polskiego Ruchu Robotniczego do 1890* (Warsaw 1890); Stanislaw Kalabinski (ed.), *Polaska klasa robotnicza. Zarys dziejow*, Vol. 1/2: *Lata 1870–1918* (Warsaw 1978).
[2] See Alan Bullock, *Hitler und Stalin. Parallele Leben* (Berlin 1991); Wolfgang Ruge, "Die Doppeldroge. Zu den Wurzeln des Stalinismus", in Rainer Eckert, Wolfgang Küttler, Gustav Seeber (eds.), *Krise – Umbruch – Neubeginn. Eine kritische und selbstkritische Dokumentation der DDR-Geschichtswissenschaft 1889/90* (Stuttgart 1992), pp. 33–43.

International Review of Social History 38 (1993), Supplement, pp. 85–103

equality and in laying the groundwork for the initial attempt at socialism that began to take shape during the First World War; and what role did the trade union movements play in trying to formalize the relations between capital and labor in the interests of the worker? The demise of the model of socialism based on a communist type of planned economy currently appears to have restored an older sense of European normality and revived earlier trends of European history. Yet it had been from these trends and in confrontation with the realities of capitalism that the vision and the alternative of a non-bourgeois society in the foreseeable future evolved. It was Marx's doctrine that first gave the labor movement a certain goal based on universal ideas, a "global mission".[3] Otherwise it could have remained a simple trade union movement. However, the unity required for this "mission" was constantly lacking. Thus, the history of the labor movement has always been one that suffered denominational, national and political division.

I would like to close these remarks by listing several major topics. These are fields of research of a dialectic social history that thinks and proceeds in a functional context and that does not isolate the history of workers and labor movements, but seeks to view these within the framework of a history of the entire society (*Gesellschaftsgeschichte*).

(1) class formation, especially that of the bourgeoisie in relation to the working class and vice versa; (2) class and gender: work, division of labor, etc.; (3) the relationship between wage labor and capital, social inequality and participation; (4) cultural processes of embourgeoisement and the limits of their impact among workers; (5) grassroots movements, labor and other movements; (6) state, classes and movements; (7) legal regulation of wage labor and class formation; (8) the achievements of organizations and institutionalization: trade unions and entrepreneurial associations, the trade unions as the prototype of modern interest representation of the dependent employee, social democracy as a modern mass party; (9) the public counter-sphere (*Gegenöffentlichkeit*), alternative societal concepts, utopias.

Synchronization and transformation of labor

The present study of class formation is based on the idea of synchronization.[4] Synchronization means to discover the simultaneity between two

[3] Ernst Nolte, *Nietzsche und der Nietzscheanismus* (Frankfurt a.M. and Berlin 1990), p. 8.
[4] See Hartmut Zwahr: "Zur Synchronisierung des Entwicklungsgangs von Bourgeoisie und Proletariat als Forschungsproblem und Aufgabe", *Beiträge zur Geschichte der Arbeiterbewegung* 23 (1981), pp. 803–824; Jürgen Kocka (ed.), *Arbeiter und Bürger im 19. Jahrhundert. Varianten ihres Verhältnisses im europäischen Vergleich* (Munich 1986). On the terminology (*Bürgerlichkeit, Entbürgerlichung*), see Jürgen Kocka, "Bürgertum und Bürgerlichkeit als Probleme der deutschen Geschichte vom späten 18. zum 19. Jahrhundert", in Jürgen Kocka

agents, that is, to proceed in a manner that synchronously, simultaneously and concurrently explores the actual give and take between these inter-acting agents instead of isolating them from one another. With regard to class formation among wage laborers and entrepreneurs, including other bourgeois groups, this means studying a pair of opposites as a unit and as interacting agents. This also means describing the capital relation as a fundamental economic given, as well as a power system, which is under-going constant transformation – socially, mentally, intellectually, culturally and politically. This is because wage labor in capitalism arises primarily as a function of capital.[5] It is included in the historical development of private property, usually originating in a feudal framework. Not until the defeudalization of labor did the classes of bourgeois society evolve. The participants could not flee from this fundamental setting as long as they operated within it. Therefore, they were also not free in their decision-making but bound to one another. However, it is still not commonplace in the economic and social history of either workers or entrepreneurs thoroughly to study the synthesis and interaction of these antipodes.

In modern history, the major transformation of labor to free labor,[6] brought about by revolution, reform, or both in the transition to capital-ism,[7] did not alter the fact that working methods were still based on manual labor. It overcame the partially feudal, partially corporate, partially privil-ege-based, non-economic restraints, freed the capital relation and created both inside and outside of this relation the principal prerequisites needed for a transformation to modern industrial labor. Industrial capitalism, however, evolved without the intervention of political force. This was limited for the most part to a temporary protective function as industries were established and credit granted. During the transition from manual labor to mechanization, the umbilical cord that linked the machine labor-ers of the capitalist era to the wage laborers of earlier centuries of Euro-pean history was cut. But it was not only the unpropertied who left the pre-class state and entered into the reality of class formation in industrial capitalism.[8] All around them and before their eyes, large groups of both burgher and proto-industrial rural dwellers were being wrenched out of

(ed.), *Bürger und Bürgerlichkeit im 19. Jahrhundert* (Göttingen 1987). Also see the editor's introduction.

[5] See Hartmut Zwahr, "Zum Gestaltwandel von gewerblichen Unternehmern und kapitalab-hängigen Produzenten. Entwicklungstypen gewerblicher Warenproduktion in Deutschland", *Jahrbuch für Geschichte* 32 (1985), pp. 9–64.

[6] Karl Marx, *Das Kapital*, Vol. 1, in Marx/Engels *Werke*, Vol. 23 (Berlin 1988); Max Weber, *Wirtschaft und Gesellschaft. Studienausgabe* (Tübingen 1980), pp. 70 ff. (on free and unfree labor).

[7] Hartmut Zwahr, "Die Konstituierung der Arbeiterklasse in revolutionsgeschichtlicher Sicht", in: *Proletariat und bürgerliche Revolution (1830–1917)* (Berlin 1990), pp. 33–55.

[8] See Jürgen Kocka, *Weder Stand noch Klasse. Unterschichten um 1800* (Bonn 1990); Jürgen Kocka, *Arbeitsverhältnisse und Arbeiterexistenzen. Grundlagen der Klassenbildung im 19. Jahrhundert* (Bonn 1990).

corporate constraints, artisan independence, as well as earlier forms of capital dependency by the political transformation and the demise of feudalism. This was proletarianization, the fate of large numbers of people whose station in preceding centuries had been far above those of urban day laborers, the packers, artisans, masons, carpenters, and those dependent on wages in general. Next came the integration into the still developing system of profit-seeking and free labor characteristic of industrial capitalism. The labor power of these people was essential for capitalist industrialization, not only since industrialization developed at a different pace in the various important branches of industry, but also because it evolved in close relationship with artisan and pre-industrial forms of production. Women and girls also joined the labor force to an unprecedented degree. Mechanized spinning mills became the pilot industry of the Industrial Revolution on the European continent. In Germany the first regions affected were Saxony[9] and the Rhineland.[10] Therefore it was the specific manner in which class formation occurred within light industry (see below) that marked the beginning of the history of German workers and the working class. An example of this would be the strike of roughly 2,000 cloth mill workers in and around Lennep (Bergisches Land) for higher wages, shorter working hours, negotiated contracts, and the right to elect foremen.[11]

The competition from the factories had forced most of the cloth weavers of the region to give up their trade. In the factories they experienced how the traditional artisan labor lost its commodity value and how the commercialization of labor depended on the transition to industrial labor, which went hand-in-hand with unusual, painful forms of control. The workers complained that the machine is "not the tool of workers, but the worker [is] the tool of the machine, the slave of awe-inspiring mechanics" (expressed in the words of an artisan). In conjunction with such dequalification, the clothmakers also experienced an estrangement from the purpose of human labor and of life as a whole. "The machine makes any skill superfluous and only requires a dull mechanic supervision." – "We are not allowed to be hungry until the bell rings [. . .] Should hunger strike too soon, that is considered disruptive and is not tolerated." The industrial order replaced the natural order; with the destruction of the household unit of production, a familiar cohesion of life was destroyed. The conflict

[9] See Rudolf Forberger, *Die Industrielle Revolution in Sachsen 1800–1861*, Vol. 1/1: *Die Revolution der Produktivkräfte in Sachsen 1800–1830* (Berlin 1982); Vol. 1/2: *Übersichten zur Fabrikentwicklung* compiled by Ursula Forberger (Berlin 1982).
[10] See Gerhard Adelmann (ed.), *Der gewerblich-industrielle Zustand der Rheinprovinz im Jahre 1836* (Bonn 1967).
[11] See Dieter Dowe, "Der Arbeitskampf in den Tuchfabriken des Kreises Lennep (Bergisches Land) 1850", in Klaus Tenfelde and Heinrich Volkmann (eds.), *Streik. Zur Geschichte des Arbeitskampfes in Deutschland während der Industrialisierung* (Munich 1981), pp. 31–51.

between capital and labor shifted from the relations between workers in home industries and the merchants and *Verleger* to the factory. Once residential dwelling and workplace had been separated, the factory became the place where the conflict between capital and labor erupted. Strikes and lock-outs brought the conflict to a dangerous, pre-revolutionary head. Entrepreneurs and wage laborers now treated both victory and defeat as part of a bilateral process of learning. This is sufficient reason to avoid any separation of such phenomena in social history and to present relations within capitalism in a synchronized and comparative fashion.

Types of class formation in the capital relation

When comparing the genesis of entrepreneurs and wage laborers, a distinction can usually be made between a type of class formation particular to light industry and one characteristic of heavy industry.[12] Within these two types of industry and their affiliated branches, to a certain extent entrepreneurs and wage laborers born to the working class are to be found. They represented a variation of class formation that began as a partnership and led to social inequality. During this change, patriarchial forms of social intercourse were discarded, although some aspects persisted.[13]

The antipodes of the capital relation in light industry, especially in the textile trade

At the heart of the manner in which class formation developed in light industry lay the earlier dependencies of the producer in proto-industrial contexts. Several aspects about the interdependent social groups reveal an identical or at least very similar degree of economic, social and political maturity. Abilities, value consciousness, etc. had sprouted from the same root, the same strand of development. An imagery that could be used to characterize the participants in any particular moment of conflict or conflict-avoidance would be that of a pair of wrestlers of equal weight and experience.

When the origins of non-agrarian entrepreneurs and wage laborers are studied, it is clear (as Germany illustrates) that employers born to the entrepreneurial class dominated. With the exception of mechanical engineering and those branches of production that grew primarily out of artisan crafts, one might assume that such a dominance existed in both light and heavy industry. On the entrepreneurial side there were indeed family and business links between both types of industry. With regard to wage laborers, however, what stands out are only the obvious differences. It is not

---

[12] See Zwahr, "Gestaltwandel", pp. 52–59.
[13] See Jürgen Kocka, "Traditionsbindung und Klassenbildung. Zum sozialhistorischen Ort der frühen deutschen Arbeiterbewegung", *Historische Zeitschrift* 243 (1986), pp. 333–376.

possible to find a similar hereditary element among wage laborers in the initial stages of class formation. Wherever capitalism evolved from the triad of manufacturing, capital-dependent craft and factory, the two inter-acting social groups possessed a similar social and mental maturity. This did not exist in the emerging centers of heavy industry during this period.

Pre-industrial entrepreneurs preferred to live in cities and large indus-trial villages; their financial institutions were located in the cities, which were at the same time the leading commercial centers of industrial regions. The cities had profited from the surplus of the proto-industries that flour-ished and expanded throughout the eighteenth century. The capital needed to make the first industrial investments accrued in the cities. In turn, most of these investments were made in traditional regions of export trade. These included the Silesian *Eulengebirge* (linen weaving; in 1844 the site of the Silesian weavers revolt), the later industrial region of the *Vorerzgebirge* (cotton weaving, mechanical spinning mills, mechanical engineering),[14] the Saxon *Vogtland* (weaving, lace manufacturing), the *Schönburgische Rezeßherrschaften* of Saxony (cotton weaving),[15] the south-east of *Oberlausitz* (linen weaving),[16] the *Bergische Land*: Barmen and Elberfeld (cotton weaving), the metal-producing region of Solingen,[17] Krefeld (silk weaving).[18] At the turn of the eighteenth to the nineteenth century, these regions were dominated by entrepreneurs born into the class. For the most part, they came from families of merchants and *Ver-leger*, some of which, in turn, had come themselves from families of small manufacturers. Examples of the type of class formation to be found in light industry outside of Germany include the silk weaving region around Lyon,[19] the English textile regions, the textile region of Lodz in Russian

---

[14] See Rudolph Strauss, *Die Lage und die Bewegung der Chemnitzer Arbeiter in der ersten Hälfte des 19. Jahrhunderts* (Berlin 1960); on Saxony, see Hartmut Zwahr, "Die deutsche Arbeiterbewegung im Länder und Territorienvergleich 1875", *Geschichte und Gesellschaft* 13 (1987) 4, pp. 464–471; Gerhard A. Ritter, "Das Wahlrecht und die Wählerschaft der Sozialdemokratie im Königreich Sachsen 1867–1914", in Gerhard A. Ritter (ed.), *Der Auf-stieg der deutschen Arbeiterbewegung. Sozialdemokratie und Freie Gewerkschaften im Partei-ensystem und Sozialmilieu des Kaiserreichs* (Munich 1990), pp. 49–101.

[15] See Hans-Albrecht Grohmann, "Kapital und Lohnarbeit in den Schönburgischen Rezeßherrschaften. Zur Konstituierung von Bourgeoisie und Arbeiterklasse in einer deutschen Exportgewerbelandschaft 1830–1852", Ph.D. thesis (Leipzig 1988).

[16] Heinz-Dieter Fleißig, "Untersuchungen zur Klassenkonstituierung der Bourgeoisie in der südlichen Oberlausitz zur Zeit der industriellen Revolution unter besonderer Berücksichti-gung der ökonomischen Konstituierung und deren Grundlagen im Textilgewerbe", Ph.D. Thesis (Dresden 1988).

[17] See Rudolf Boch, *Handwerker-Sozialisten gegen Fabrikgesellschaft. Lokale Fachvereine, Massengewerkschaft und industrielle Rationalisierung in Solingen 1870–1914* (Göttingen 1985).

[18] See Peter Kriedte, *"Eine Stadt am seidenen Faden". Haushalt, Hausindustrie und soziale Bewegung in Krefeld in der Mitte des 19. Jahrhunderts* (Göttingen 1991).

[19] See Yves Lequin, *Les ouvriers de la région Lyonnaise (1848–1914)*, Vol. 1: *La formation de la classe ouvrière régionale*, Vol. 2: *Les interests de classe et la république* (Lyon 1977).

Poland,[20] and the Russian textile regions (such as the Ivanovo-Kineshma region).[21] With regards to the development of the artisan crafts, proto-industry, decentralized and centralized manufacturing, and finally the factory, the urban–rural comparison of class formation[22] clearly indicates a certain balance in the developmental pattern of entrepreneurs and wage laborers.

In a certain historical-political milieu, all those conflicts surfaced that were to accompany the industrial-capitalist type of production. Sooner or later, the factory and the factory system became predominant. They began to destroy pre-industrial, long established methods of production and ways of living. The guilds were alarmed as the new force of the industrial bourgeoisie penetrated their existence from without, so to speak, and left artisan labor at the mercy of competition. They fought against a form of production that, in their opinion, "still dangled in a very uncertain legal state"[23] from which the market relationships of the industrial bourgeoisie developed. As the united Leipzig guild masters warned in a petition to the Landtag, England's manufacturing and factory system also started

in very small spots where there were no guilds, in Manchester, Birmingham and Liverpool, and with time, these boroughs came to be counted among England's most important cities. Manufacturing in our fatherland has developed in a similar manner. It also started in small cities and areas where no important guilds existed, and in turn these communities grew and expanded and were profitable to their inhabitants.[24]

For the first time, many journeymen in the guilded crafts discovered that being wage-dependent was no longer merely a short step toward petty bourgeois independence, but a permanent way of life. The overcrowding of the crafts became a mass phenomenon. Master craftsmen were deciding in ever-growing numbers not to have their sons learn the trade of their fathers. Many quit when they could no longer lower the prices of their

[20] See G. Missalowa, *Studia nad powstaniem lodzkiego okregu przemyslowego 1815–1870*, Vol. 1: *Przemysl* (Lodz 1964); Vol. 2: *Klasa robotnicza* (Lodz 1967); Vol. 3: *Burzuazja* (Lodz 1975).

[21] Daniel Mandes, "The Ivanovo-Kineshma Region Working Class. A Case Study of the Russian Labour Movement in the Province, 1914–1917", paper presented at a colloquium on comparative labor history, Cortona, June 1986.

[22] On this topic, see Hartmut Zwahr, "Zur Genesis der deutschen Arbeiterklasse. Stadiale und regionale Entwicklungsformen des deutschen Proletariats im Vergleich", in: *Zur Entstehung des Proletariats* (Magdeburg 1980), pp. 25–49; *idem*, "Arbeiterbewegung im Länder- und Territorienvergleich", pp. 448–507; *idem*, "Der Übergang der Arbeiterbewegung in die Provinz. Einsichten am Beispiel Deutschlands, 1848–1900", in: Rudolf G. Ardelt and Erika Thurner (eds.), *Bewegte Provinz: Arbeiterbewegung in mitteleuropäischen Regionen vor dem Ersten Weltkrieg* (Vienna and Zurich 1992), pp. 63–86.

[23] See *Petition, überreicht der Königlich-Sächsischen Ständeversammlung von den endesunterschriebenen Innungen und Personen der Stadt Leipzig im Jahre 1839*, p. 14.

[24] *Ibid.*, pp. 83f.

goods to match those of cheaply manufactured goods. Others, such as the linen weavers, clothmakers, and knitters, had to resort to sweating.

The "bourgeoiseness" (*Bürgerlichkeit*) in light industry could not do without free labor, competition and a national market. Its success led to the proletarianization of large segments of the pre-industrial classes and changed workers' images of themselves. "Anti-bourgeoiseness" (*Antibürgerlichkeit*) became part of increasingly radical protests. People of petty bourgeois origin, unlike those of agrarian origin, began to consider civil values and ideals for the first time in a perspective that was to transcend bourgeois society.[25]

Particularly in the villages and cities of the older regions of export-oriented industries, working conditions under pre-industrial and, later, industrial capitalism and its various mixed forms produced a type of worker unknown to agrarian regions. Nor did he or she exist in the central regions of heavy industry at the time. This type of person introduced into the labor movement abilities and experiences, an already strong urban culture and way of life, self-confidence, a desire to live humanely and, in the opinion of a minority, to govern society. He or she helped create this first major mass movement of modern times. Wilhelm Liebknecht described one such worker-socialist who stemmed from the long evolution of capital-dependent, producing families, namely Christian Hadlich. Born in 1831 as the son of a stocking knitter master in Hirschberg (Silesia), Hadlich had become a journeyman in his father's trade.

In Christian Hadlich I met a type of person for the first time in Germany that I would later meet often in the Saxon *Erzgebirge* and *Vogtland*: from the brown, lively eyes radiated intelligence and great kindness, the body weak – the result of degeneration caused by several generations of hunger and deprivation – the countenance the expression of painful comprehension, deep reflection and a probing awareness of human misery, which he himself had experienced and felt in the suffering of others [. . .]. I do not know what year he came to Leipzig. From casual remarks one can deduce that he was there in 1848 and 1849 at least temporarily, and that he then belonged, or at least frequented the former workers' association, which had a strong "communist bias". When I arrived in Leipzig, he was already one of the most active board members of the workers' education association [. . .]. He was the soul of the association, to which he devoted all thought and deed. We quickly became friends. And he was the first of my new associates to declare himself wholeheartedly for socialism.[26]

Other workers in Leipzig and comparable cities, among them a good many sons of peasants, fought with grim determination to become civil servants for the railroad or the postal service.[27] Petty bourgeois enterprises, such

---

[25] See Hartmut Zwahr, "Verbürgerlichung und Entbürgerlichung beim Übergang zum Industriekapitalismus. Ein sächsisch-polnischer Vergleich", *Neues Archiv für sächsische Geschichte*, forthcoming.

[26] Wilhelm Liebknecht, *Erinnerungen eines Soldaten der Revolution* (Berlin 1976), pp. 323f.

[27] See Susanne Schötz, "Zur Entstehung und Beamtung von Postpersonal. Das Beispiel Leipzig", *Jahrbuch für Regionalgeschichte* 12 (1985), pp. 172-188; idem, "Städtische Mittel-

as that of small-scale, fresh produce retailer or pub owner, also offered chances to enter into an occupation with opportunities to improve one's lot.[28] Sons of peasants and agricultural laborers were very rarely among the first and second generations of the pioneers of the social democratic labor movement. Whereas the sons of artisans who became wage laborers usually experienced proletarianization as a social decline, the sons of peasants who went to the cities and became wage laborers appear to have found more avenues for social advancement than has been generally thought. They also endured dependencies that those from the lower urban social strata either completely refused to accept or only reluctantly put up with. Biographical evidence clearly shows these differing approaches to life.[29] For the most part, it was the fate of the artisan to experience "debourgeoisement" (*Entbürgerlichung*). Where this was transformed into the anti-bourgeois sentiments that were to become so vital to the early social democratic-socialist labor movement, these same people also possessed education, ideals, a longing for utopia, and a political culture rooted in bourgeois origins. From this they acquired an important set of emancipating ideas and behavior, which must also be seen primarily as a bourgeois inheritance.[30] The republicanism espoused by large segments of the working class, such as Bebel found in the 1860s in the kingdom of Saxony,[31] is rooted in the 1848 revolution. To a degree, this remaining spark of permanent politicization fueled the fires of socialist republicanism. How easily the worker-socialists moved in the red-tinged imagery of the socialist vision! Both the profession of faith and the commitment it earned from the masses are to be considered as achievements of the social democratic movement which would create a new culture based on earlier traditions.[32]

We also come across the capital-dependent, artisan type of producer in the small-scale metal industry of the *Bergische Land* and the Prussian Mark. There he or she established a specific type of labor movement that

schichten in Leipzig während der bürgerlichen Umwälzung (1830–1870), untersucht auf der Grundlage biographischer Massenquellen", Ph.D. thesis (Leipzig 1985).
[28] *Ibid.*
[29] Susanne Schötz, "Karriereverhalten in Umbruchzeiten: Zur Rekrutierung von Leipziger Kleinbürgergruppen während der industriellen Revolution (1830–1870)", in Georg G. Iggers (ed.), *Ein anderer historischer Blick. Beispiele ostdeutscher Sozialgeschichte* (Frankfurt a.M. 1991), pp. 56–69; idem, "Zur Konstituierung 'kleiner' Selbständiger während der bürgerlichen Umwälzung in Leipzig. Ein Beitrag zur messestädtischen Sozialgeschichte", *Jahrbuch für Geschichte* 38 (1989), pp. 39–94.
[30] See Hartmut Zwahr, "Konstitution der Bourgeoisie im Verhältnis zur Arbeiterklasse. Ein deutsch-polnischer Vergleich", in Jürgen Kocka (ed.), *Bürgertum im 19. Jahrhundert. Deutschland im europäischen Vergleich*, Vol. 2 (Munich 1988), pp. 178ff.
[31] See August Bebel, "Aus dem Anfang der Arbeiterbewegung", in: *Die Gründung der Deutschen Sozialdemokratie* (Leipzig 1903), p. 8.
[32] See Hartmut Zwahr, "Namen, Symbole und Identitäten Geächteter im 19. Jahrhundert", in Manfred Lechner and Peter Wilding (eds.), *"Andere" Biographien und ihre Quellen. Biographische Zugänge zur Geschichte der Arbeiterbewegung. Ein Tagungsbericht* (Vienna and Zurich 1992), pp. 27–35.

was supported through the organization of craft associations.[33] In addition to these, the German Metal Workers' Association became the most important industrial trade union beginning in 1891. The breakthrough to a mass union was due to the flood of skilled wage laborers. It occurred despite the resistance put up by the united front of the "old working class" in the craft unions. In this conflict, capital-dependent piece workers clashed with machine-dependent factory workers. The older "artisan socialists" criticized the direction that technological development in capitalism was taking. They believed that eventually a working class would emerge that would lose the ability "to one day confront the masters in the factory and in society and to organize production on their own".[34]

The logic of capitalism, as it emerged in a fully developed form in textile production from within the triad of manufacturing, crafts dependent on capital, and the factory system, was actually one of the strongest forces behind the embourgeoisement during the transition to industrial capitalism. In her statistical studies on Germany in the period after customs unification, the economist Gertrud Hermes claims that this was to be of great importance for the country. "The textile trades were the strongest industrial power to oppose the large landowners."[35] She notes that this industrial sector also supplied Ferdinand Lassalle and Friedrich Engels the financial means "to complete their life work". The textile industry was the first industry to press for civic ideals and practices in Germany and elsewhere. It also pioneered various new frontiers of bourgeois pursuit. Contrary to the sector of mining and smelting industry, which often evolved from large landowning, this industry did not have roots in an earlier feudal past. There is no evidence that the state bureaucracy exercised any supervision over the textile industry comparable to that of mining or, in fact, its control over the German railways. Once freed from the shackles of a system of state control and special privileges, industrial textile production was subjected to strong pressure from international competition. As a result of this, adaptation to everything that constituted an international industrial "bourgeoiseness" was especially urgent. Manufacturers demanded rights of representation and constitutional rights, trade and manufacturing legislation, credit institutions for industry, protection for inventions and patterns, trade schools and training programs, a revamping of the transportation system, an infrastructure beneficial to industry, and much more. The logic of capitalism and its impact on industrial production and reproduction finally deprived the artisan-bourgeoisie, the *Handwerker-Bürger*, of its longing for a life in a free, classless society of citizens. However, in the view of the leading members of the economic

[33] See Boch, *Handwerker-Sozialisten*, pp. 79ff.
[34] *Ibid*.
[35] Gertrud Hermes, "Statistische Studien zur wirtschaftlichen und gesellschaftlichen Struktur des zollvereinten Deutschland", *Archiv für Sozialwissenschaft und Sozialpolitik* 63 (1930), p. 136.

bourgeoisie, the *Wirtschaftsbürger*, this was an unavoidable step down the "English road".[36]

The antipodes of the capital relation in heavy industry

With regards to the sector of heavy industry, we discover a type of class formation in which the interacting social elements are very unequal, indeed extremely unequal. When the location of iron and coal deposits dictated it, industrial plants and factories sprung up in the middle of nowhere, so to speak. The central regions of heavy industry in the German economy gradually evolved like this in Silesia, the Rhine and Ruhr valleys, and the Saar. The majority of the investors had been born into entrepreneurial families. The biographies also trace their lineages to the entrepreneurial dynasties of earlier kinds of urban trade centers, although individual cases cannot be discussed here. Contrary to the entrepreneurs, most of the workers in the coal mines and smelting foundries came from villages. They came from peasant families and from families who belonged to the poorest in the villages. All of these people, including the tens of thousands of Poles in the Ruhr region,[37] arrived in the developing industrial regions and mining colonies with a great willingness to adapt. As a rule, they respected state authorities much longer and attempted to maintain a way of life customary to village life. Catholic pastoral care knew how to integrate these miners and foundry workers into a new environment of heavy industry. Originally, this type of worker contributed little to the social democratic labor movement.[38] The experience of the First World War wrenched a greater part of the younger generation out of the traditional societal order. Hence, entrepreneurs and wage laborers squared off like a poorly matched pair of wrestlers, to continue the metaphor. The parity between textile entrepreneurs and the workforce in the industrial regions of Russian Poland was also very unequal ever since the formerly subservient peasants and their sons from the large estates had lost their employment through agricultural reform, and vast numbers of them had become unskilled or semi-skilled factory workers.[39]

---

[36] See Rudolf Boch, "Von der 'begrenzten' zur forcierten Industrialisierung. Zum Wandel ökonomischer Zielvorstellungen im rheinischen Wirtschaftsbürgertum 1815–1845", in Hans-Jürgen Puhle (ed.) *Bürger in der Gesellschaft der Neuzeit. Wirtschaft – Politik – Kultur* (Göttingen 1991), p. 149.

[37] On this topic, see Christoph Kleßmann, *Polnische Bergarbeiter im Ruhrgebiet 1870–1945. Soziale Integration und nationale Subkultur einer Minderheit in der deutschen Industriegesellschaft* (Göttingen 1978).

[38] See Klaus Tenfelde, *Sozialgeschichte der Bergarbeiterschaft an der Ruhr im 19. Jahrhundert* (Bonn 1981); Klaus Tenfelde and Helmuth Trischler (eds.), *Bis vor die Stufen des Throns. Bittschriften und Beschwerden von Bergleuten im Zeitalter der Industrialisierung* (Munich 1986); for a more comprehensive study, see Gerhard A. Ritter and Klaus Tenfelde, *Arbeiter im Deutschen Kaiserreich 1871–1914* (Bonn 1992), pp. 298ff., 390ff.

[39] See Zwahr, "Konstitution der Bourgeoisie", pp. 158f., 173f.

At this point it needs to be demonstrated, briefly, that entrepreneurs and wage laborers of working-class origin sprung from the same social turf. The actors of future capitalism resembled one another like two peas in a pod. Social inequality stemmed from a state of sameness. The original social balance can be best demonstrated (and biographically best illustrated) in the field of mechanical engineering. The founders (inventors, builders, industrial pioneers) usually had a background in the crafts. They sought occupational training as wage laborer-journeymen in the developing industrial plants (manufacturing factory at the time still meant building machines and appliances each individually, no production line assembly). They became foremen, masters, and factory managers before they dared to become self-employed. They took this step with little capital of their own, but with a great deal of ability and a strong will to work hard. As masters of their craft, they became experts and drew to their side friends, acquaintances and colleagues from the ranks of skilled workers both in the factories and the artisan shops. In the original plant, a type of production democracy temporarily prevailed. This fell apart as the dynamics of capitalism began to polarize and to dominate those involved in production. The production democracy of social equals, to remain with a concept that is perhaps a bit too "strong", was replaced step-by-step by personal power. Work regulations were introduced that clearly assigned duties and stipulated restrictions within a framework of hierarchical, authoritative management and subordination. It heralded the beginning of class divisions among the groups involved in production.

The most prominent of all known examples of this is Chemnitz. In the mid-1860s, numerous machinists refused to acknowledge factory regulations that had been drafted by the largest entrepreneurs in accordance with Saxon trade law. They also refused to submit to the master-of-the-house stance taken by former comrades, the social climbers of newly acquired wealth. They left their jobs and founded the German Machinists' Company (*Deutsche Maschinenbau-Arbeiter-Kompanie*), organizing it as a volunteer association.[40] More than one hundred production workers attempted to replace bourgeois management with the cooperative self-administration of wage labor. Although this experiment in self-determination failed, it deserves attention. It reveals an elementary need for work relations devoid of power struggles and based on cooperation, but it also illustrates the fundamental difficulties that arose for a plant managed on a cooperative basis in a market economy. The original partnership was replaced by relationships dominated by power. This was paralleled by a concentration of capital and the transformation of the earlier artisan-entrepreneur into a "factory boss" as a result of market conditions.

---

[40] See Ernst Hofmann, "Die Deutsche Maschinenbau-Arbeiter-Kompanie in Chemnitz (1863–1867)", *Jahrbuch für Wirtschaftsgeschichte* 1983-III, pp. 77–105.

Bases of class formation

The social basis of class formation[41]

The social basis of class formation was a given already during the phase when an enterprise was being established, that is during the economic formation of a particular form of capitalism. Clearly discernable patterns of recruitment, characteristic marriage circles, milieus, etc., were typical of the social profile for both wage laborers and their entrepreneurial counterparts. For example, the marriage circles of entrepreneurs in both light and heavy industry, with the exception of artisan-types, were primarily restricted to the merchant and industrial bourgeoisie. Usually the wives shared the same bourgeois social background as their husbands. Consequently, the process of embourgeoisement was founded on a stable social base. The same also holds true for the marriage patterns of wage laborers from the same proto-industrial environment. For example, it can be presumed that a high percentage of the workers of the industrial region of the *Erzgebirge* at the turn of the nineteenth to the twentieth century were born into working-class families. Compared with the social formation of the bourgeoisie, it becomes evident that class affiliation and class origin were paralleled to a significant degree for both groups. Perhaps it must even be inferred that certain traits, such as rationality, work attitudes, and self-confidence, which are characteristic of both entrepreneurs (based on property, achievement, family tradition) and workers (based on the value-generating function of wage labor and on a claim in society earned through achievement), correspond to a specific dialectic of capitalism.

The economic basis of class formation

A second basis of class formation is the economic one. It should also be studied and presented in the context of a concrete relationship between the two groups of actors. At the same time, however, the participants should and must be measured against identical standards. The following is a rough outline of the method that should be applied. It is a feasible method, and I assume[42] that its application would make a new sort of integrative social history possible in case studies, and later in more general, broader based research. The point is that entrepreneurs and wage laborers are both the producers and sellers of commodities in capitalism. This is one way to approach the constitution of class. In particular, it can be asked how both groups identified and pursued their interests within the given

---

[41] See Hartmut Zwahr, *Zur Konstituierung des Proletariats als Klasse. Strukturuntersuchung über das Leipziger Proletariat während der industriellen Revolution* (Berlin 1978, Munich 1981), pp. 115–203.

[42] Hartmut Zwahr, "Konstitution der Bourgeoisie", pp. 149–186.

framework of production and which means and methods they used in order
to do this. Additional attention should also be given to the factors of
parity and simultaneousness, or the lack thereof, and how congruence
and incongruence of interests relate to these factors and to the pursuit of
functionally comparable interests. Two areas are to be examined in each
field of study concerning the economic basis of class formation: first, entrepreneurs and wage laborers as owners and producers; second, both groups
as the sellers of commodities.

Entrepreneurs and wage laborers as owners and producers

The entrepreneur was the leading figure of production in the capital relation. As the owner of the means of production, commodities, and labor
assets, as the buyer of labor power and the procurer of commodities, and
as the hegemonic partner in a labor and power relationship, the entrepreneur was dependent on the wage laborers, who not only produced the
commodities but who were the producers of their own labor power as
well. The constitution of a bourgeoisie is based on material and conceptual
foundations. It can be said that the material foundations originated principally from the system of production. To a great degree, both the bourgeoisie and the working class derived their self-image as well as the basis
of their diverging interests from the production of commodities: the bourgeois as founder, organizer, financer, innovator, who pursued profit-
oriented productivity; the worker as the immediate producer of society's
means of existence, which were socialized through private profit-seeking.
Workers who had reached a certain level of class consciousness derived
from this fact their rights to have a share of the product, to control production, and finally to be hegemonic. "The interest of workers and employers
do indeed coincide", stated the Saxon industrial writer Wieck, "yet their
related demands are not uniform. In this sense they diverge abruptly."[43]

At the heart of the history of entrepreneurs and enterprises was the
pursuit of profits through the maximum exploitation of capital, specifically
property, and the creation of conditions aiding exploitation for the purpose
of industrial growth. This concept, understood as forced industrialization,
corresponded to a new understanding of industrialization and had emerged
within Germany from the debate among the Rhenish economic bourgeoisie.[44] Material and conceptual origins of the bourgeoisie developed in
both ways. In contrast to this, the economic interests of the working class
were directed toward the development of individual labor power and its

[43] Quote taken from Siegfried Moltke and Wilhelm Stieda (eds.), *Albert Christian Weinlig
in Briefen von ihm and an ihn* (Leipzig 1931), pp. 296f. (letter dated 30 April 1848).
[44] See Rudolf Boch, *Grenzenloses Wachstum? Das rheinische Wirtschaftsbürgertum und seine
Industrialisierungsdebatte 1814–1857* (Göttingen 1991).

best possible valorization as a commodity. These owner interests conflicted with those of the entrepreneur.

The entrepreneurs in the early stages of capitalism viewed workers primarily as the owners of labor power. Workers had to be able-bodied and profitable. From this arose certain requirements concerning qualification and training and a limited provision of education. Workers needed to be in a position to feed themselves and others. The entrepreneurs presented themselves as providers and benefactors. The workers were dependent on the market, and as such they resembled the entrepreneurs. They were subject to entrepreneurial calculation and received a price in line with real market conditions. They were persons who could endanger order and property should basic needs not be satisfied. From this came the recognition that it was necessary to secure a minimum income, in those cases where this was not conceded for other reasons, and a bourgeois need for security, discipline and socialization. The entrepreneur assumed the role of teacher and public educator.

Wage laborers were seen as the objects of capital valorization, and entrepreneurial motivation for helping them ranged from a sense of Christian responsibility and philanthropy to the calculated maintenance of minimal requirements of existence. The hard-working were promised advancement and entrepreneurial embourgeoisement. Yet, it was not the mindset of the entrepreneurial bourgeoisie that first elevated the worker to a subject of history that achieves a societal position according to its position as a productive force. It was fine for workers to valorize their property in wage labor, but not to become "citizens" of equal standing, perhaps through embourgeoisement. For a long time, embourgeoisement was closely guarded through the goals specified by bourgeois hegemony.

As a rule, the perspectives of the "labor question" changed as the working class evolved from its "raw state" and began to demonstrate its autonomy. Stated with some exaggeration, it was not until the working class developed anti-bourgeois behavior that it became worthy of integration into bourgeois/civic society. This process of integration was restricted not only by the bourgeois image of society, but also by way of the market dependency and the position of a class that supported itself with wages earned chiefly from manual and machine labor. As the owner of labor power, it was not in a position to protect and utilize this property in a manner typical of the entrepreneurial bourgeoisie. How many hurdles had been placed before it ever since it attempted to enter the labor market as an organized force! And yet in principle, it had, in its role as an owner, done nothing differently from its entrepreneurial counterpart.

Entrepreneurial and worker interests could join forces in a movement of occupational training in artisan associations, in Sunday schools, trade schools for improvement, and workers' education associations. The view that knowledge, perceived as civic education, meant power, undeniably has enlightened origins. One Chemnitz '48er thought that the "fully developed industry" represented a power that forced the worker "to think" and thus made him "independent in thought and action".[45] The positive attitude toward steady work, the typical tendency to conduct one's life rationally and methodically, and the autonomous perception of interests had already began to flourish in the proto-industrial beginnings in which miners, weavers, knitters, lace-makers, etc. were included. Compared to this, the attitude of people in feudal labor relations tended to be more destructive and disobedient.

Such a comparison can only be outlined here. It is not possible to go into any further detail, and yet the entire scope of possible variations should also be considered in the following section.

Property valorization through the sale of commodities

The entrepreneur seeks the market for the purpose of profit, the wage laborer for the purpose of securing his or her existence by selling labor power for wages. If one compares them both as sellers of commodities, then in the case of the former, the individual is separate from the commodity, whereas in the case of the latter, the individual and the commodity are inseparably linked. Therefore, the worker is in a disadvantageous position while negotiating the work contract as compared to the seller of any other commodity. The person who buys the use of labor power takes possession of the individual selling it. In this context, he or she determines temporarily the use of people for capital valorization and at the same time attains authority over the wage laborer's person. For example: In the early industrial spinning factory, the labor power was kept in a servant status (primary patriarchalism). City ordinances protected this form of personal power not only against entrepreneurs who wished to entice workers from there, but also against wage laborers who wished to escape. Consequently, the workers were still in a fairly strong position in the textile mills of the early phase of industrialization, otherwise the entrepreneur would not have constrained them in this way.

In the second half of the nineteenth century, the relationship began to change. In the end, many working men and women had become disposable and exchangeable. Firing became a strong means of coercion. Out of the servant-like constraints on wage laborers arose a core of workers who were fairly safe from unemployment. The purpose of this rather crude outline is to demonstrate a methodological problem. This consists of examining and depicting property valorization on both sides of the capital relation through an analysis of the means and methods used by the entrepren-

---

[45] Quote cited in Ernst Hofmann, "Die Entwicklung der Arbeiterbewegung in Chemnitz zwischen 1862 und 1866", *Beiträge zur Heimatgeschichte von Karl-Marx-Stadt* 25 (1982), p. 16.

eur and the wage laborer in selling their specific commodities. For example: in the textile industry of the kingdom of Saxony, but not only here, an interest group for the trade emerged that was based on the tradition of linking the interests of entrepreneurs and wage laborers. Until 1848 it operated on the level of the "fatherland" (that is, Saxony), and afterwards on the "German" level (that is, national). The new form of interest consolidation illustrates protectionists in action. As the advocates of a strategy of national embourgeoisement, they directed the basic needs of the workers towards the path of state help. The alliance of spinning factory owners brought about the first statewide wage agreements. It also consolidated the practice of managerial authority. Along the lines of civic education, this was experienced by the workforce as "despotism" and "white slavery". The "subjugation of the free spirit" appeared to be incompatible with human dignity.[46] The victims measured the industrial bourgeoisie against the civic ideals of liberty, equality and fraternity.

In this example of an alliance within a branch of industry, the textile entrepreneurs first departed from the principle of a free market economy, without granting the men and women of the working class the same opportunity. The demand for maximum customs protection and higher prices in the domestic market reflected the entrepreneurs' interests; it could also have led to an improvement in the price of working-class labor power. Because the entrepreneurs had linked worker interests to state help, the workers instead lagged behind economically as sellers of commodities. They still did not have an equally effective strategy of commodity valorization in a developing market-oriented society. With this in mind, strikes and trade unionization should be seen as developments that corresponded in good measure to the branch alliance of the entrepreneurs or comparable interest associations. In that way, simultaneities and dislocations of social and economic action can be related to processes of class formation, interaction and changes in the contextual framework. It was solely for this purpose that the very fragmentary examples presented here were even included. They relate not only to the factors that encouraged class formation, but also to those that led to class de-formation (to borrow Jürgen Kocka's term) on the economic, social, and political level.[47]

The political basis of class formation

The emerging bourgeois/civic society was the result of defeudalization and embourgeoisement. Modes of thought of the new middle class were incorporated to some degree in all classes and social groups. Even the working class can be considered to be a product of civic society since it

[46] "Arbeiterzustände", *Dresdner Tageblatt*, 31 January 1847.
[47] See Jürgen Kocka, *Lohnarbeit und Klassenbildung. Arbeiter und Arbeiterbewegung in Deutschland 1800–1875* (Bonn 1983), p. 30.

absorbed very many of its elements. If it had not done this, the working class would not have been able to function in a system based on capital valorization through profit maximization. Yet in the view of the majority of at least the original entrepreneurial bourgeoisie and *Bildungsbürgertum*, the sphere of production was the only one in which the working class was permitted to resemble the bourgeoisie. A comparison of bourgeois elites across Europe reveals how great the consensus on this was. The fact that workers refused in the first half of the century to be content with the place in society assigned them by the nobility and the bourgeoisie is linked in a very elementary manner with their own application of civil values. This adaptation of civil values enabled them to view themselves and the position of their own class from the perspective of the ideals of liberty, equality and fraternity. At the same time, class position, exclusion and delimitation made possible the formation of the working class into an independent historical subject (with smooth transitions to the politics of other classes and strata). This did require that the working class assimilate civil values not only in the national context but also in the international context of the bourgeois epoch.

Class interests led workers not only to assimilate a modified form of bourgeois achievements but also to include them into their own basic value system. In this way they achieved their own set of goals and political education. They began to apply these practically. During this entire period, forms of self-help can be traced, such as trade unions and cooperatives, while a minority, whose political influence was growing, sought political solutions of a more fundamental nature and supported the creation of a socialist party. The bourgeois vision of the liberated individual, who is assimilated into a society of liberty, equality and fraternity, was projected onto the classless, socialist society of the future. It was linked with the vision of a "new" man. Without this prerequisite stage of embourgeoisement and the subsequent anti-bourgeoise effects, the labor movement would have not been able either to find acceptance of such an anticipated future or to lay the groundwork for its realization. A new element was the perspective of internationalism, then hardly evident among the bourgeoisie. In capitalist society, socialization and solidarity occurred on a national premise, later to become a nationalistic one on the eve of the First World War.

The formation and modernization of bourgeois society in the countries of central and western Europe prior to the First World War are not conceivable without the pressure for societal change exerted by the labor question first in England and then on the Continent beginning in 1830 and especially from mid-century onward. However, within capitalism the pressure posed by the masses of wage laborers was not dysfunctional; in fact, in many ways it helped to optimize the system. This happened in the factories as well as at the community and state levels. To a great degree, cooperative self-help developed at the same time. The steady growth of real income and the increase in political participation were both trends that not even the formidable First World War could permanently disrupt. "The labor movement and prewar bourgeois society. An attempt to take stock of a century" should be the topic that would follow the considerations presented here.

Translated by Donah Geyer and Marcel van der Linden

History of Symbols as Social History?

Ten preliminary notes on the image and sign systems of social movements in Germany

GOTTFRIED KORFF

I

The last two centuries have produced, transformed and destroyed a myriad of political symbols of a linguistic, visual and ritual form. Between, say 1790 and 1990 the political sphere witnessed both an explosion in the generation of symbols and a radical decline of symbols. This calls for explanations.

Mary Douglas and Serge Moscovici have provided insightful reflections on the theory and history of political symbols of modern social movements. In Moscovici the analysis of symbols is part of a political psychology which aims to interpret the behaviour and conceptions of nineteenth- and twentieth-century mass movements.[1] Moscovici's basic premise is that, due to the emergence of new forms of collective conditions of existence, society's perception of itself has been determined since the French Revolution by the image of the mass, by the concept of political mass movements. The extent of the revolutionary processes which determined and accompanied the progress into modernity, and the political reaction following them, were defined by the category "mass" by those directly involved as well observers. The "mass" was not just a category but also a strategy: the "mass movement" and the "mass action" were seen as the goals of political action. Reaching this goal required collective representations in the form of linguistic, visual and ritual symbols. Signs, images and gestures created and consolidated collective identities.[2]

Political symbols are means of communication in a mass society. Symbols enable the development of group identities and the contraction of linguistic communication processes.[3] Nineteenth-century French literature, which, unlike that of other European countries, often set up "society" as the hero of novel, offers impressive insights into the use and significance of new political signs and symbols, of flags, clothing and gestures.[4] A prime example is provided by the five volumes of Victor Hugo's *Les Misérables* (1862), which describe in precise detail the political symbols of the period

[1] Serge Moscovici, *The Age of the Crowd. A Historical Treatise on Mass Psychology* (Cambridge 1985).
[2] Lynn Hunt, *Culture and Class in the French Revolution* (Berkeley, 1984).
[3] Bernhard Giesen, *Die Entdinglichung des Sozialen* (Frankfurt/M., 1991), p.240.
[4] See Wolfgang Kemp, "Das Bild der Menge, 1789–1830", *Städel-Jahrbuch*, NF 4 (1973), pp. 249–270.

International Review of Social History 38 (1993), Supplement, pp. 105–125

between 1815 and 1830 covered by the novel. The same is the case in Emile Zola's *Germinal* (1885), which depicts the emerging symbolic orientations of the politicizing French working class.

II

Moscovici points to formal structural elements and relations of modern society to explain the rise and consolidation of specific political symbols in the nineteenth and twentieth centuries. Mary Douglas, on the other hand, primarily locates symbolic understanding in the society's class structure, in the social hierarchy of "industrial societies".[5] This allows her to explain not only the emergence, but also the differentiation and erosion, of political systems. In her analysis Douglas relies on the work of the sociolinguist Basil Bernstein, and in some sense she argues along sociolinguistic lines. The lower classes of urban industrialized society, the bedrock of social movements, are not integrated into the system of political discourse of bourgeois society because they are restricted in their linguistic behaviour and their political articulacy. The restricted language code is compensated by highly ritualized communication types, which are emotional and affective rather than logical and discursive. Restricted language code and ritual are correlated to each other. The rituals, Douglas observes, are used to adorn and strengthen the group cultures. The non-discursive behavioural logic of the lower-class collective has to rely on symbols to enable it to fit into the political scheme of general society. At the same time cultural and social self-images and collective identities are developed. Collective identities, however short-lived they may be, derive a consistency through their sign and image systems, and thus fit recognizably into a social reality.

Douglas' considerations not only place political symbolism in a social context, in the class structure of a society, but also in a historical context. She observes a gradual decline of symbolic orientations in industrial society, caused by a reduced receptivity to symbols, due in turn to a steady extension of discursive forms of communication in western industrial society.[6] Increasingly symbolic forms are replaced by linguistic forms. It may be that in her analysis Douglas has been too much influenced by a "simple" ethnological conception of symbolism – something to which, according to Victor Turner, ethnologists and anthropologists often succumb because they tend to miss the "watershed division" between "symbolic systems and genres belonging to cultures which have developed before and after the Industrial Revolution"[7] – and that she has therefore not given sufficient

[5] Mary Douglas, *Natural Symbols. Exploration in Cosmology* (London 1970), esp. "To Inner Experience", pp. 40–58.

[6] *Ibid.*, p. 63 and p. 55

[7] Victor Turner *From Ritual to Theater. The Human Seriousness of Play* (New York, 1982), p. 30.

Figure 1. "A Salute to the May day celebration." May Day postcard from circa 1910

weight to the increased power of symbols deriving from the greater aesthetic sophistication and the impact of the mass media and to their "ludic"
and "experimental" significance in the reality of modern society (and even
more so of post-modern society). Symbols are not only the expression of
a restricted (i.e. non-linguistic culture), but also the expression of a "ludic"
culture, which means that political symbols still remain part of our image
worlds even after they have lost their political significance. This is evident
particularly in the history of symbols of the left. Political symbols no longer
seem necessary as orientation signs, but they are still known. That explains
their random, playful or "ludic" usage. Not infrequently political symbols
mutate into do-it-yourself and play elements of subcultural groups and
thus lose their political significance and instrumentality. The hammer-and-
sickle emblem becomes a fashion accessory.[8]

III

In conjunction with Moscovici's model Douglas' observations offer an
explanation of the rise and decline of political symbols, particularly those

[8] See also Gottfried Korff, "Notizen zur Symbolbedeutung der Sichel im 20. Jahrhundert",
in Silke Göttsch and Kai Detlev Sievers. (eds.). *Forschungsfeld Museum. Festschrift für
Arnold Lühning zum 65. Geburtstag* (Kiel, 1988), pp. 195–225, esp. pp. 212f. On the sale
of "socialist" symbols during and following the dissolution of East Germany, see Monika
Flacke-Knoch, "Die verkaufte Biographie", in *Bilder vom Neuen Deutschland: Eine deutsch–
deutsche Ausstellungscollage*, exhibition at the Kunsthalle Düsseldorf, 13–22 July 1990
(Düsselford, 1990), p. 25.

of the nineteenth and twentieth-century social movements. Symbols, we know, extend well beyond the reach of verbal understanding. They are of key importance above all in environments characterized by linguistic and other restrictions. This means that the role of symbols and signs in identity and group formation will be particularly significant within social groups that are disadvantaged in their verbal, cognitive and intellectual development because of a restrictive working life, living conditions and forms of communication. Richard Hoggart put the situation of working people succinctly: "They had little or no training in the handling of ideas or in analysis."[9] A similar point is made by Paul A. Pickering in his essay "Class without Words", which investigates the role of symbolic forms of communication in the British Chartist movement.[10] As the masses pushed towards political articulation, symbols and expressive signs played an important role in the forging of identity and unity. This applies especially in the first half of the nineteenth century, when there existed as yet no other media and institutions for social communication like political associations and parties.

Max Weber was the first to note the irrational, emotional behaviour of the politically unorganized mass, "irrational mob rule", as he called it.[11] For him it is irrational because it is unformed or unmediated, neither by parties as "organized political interest groups" nor by intentional symbols. Weber sees symbols as transitional forms, as transitory media, as communicative aids in the creation of "communal action based on agreement", which is distinguished from "uniform mass action" and "mass-determined action" by a sense of purpose. A precondition for the rise of political action groups is the organization of a "plurality of people by means of similar purposive usage of specific externally similar symbols."[12] Since they support political activities in a suggestive and affective way, symbols become obsolete as the rationality potential grows in the parties. Parties, according to Weber, are concerned with the realization of "specific political goals."' The unorganized mass on the street – suspect as far as Weber was concerned because it tends towards "coups, sabotage and similar excesses"[13] – forms and directs itself in its aims by means of symbols, images and signs. In so doing it develops politically mature and functional organizational structures, which in the long term make symbols redundant. The politics of democratization and mass communication is determined by the word, a trend which is also encouraged by the technical media.

---

[9] Richard Hoggart, *The Uses of Literacy: Aspects of Working Class Life with Special Preference to Publications and Entertainments* (Harmondsworth, 1958), p. 102.
[10] Paul A. Pickering, "Class without Words: Symbolic Communication in the Chartist movement", *Past and Present*, 112 (1986), pp. 144–162.
[11] Max Weber, *Wirtschaft und Gesellschaft: Grundriss der verstehenden Soziologie* (Tübingen 1972), p. 868.
[12] Max Weber, *Soziologie: Weltgeschichtliche Analysen: Politik*, third edn. (Stuttgart 1964), p. 127; see also Giesen, *Die Entdinglichung des Sozialen*, p. 207.
[13] Max Weber, *Wirtschaft und Gesellschaft*, p. 839.

Figure 2. Cover page illustration of the May 1904 issue of *Vorwärts*

Unlike Weber, Robert Michels observes the rise of a "new" irra-
tionalism as a result of the ideologization of politics, and he has described
this in relation to party symbols and rituals.[14] And indeed, symbols should
be seen in relation to the political ideologies of the nineteenth and especially the twentieth century – the "age of ideologies", as Karl Dietrich

---

[14] Robert Michels, *Zur Soziologie des Parteiwesens in der modernen Demokratie: Untersuchungen über die oligarchischen Tendenzen des Gruppenlebens* (Stuttgart, 1970), pp. 57–64
("Das Verehrungsbedürfnis der Massen"), and "Psychologie der antikapitalistischen Massenbewegungen", in *Grundriss der Sozialökonomik*, vol. 9, part viii (Tübingen, 1926), pp. 343–
349 ("Das Bedürfnis nach Symbolik").

Bracher has called it.[15] Symbols play a key role in the propagandistic dissemination of ideologies. They abbreviate and simplify the contents and the message of political statements and thus make them memorable and socially effective. The fact that in the context of the ideologies of the nineteenth and twentieth centuries many observers talk of "new religions" and "new myths" shows that political styles still have symbolic potencies in the "disenchanted" world. This is why the irrational political mobilization of the masses after the First World War in support of ideologies produced a wealth of political symbols, emblems and metaphors.

IV

The history of political symbols in mass society should be analysed, then, from two perspectives: one concerned with the emergence, development and consolidation of specific symbols (in short, the political and ideological perspective); and a second concerned with their general impact, their conceptual transformations and informalizations (what might be called the ethnological perspective). When symbolic behaviour is analysed solely in political science terms, important dimensions are ignored. It is true that political symbols play an essential role in the system of power and domination (as outlined by Murray Edelman).[16] But they also have an "elementary" function, as it were, insofar as they offer guidelines for the relationship between people, society and politics. Political symbols satisfy a need not only for building political identities and transmitting ideology, but also for clarity, security and confirmation, because modern society has become complex and incomprehensible, particularly in the political sphere. This has happened as a result of processes which are perceived as contrary and contradictory: objectification and ideologization, "disenchantment" and mythologization, individualization and collectivization, and so on. Symbols satisfy the individual's need for non-rational identification in mass society. If there exists a structural need for symbols in modern societies (a need which, contrary to what Weber expected, disenchantment has intensified rather than diminished), then the issue of symbols should be addressed not merely in relation to political organizations, movements and ideologies, but also in the context of a cultural anthropology of aesthetics, an ethnology of sensual, non-discursive communication in industrial society.[17]

A survey of the historical, ethnological and sociological analyses of the symbols in industrial societies – which considering the political significance of the subject matter are rather few in number – gives the impression of

[15] Karl Dietrich Bracher, *Zeit der Ideologien: Eine Geschichte politischen Denkens im 20. Jahrhundert* (Stuttgart, 1982).
[16] Murray Edelmann, *Politics as Symbolic Action. Mass Arousal and Quiescence* (Chicago, 1972).
[17] See Alfred Lorenzer, *Das Konzil der Buchhalter: Die Zerstörung der Sinnlichkeit: Eine Religionskritik* (Frankfurt/M., 1981).

an ever evolving usage of linguistic, visual and gesticulatory symbols.[18] It is clear that there was an inflation of symbols in the second half of the nineteenth century and the first half of the twentieth century and a deflation of "organized" political symbols, though not of symbols in general, in the second half of the twentieth century.

An iconographic analysis of the history of symbols of the German labour movement produces a similar picture. The period during which consistent symbols were elaborated and established lasted until around 1870, with a characteristic juxtaposition and opposition of transitional forms and innovations. Symbolic and ritual forms were consolidated, officialized and ceremonialized in the last third of the nineteenth century and up to the outbreak of the First World War. In the period after the First World War new symbols were invented and created and older ones developed further and transformed. All this occurred in a productive, symbol-generating dialogue among the parties of the left, but in part also in opposition to the emergent symbolic language of fascism (not just in Germany).

It was with good reason that Walter Benjamin spoke of the conflict between aestheticized politics and politicized aesthetics during the Weimar Republic, a conflict he considered resolved in 1933 in favour of the aestheticization of politics.[19] In the final years of the Weimer republic and during the Third Reich technical advances in mass information and suggestion also came into a play, a phenomenon which has as yet been scarcely analysed.

After 1945 we find specific elements in Western Europe which had been absent from the earlier phases. There occurred an erosion, or more precisely, a diffusion of the proletarian and socialist symbolic legacy, caused by the end of the proletariat on the one hand and the rapid rise of the mass media and the emergence of new styles of consumption on the other. In the communist countries of Central and Eastern Europe the use of political symbols was highly organized and centrally directed. Symbols were deployed extensively, but because their use was institutionalized within a context of political and ideological block formation, they also lost their dynamic power.[20] In 1989–90 the communist imagery, slogans and symbols collapsed as quickly as the political regimes themselves.

V

The point is proved by the history of the red flag, May Day and the clenched fist. These three symbols belong to different phases of the labour

---

[18] An overview is provided by Rüdiger Voigt (ed.), *Symbole der Politik, Politik der Symbole* (Opladen 1989).

[19] Walter Benjamin, *Das Kunstwerk im Zeitalter seiner technischen Reproduzierbarkeit* (Frankfurt/M., 1963), pp. 48–51.

[20] Ralf Rytlewski, Birgit Sauer and Ulrike Treziak, *Politische Kultur in Deutschland: Bilanz und Perspektiven der Forschung* (Opladen, 1987), pp. 247–257.

Figure 3. "We attack." May Day postcard from 1931

movement. The red flag represents the early labour movement before
and during the 1848 revolutions and before the foundation of the Social
Democratic Party of Germany (SPD). It has of course accompanied the
labour movement in changing forms until the present day. May Day represents the labour movement at the height of its organized development
in the last decade of the nineteenth century, when the streets in Germany
had been reconquered for the politics of the masses after the repeal of
the Anti-Socialist Law. May Day became the triumphal public act of the
proletarian class. The clenched fist originated in the turbulent early years
of the Weiman republic and became a symbol initially of the communist

half of the devided labour movement. It was adopted by the "Iron Front" (albeit in combination with the slogan "Freedom!") and later became, particularly through its adoption by the Popular Front in France and during the Spanish Civil War, the international socialist sign of recognition and ceremonial greeting. After 1933 the Nazis either proscribed or destroyed the socialist symbols or "nationalized" them, thereby destroying them in two ways, by liquidation and transformation (a precondition of the Nazi appropriation). An impressive series of photographs of Walter Ballhaus illustrates the opposition of the red flag and the swastika during the occupation of the trade union headquarters in Hanover on 2 May 1933. One of the photographs shows how the swastika flag is raised; a second shows the burning of the red flag and its remains as a heap of ashes.[21]

The origins of the red flag indicate how much the socialist prolaterian symbols were generated in the tension between spontaneity and organization.[22] They also, incidentally, bear witness to the strongly international orientation even of the early labour movement. The colour red as a republican-socialist symbol has its roots in the Jacobin tradition of the French revolution, as we know from the thorough work by Maurice Dommanget.[23] Red appeared on the political stage, first sparingly, then more frequently, in the period leading up to 1848 ad during the revolutions of that year as the symbol that distinguished the proletarian activists from the bourgeois and petty bourgeois elements among the revolutionaries. It was the "new masses", those collectives which defined themselves as "neither estate nor class", which rallied around the red flag. But the symbol had to be created first. Many reports indicate that the flags of socialist red emerged spontaneously, in the course of political activities, as the product of symbol-creating *bricolage*. The red flag is a symbol "born in struggle" during the events of 1848 and the campaign for constitutional reforms in Germany. In future the colour red would terrify the bourgeoisie.[24] It was adopted by the Lassalle-led labour movement and the Paris Commune, which further strengthened its fear value. The purpose of the new symbol was to delineate the left from the strategic logic of bourgeois and petty bourgeois groups and to encourage action. It should be borne in mind here that because this symbol emerged out of political action, it was not planned or

---

[21] Walter Ballhaus, *Licht und Schatten der dreissiger Jahre: Foto-Dokumente aus dem Alltag* (Munich, 1985) pp. 159f.

[22] See Gottfried Korff. "Rote Fahnen und Tableaux Vivants: Zum Symbolverständnis der deutschen Arbeiterbewegung im 19. Jahrhundert", in Albrecht Lehmann (ed.), *Studien zur Arbeiterkultur* (Münster, 1984), pp. 103–140.

[23] Maurice Donmanget, *La Revolution de 1848 et le drapeau rouge* (Paris, 1948) (Collection Spartacus 2/17); Gabriel Perreux, *Les origines du drapeau rouge en France* (Paris, 1930).

[24] In the annotations to Alfred Rethel's "Auch ein Totentanz" (1849) the "hero of the red republic" is represented as the harbinger of destruction. This caused Rethel's series of woodcuts to be regarded as anti-revolutionary conservative propaganda. A plausible reinterpretation has recently been offered in Peter Paret, *Kunst als Geschichte: Kultur und Politik von Menzel bis Fontane* (Munich, 1990), pp. 124–154.

directed in any way: it acquired its contours from a specific local interplay of spontaneity, ritualism, protest and programme.

Because they originated in the course of political activity, the red flags flying on the barricades or carried at demonstrations were often a matter of improvisation. Improvisations on the red theme appeared time and again in 1948–49; adapted clothing, torn-up bedlinen, red-dyed straw mattresses. "In some cases women's underwear tied to a pole sufficed as a means of influencing and enthusing the masses", Robert Michels observed.[25] This points to the interplay of political meaning and spontaneous, almost wild, usage in a local revolutionary act which was characteristic of the red symbol's development.

The role of red stabilized during the "cold" phrase of the Lassalle movement. During the German Empire the red flag lived a kind of double life. On the one hand it was a ceremonialized emblem, partly heavily adorned with a mixture of traditional and new ornaments; on the other hand it was a "wild" agitation tool a rag signifying movement. The decorative ceremonial flag was, as Michels described in the same passage, "kept in the secure rooms of the movement's sanctuaries." The wild flag, however, continued to be raised on buildings during night-time actions and thus gave expression, as a "spontaneous" sign, to the courage, vigour and dynamism of the labour movement.

VI

The first time May Day was celebrated as the international festival of labour was in 1890.[26] The labour movements in Europe had widely different strengths and organizational structures, and the nature of the May Day celebrations varied accordingly. The ambivalence of holiday and day of struggle gave May Day a unique character, but also a special elasticity which stimulated different presentational forms. In linking struggle and celebration, May Day laid claim to an epochal and international perspective. That had been the intention of the international workers' congress in Paris in 1889, which on the occasion of the centenary on the French Revolution had sought to renew the elan of the *fêtes révolutionnaires* and thus establish the workers' movement as the "true heirs" of the revolution.

May Day demonstrated both the political and the cultural claim of the labour movement. The eight-hour day was a demand for co-determination

---

[25] Robert Michels, *Zur Soziologie des Parteiwesens*, p. 344

[26] On the significance of May Day, see Gottfried Korff, "Seht die Zeichen die euch gelten, Fünf Bemerkungen zur Symbolgeschichte des 1. Mai" in Inge Marssolek (ed). *Zur Geschichte des 1. Mai* (Frankfurt/M. and Vienna, 1990), pp. 15–39; Verein zum Studium sozialer Bewegungen (ed.), *100 Jahre Erster Mai: Beiträge und Projekte zur Geschichte der Maifeiern in Deutschland: Ein Tagungsbericht* (Berlin, 1989); Andrea Panaccione (ed.), *The Memory of May Day: An Iconographic History of Origins and Implanting of a Workers' Holiday* (Venice, 1989).

and self-determination in one. It was to increase the amount of leisure time and thus offer more freedom, greater human dignity and scope for cultural activity. The May Day celebrations showed what the labour movement had learnt since its beginnings, above all during its organized phase, in terms of imagination, strategy, discipline and direction. May Day allowed the public presentation of the workers' condition, not as a mode of existence, but rather as an enjoyable interactive activity (involving the whole family) which articulated the movement's demands for social justice and cultural freedom. May Day was the socialist labour movement's successful attempt at self-representation.

With the hindsight of history the transfer of the May Day activities to the following Sunday may appear as a sign of a lack of political energy, as conflict avoidance. But from the viewpoint of the celebrating masses it was precisely the cultural and entertaining elements which made "our very own festival" (Kurt Eisner's phrase)[27] into an effective medium for confident socialist politics. And, as already mentioned, the ideology of the celebration dovetailed with the political demand for the eight-hour working day, which had been the starting point of the May Day movement and to which it was dedicated in its early decades. Leisure time was seen as culture time, as an opportunity for educational and cultural self-realization.

The pivotal significance of May Day's festive character was tapped not least through the spring and rebirth metaphor. This was an integral part of the May Day rhetoric and iconography.[28] Two association complexes play a role here: the awakening, budding and forward-pointing aspect of nature reborn on the one hand, and on the other the airy, free and natural aspects which were so poignantly at odds with the drudgery of factory work and the deplorable living conditions of the proletariat. The symbolic elements gave the holiday a great dynamism in the decades before the First World War. This was able to assert itself effectively even when the celebrations were impeded by drastic or subtle repressive measures or were controversial within the labour movement itself.

The natural elements of the May Day iconography corresponded to the nature-related rituals exercised in practice. Forest walks, excursions, gatherings in open-air restaurants and Sunday dances were as much a part of May Day as the marches and political demonstrations. Dress was also used to symbolize the transcendence of the everyday reality. At May Day events workers would wear their best suit, tie, hat and overcoat and pin a red carnation in their buttonhole.

[27] Kurt Eisner, "Festlicher Kampf", in *Gesammelte Schriften*, vol. 2 (Berlin, 1919), pp. 92–96.
[28] Klaus-D. Pohl, "Allegorie und Arbeiter: Bildagitatorische Didaktik und Repräsentation der SPD 1890–1914: Studien zum politischen Umgang mit bildender Kunst in den politisch-satirischen Zeitschriften 'Der wahre Jacob' und 'Süddeutscher Postillon' sowie in den Mai-festzeitungen", doctoral dissertation, University of Osnabrück (Osnabrück, 1986).

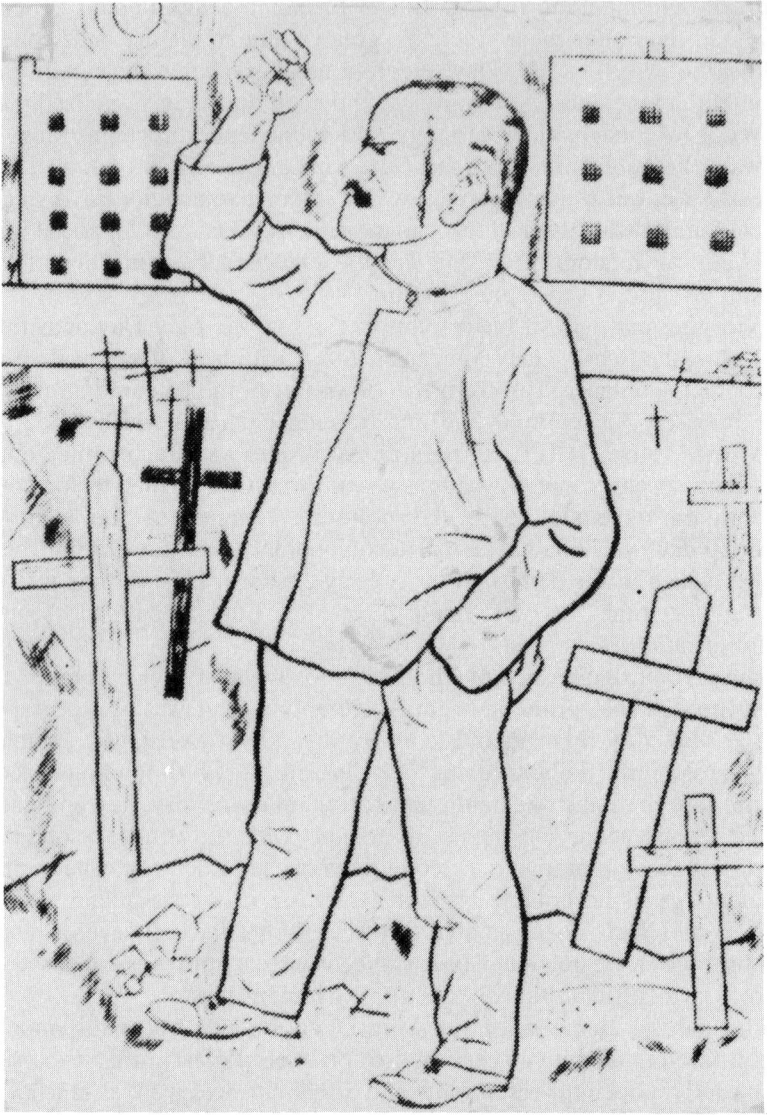

Figure 4. George Grosz: Over the tombs of March: Beware! (1922)

VII

The spring-like character of May Day was lost in the Weimar Republic. In fact the festival's whole iconography and choreography was transformed. Like other symbols of the labour movement, May Day suffered from a loss of socialist utopian sentiment. The joyful aspect disappeared, harder contours came to the fore.[29] One reason for this was certainly the SPD's participation in government at local, regional and national level, which confronted socialist ideals with political realities. In addition, and linked to it, there was the division of the labour movement. Through competition and friction this division did, however, have a productive and creative effect on symbol development. New symbols were created or adopted from elsewhere and put at the core of new rituals, signs and gestures. The hammer-and-sickle emblem was adopted from the newly formed Soviet Union. A new development was the "clenched fist", which became the ritual greeting of the Red Front and was used as a distinguishing offensive symbol against the social democratic labour movement. Two points should be stressed in relation to the fist symbol: first, it came about as a deliberate creative act by an artist, a fact which clearly illustrates the labour movement's proximity to the artistic avantgarde; and second, it played a prominent role as a defining symbol in street demonstrations (the kind of action which typified the style of demonstrating during the Weimar republic). The Red Front's fist emblem was designed by John Heartfield on the basis of a drawing by Georges Grosz. Out of a latent elementary expression of anger he created a fixed symbolic form which as a gesture and an image was easy to transmit. The fist was a response to the greeting of Mussolini's fascist movement which emerged soon after the First World War and was later adopted by the Nazis.

Together with the slogan "Red Front!" the fist became the hallmark of the communist-oriented working class. It became a gesticulatory component of the street marches which marked the "symbol war" of the 1920s. The marches escalated into open street terror, an extension which was latent in the symbolic-affective "struggles" of the demonstration culture. The notorious street brawls of May 1929 were part of this, as was the "struggle for Berlin" organized by Joseph Goebbels.[30] Towards the end of the republic the "symbol war" degenerated into the "logic of the heavier stick" (in the words of Carl von Ossietzky).

Other socialist symbols succumbed to the symbol war, including the red flag, May Day, and the workers' education movement. Both left-wing parties created their own flag and May Day rhetoric, and their own May Day iconography and choreography. Once again influenced by the art of the avantgarde, both established their own education and cultural networks, with in part fascinating results. Piscator, Brecht, Hindemith, Weill,

---

[29] Gottfried Korff, "Roth Fahnen und geballte Faust: Zur Symbolik der Arbeiterbewegung in der Weimarer Republik", in Peter Assion (ed.), *Transformationen der Arbeiterkultur* (Marburg, 1986), pp. 86–107.

[30] Joseph Goebbels, *Kampf um Berlin* (Munich, 1932); Gerhard Paul, *Aufstand der Bilder: Die NS-Propaganda vor 1933* (Bonn, 1990). The street fights could in turn generate symbols and symbolic figures: examples are the Nazi cult figure Horst Wessel and the Horst Wessel Lied.

Figure 5. Emblem, of the *Rote Frontkämpferbund* with the fist by John Heartfield (1927)

Eisler, Heartfield and Grosz all made major contributions to the cultural history of the Weimar Republic. Never before and never since has the link between the labour movement and avantgarde art been closer and more productive than in the 1920s. The loss of utopia was to some extent compensated by the competition over symbols and the artistic impulses, which helped to mould the much admired dynamism and energy of "left-wing" culture in the Weimar Republic.

Towards the end of the Weimar Republic the new mass media began to have an impact. They also gave new impulses to working-class culture. But they did not present a productive challenge, as Benjamin, Eisler and Brecht imagined and predicted, because after the Nazi takeover in 1933 the mass media were "streamlined" and manipulated to give a totalitarian direction to all aspects of public life.

VIII

A large number of workers' symbols survived during the Nazi period because in the early years of the dictatorship many of the well-known social symbols were remodelled for a fascist application. Not all of it was a case of usurping the proletarian socialist heritage, however, since a number of political symbols of the left (the marches, uniforms and the ceremonial greetings, among others) were derived from the signs and gestures of Italian fascism. The fascist conception of symbols was based on form but above all on functional aspects, the blatantly manipulative intention which Benjamin described as the intention to "aestheticize politics". The Third Reich's didacticism proved effective, as was the instrumentalization of mass-media techniques, with authentic means of communications bracketed with media strategies. Using the example of Nazi symbols Saul Friedländer and George L. Mosse have described with great insight the coupling of individual and mass-psychological motivations into an instrument of domination.[31] The symbols were used to "stage a dramatic production of the community", in which the social contradictions of modern society were to be resolved through harmonization and manipulation.[32] The political messages embedded in the symbols and identities of the social movements which had arisen in the mid-nineteenth century (parties, associations and unions) were defused and "nationalized". Justified in terms of the demands of "the people", the whole population was permanently mobilized by means of a system of direction and ritual, enhanced and at times picturesquely decorated with the traditional symbols.[33]

Compared to the symbols of the Nazi era, those of the two German states after the Second World War have been very inadequately studied. Remarkable, particularly in West Germany, was a dissociation and abstention from symbols, rooted in an aversion to the political collectivisms of the Nazi era, particularly its community ideology. In addition we encounter the phenomenon which has been described as the end of the proletariat.[34] A confident and articulate labour movement, with all its symbols,

---

[31] Saul Friedländer, *Reflets du nazisme* (Paris 1982); George L. Mosse, *Nationalism and Sexuality. Respectability and Abnormal Sexuality in Modern Europe* (New York, 1985).

[32] Rainer Stommer, *Die inszenierte Volksgemeinschaft: Die "Thing-Bewegung" im Dritten Reich* (Marburg, 1985).

[33] On the invocation of the "people" (*Volk*) as an instrument of domination, see Bracher *Zeit der Ideologien*, pp. 164f.

[34] Josef Mooser, *Arbeiterleben in Deutschland 1900–1970: Klassenlage Kultur and Politik* (Frankfurt/M., 1984); Ulrich Beck, "Jenseits von Stand und Klasse? Soziale Ungleichheiten, gesellschaftliche individualisierungsprozesse und die Entstehung neuer sozialer Formationen und Identitäten", *Soziale Welt*, special volume (1983), pp. 35–74.

Figure 6. The European Socialist parties' fist holding a carnation

seemed no longer plausible, not least because the social movements were incorporated into the structure of mass-membership of people's parties. Individualization processes, enhanced by private media consumption, not only dissolved political blocks but also mental preconceptions.[35]

[35] Klaus Tenfelde, "Ende der Arbeiterkulter: Das Echo auf eine These", in Wolfgang Kaschuba, Gottfried Korff and Bernd Jürgen Warneken (eds.), *Ende oder Veränderung: Arbeiterkultur seit 1945* (Tübinger, 1991).

We must wonder whether the orientation on political symbols has not been replaced by a powerful orientation on consumption, with the aesthetic of commodities taking over the function of guiding symbols in Douglas' sense. (Another phenomenon can in fact also be observed, namely the transformation of the social movements' symbols into consumer articles or fashion accessories: the hammer and sickle as ear-rings, the fist as wall decoration, and May Day as a special folkloric event.)[36]

Pluralization, differentiation and privatization of the "mass" – the concentration of these processes may lead to what may be called the end of "collective political symbols". There can be no question of an end to a symbolic orientation in general, as studies of young people's perceptions or the work of Pierre Bourdieu's on the aesthetics of distinctiveness show.

IX

The European version of the youth revolts and "student revolutions" of the late 1960s and early 1970s contributed in no small measure to the erosion of left-wing political symbols. These movements related to the "heritage" of symbolic forms in part-creativity and playfully (especially in France) and in part rigidly and protectively (especially in West Germany). In general the heritage was used eclectically, and the impact of the inherited symbols was inflationary. This applied to emblems, rituals as well as words and slogans. The student and youth rebellions encouraged a trend towards the uncoupling of symbol systems from their previously relatively strong political links (to organizations, parties and associations). The political symbols lose their roots without, however, establishing themselves in their new environments, which was impossible not least because these were highly unstable ideologically and organizationally. The organizational uncoupling of left-wing political symbols by the 1968 generation fostered the random use of the semiotic heritage and opened it up to commercialization. New forms, like the Easter demonstrations (against the arms race etc.) failed to gain a structural permanence or have a lasting impact.

In the communist states of Central and Eastern Europe the heritage was administered by the state and prescribed as political decoration. In this way political symbolism succumbed to the mechanism of a centrally manufactured ritual public sphere which left no scope for dynamic and creative developments.[37] The red flags and red carnations were for waving during the May Day marches, which were celebrated as state occasions.

---

[36] See the discussion of the contemporary relevance of May Day at at seminar on working-class culture held in Tübingen in 1989, pubnlished in *ibid*. See also the more recent Inge Marssolek, "100 Jahr 1. Mai: (k)ein Grund zum Feiern", *Journal Geschichte*, 5/1990, pp. 12–23.

[37] Michael Hoffmanm, "Vom Schwung der Massenfeste: Uberlegungen zur wirksameren Gestaltung traditioneller und neuer Feiertage", *Kultur und Freizeit*, 24/11 (1986), pp. 22–25, and 24/12 (1986), pp. 27f.

Figure 7. Anti-socialist poster from the French elections in Spring of 1993

The clasped hands of the 1848 labour movement became, in distortion of the iconographic tradition, the symbol of East Germany's Social Unity party (SED). No new symbols were created, with the exception of the hammer and compass on the East German coat of arms, which was closely linked to the Soviet hammer and sickle motif.

The revolutions of 1989 brought an abrupt end for several symbols, either through public abolition (state and party emblems) or private distancing (the red flags, forms of address like the familiar *Du* among party comrades). Within the space of a few months the dissolution of the GDR and the other communist regimes completed a change which had been occurring gradually in Western Europe since the Second World War. Political symbols – some of which had a more than century-long tradition –

Figure 8. Fabric design featuring a hammer and sickle at a New York fashion show in the mid-1980s

were transformed into "ludic" elements. The flags waved at the marches became party decorations, and SED badges became fashion accessories. The "ludic" reinterpretation of the symbols to some extent certainly amounted to a demonstrative distancing from the despised previous system.[38] At the same time, however, East German symbols continue to be used in political contexts, both organized and unorganized or "wild". An example of the latter was the use of the hammer and sickle and red flags during the squatter riots in Berlin in the autumn of 1990; and in an example of organized use, the Party of Democratic Socialism, the SED's successor, gave prominent display to the colour red at its 1990 May Day rally in front of the Berlin Reichstag.

X

Symbols are abbreviations for ideologies. If it is true that in the last decade of the twentieth century Europe has entered a post-ideological era, then we have here another reason for the demise of the political symbols of social movements. Symbols are simplified objectifications of ideologies, and indeed, the history of the symbols of social movement is closely interlinked with the history of political ideologies in the twentieth century. Political symbols flourished in the wake of revolutions and dictatorships in the first half of this century. And the waning of ideological commitment after the Second World War had led to a contraction in the use of political symbols, initially in the 1950s and especially since the mid-1970s. (Interestingly, the ideologically charged interlude of the late 1960s did not have a regenerative effect, but actually contributed to the decline of political symbols.)

Political symbols also play an important role beyond the ideologies. The alternative movements and countercultures which emerge in the 1980s display a wide range of emblems and signs, albeit invariably with very limited social and temporal scope. These are temporary signs of identity, of varied political origins and each time syncretically remixed. An example is the eclecticism and syncretism of the symbols used by the squatter groups and their autonomous and anti-establishment successors in the inner cities. The protest cultures within industrial society employ a wide range of symbols, including the black of anarchism, swastikas, hammer-and-sickle as well as archetypal images (snakes and dragons). Their common characteristic is dissociation from the "semantic forms" typical of the "intellectual" youth rebellion of the late 1960s. That spontaneous, politically intended but short-lived symbols are currently emerging with particular intensity in a linguistically, semantically and verbally

---

[38] Gottfried Korff, "Rote Fahnen und Bananen: Notizen zur politischen Symbolik im Prozess der Vereinigung von DDR und BRD", *Schweizerisches Archiv für Volkskunde*, 86 (1990), pp. 130–160.

Figure 9. Removing the SED insignia with the fraternal clasped hands from the party's Dresden headquarters (March, 1990)

undeveloped underclass – as already observed by Karl Heinz Bohrer in the late 1970s[39] – may be linked to Douglas' class-specific socialization and outlook. In other words, symbols and rituals are still the means by which the "lower levels" of mass industrial society organize themselves and communicate. "Such non-verbal symbols are capable of creating a structure of meanings in which individuals can relate to one another and realize their own ultimate purposes."[40]

Translated by Harry Drost

[39] Karl-Heinz Bohrer, "Die drei Kulturen", in Jürgen Habermas (ed.), *Stichworte zur "Geistigen Situation der Zeit"* vol. 2, "Politik und Kultur" (Frankfurt/M., 1979), pp. 636–668.
[40] Mary Douglas, *Natural Symbols*, p. 73.

Race and the Working-Class Past in the United States: Multiple Identities and the Future of Labor History

DAVID ROEDIGER

In concluding his 1935 masterpiece, *Black Reconstruction in America*, W.E.B. DuBois observed:

The most magnificent drama in the last thousand years of human history is the transportation of ten million human beings out of the dark beauty of their mother continent into the new-found Eldorado of the West. They descended into Hell; and in the third century they arose from the dead, in the finest effort to achieve democracy for the working millions which this world had ever seen. It [post-Civil War Reconstruction in the U.S.] was a tragedy that beggared the Greek; it was an upheaval of humanity like the Reformation and the French Revolution. Yet we are blind and led by the blind. We discern in it no part of our labour movement [. . .][1]

Since DuBois wrote those lines historians have made substantial strides toward portraying the drama of African-American labor history, but have only begun to appreciate how a consideration of race might change the way the broader drama of labor in the U.S. past it itself plotted. This article argues that we may now at last be on the verge of a redramatization of U.S. labor history which moves race from the margins to the center of the story and which fully historicizes and problematizes the racial consciousness of white workers, as DuBois does from the earliest pages of *Black Reconstruction*.

However, in advancing this hopeful argument, I would stress that the grounds for hope have been present before, but not fully realized. Likewise deserving emphasis are the tremendous stakes involved in a reconceptualization of race and class in the past of U.S. labor. DuBois' framing of the issue in terms of drama captures those stakes strikingly. The ability of labor historians to cast their research in terms of dramatic issues like emancipation and independence, and to penetrate the ways in which workers conceptualized those issues, depends in large measure on extending to the discussion of race and class the same sort of tough-minded analysis which has matured more quickly where the study of gender and class is concerned. The first section of this study surveys recent historiography to make a case for cautious optimism regarding the future of a labor history which fully incorporates race and gender. The balance of the

---

[1] W. E. B. DuBois, *Black Reconstruction in America, 1860–1880* (New York, 1962, originally 1935), p. 727; cf. David Montgomery, "The Conventional Wisdom", *Labor History*, 13 (Winter, 1972), p. 134.

International Review of Social History 38 (1993), Supplement, pp. 127–143

essay makes concrete the stakes involved in reconceptualizing race in the working class past by concretely examining three small but significant dramas.

The tardiness of U.S. labor historians in making the study of slavery and race central to their work is as ironic as it is regrettable. The very project of a "new labor history" initially gained its appreciation for the fact that masses of working people make their own history not so much through witnessing significant trade union insurgencies as through the example of the Black freedom movement. The leading figures in early attempts to rewrite working class history were profoundly influenced by DuBois and, to a lesser extent, by the Black Trinidadian historian C.L.R. James. Herbert Gutman set out a research agenda which, as Ira Berlin has written, made "study of the Afro-American family [. . .] not a detour on the road to a history of the American working class, but the center lane on the main highway".[2] Such scholars at Gutman, Harold Baron, Paul Worthman and James Green produced pathbreaking analyses of race and labor. Above all, Alexander Saxton published *The Indispensable Enemy: Labor and the Anti-Chinese Movement in California* in 1971.[3] Saxton's work, itself indispensable and unsurpassed, fully raised the question of the impact of white racial identity on unions and on white workers themselves at that early date.

Nonetheless, scholarship on race and labor failed to flower. Saxton and George Rawick did not come to be considered central figures in the new labor history as David Brody, David Montgomery and Gutman did. Fascinating studies of race and white workers, such as those by Mary Ellen Freifeld and Barry Goldberg, remained unpublished and underappreciated. Eric Foner, Sean Wilentz and Mongomery brilliantly and convincingly restored the centrality of the sectional controversy, the Civil War

---

[2] See Berlin's introduction to Herbert Gutman, *Power and Culture: Essays on the American Working Class*(New York, 1987), p. 46; the interviews with Mongomery and Gutman in MARHO, ed., *Visions of History* (New York, 1983) and "Dave Roediger Interviews George Rawick", in Don Fitz and David Roediger, eds., *Within the Shell of the Old* (Chicago, 1990). As David Brody observes, however, Gutman took a range of positions on the placing of slavery and race within working-class history. See Brody, "On Creating a New Synthesis of American Labor History", in J. Carroll Moody and Alice Kessler-Harris, eds., *Perspectives on American Labor History*: The Problems of Synthesis (Dekalb, IL, 1989), p. 216 n. 9 and Mimi Rosenberg, "An Unpublished Interview with Herbert Gutman on United States Labor History", *Socialism and Democracy*, 10 (Spring–Summer, 1990), p. 58.

[3] Saxton, *The Indispensable Enemy: Labor and the Anti-Chinese Movement in California* (Berkeley, 1971); Baron, "The Demand for Black Labor: Historical Notes on the Political Economy of Racism", in James Green, ed., *Workers' Struggles, Past and Present* (Philadelphia, 1983); Paul Worthman, "Black Labor and Labor Unions in Birmingham, Alabama, 1897–1904" in Milton Cantor, ed., *Black Labor in America* (Westport, CT, 1969); Green, "The Brotherhood of Timber Workers, 1910–1913", *Past and Present*, 60 (August, 1973), pp. 161–200; Gutman, "The Negro and the United Mine Workers of America: The Career and Letters of Richard L. Davis and Something of Their Meaning, 1890–1900" in

and Reconstruction to working-class history, but they did so largely without the same emphasis DuBois placed on the self-activity of black workers and the white racial identity of white workers.[4]

Herbert Hill may be partly correct in attributing the new labor history's failure to engage fully the questions of racial identity and racism to an excessively zealous search for a usable and inspiring past.[5] However, other factors also mattered greatly. The nearly total isolation of communist historians from the new labor history deprived younger scholars of associations with Philip S. Foner and Herbert Aptheker, two of the most knowledgeable students of race, anti-racism and labor.[6] The strong influence of Eugene Genovese's weighty studies of slavery as a precapitalist political economy tended to isolate the history of slavery from the history of wage labour.[7] Moreover, the very strength of the new history's emphasis on daily life made it less-than-quick to understand the symbolic and political importance of whiteness even to white workers who did not regularly encounter workers of different racial identities.[8]

Several recent developments open the possibility that the new labor history will at long last realize its early promise with regard to providing a full consideration of race and a critique of working-class whiteness. The novelist and critic Toni Morrison has recently observed that studies of

Julius Jacobson, ed., *The Negro and the American Labor Movement* (Garden City, NY, 1968), pp. 49–127.

[4] Barry H. Goldberg, "Beyond Free Labor: Labor, Socialism and the Idea of Wage Slavery, 1890–1920" (Ph.D. diss., Columbia University, 1979) and Mary Ellen Freifeld, "The Emergence of the American Working Classes: The Roots of Division, 1865–1885" (Ph.D. diss., New York University, 1980); Foner, *Free Soil, Free Labor, Free Men: The Ideology of the Republican Party before the Civil War* (New York, 1970); Foner, *Reconstruction: America's Unfinished Revolution, 1863–1877* (New York, 1988); Mongomery, *Beyond Equality: Labor and the Radical Republicans, 1862–1872* (New York, 1967); Wilentz, "The Rise of the American Working Class, 1776–1877: A Survey" in Moody and Kessler-Harris, eds., *American Labor History*, pp. 83–151.

[5] See, for example, Hill, "Mythmaking as Labor History: Herbert Gutman and the United Mine Workers of America", *International Journal of Politics, Culture and Society*, 2 (Winter, 1988), pp. 132–98. My own fuller reflections on race and the new labor history are found in "Labor in White Skin: Race and Working Class History" in Mike Davis and Michael Sprinker, eds., *Reshaping the U.S. Left* (London and New York, 1988), pp. 287–308.

[6] See Philip S. Foner, *Organized Labor and the Black Worker, 1819–1973* (New York, 1974); Bettina Aptheker, ed., *The Unfolding Drama: Studies in United States History by Herbert Aptheker* (New York, 1979); Melvyn Dubofsky, "Give Us That Old Time Labor History: Philip S. Foner and the American Worker", *Labor History*, 26 (1985), pp. 118–37.

[7] Brody, "Synthesis", in Moody and Kessler-Harris, eds., *American Labor History*, p. 216 n. 9 and Roediger, "Precapitalism in One Confederacy: Genovese and the Politics of History", *New Politics*, 13 (Summer, 1991), pp. 90–95. Note, however, that Genovese's practice in comparing labor under slavery and under the wage system has been more supple than his theory. See esp. *Roll, Jordan, Roll: The World the Slaves Made* (New York, 1976), esp. pp. 285–324.

[8] Rosenberg, "Unpublished Interview", p. 58.

gender relations and identity have cleared the ground for the reconsideration of racial identity within cultural studies generally.[9] Her point applies with specific force to labor history. In the last decade, gendered studies of the working-class past have proven far and away the most dramatic contributions to labor history. Studying not only women workers but the masculinity of male craft workers and trade unionists, historians have reinvigorated scholarship on unorganized workers, pioneered in sophisticated research on labor in the service industries, and convincingly connected the work experience with ideology, family, consumption, and leisure.[10] Many of these historians, including Joanne Meyerowitz, Evelyn Nakono Glenn, Nancy Hewitt, Dolores Janiewski, Vicki Ruiz, Dana Frank, Patricia Cooper and Tera Hunter, have been enormously attentive to the dynamics of race as well as to class and gender.[11]

But even when they have not discussed race extensively, historians of labor and gender have made a decisive contribution to the study of race and class. They have demonstrated, particularly in the recent work of Joy Parr, Elizabeth Faue, and Jeanne Boydston, that the consideration of class and gender is not a zero-sum game in which an increasing emphasis on

[9] Morrison, "Unspeakable Things Unspoken: The Afro-American Presence in American Literature," *Michigan Quarterly Review*, 28 (Winter, 1989), esp. pp. 2–3 and 38.

[10] A quite incomplete list of major recent works would feature Christine Stansell, *City of Women: Sex and Class in New York, 1789–1860* (New York, 1986); Susan Porter Benson, *Counter Cultures: Saleswomen, Managers and Customers in American Department Stores, 1890–1910* (Urbana, 1986); Barbara Melosh, *The Physician's Hand: Work Culture and Conflict in American Nursing* (Philadelphia, 1982); Mary Blewett, *Men, Women and Work: Class, Gender and Protest in the New England Shoe Industry, 1780–1910* (Urbana, 1988); Alice Kessler-Harris, *A Woman's Wage: Historical Meanings and Social Consequences* (Lexington, KY, 1990); Ava Baron, ed., *Work Engendered: Toward a New History of Men, Women and Work* (Ithaca, NY, 1991); Jacqueline Dowd Hall, "Disorderly Women: Gender and Labor Militancy in the Appalachian South' in Ellen Carol DuBois and Vicki L. Ruiz, *Unequal Sisters: A Multicultural Reader in U.S. Women's History* (New York and London, 1990), pp. 298–321. Kathy Peiss, *Cheap Amusements: Working Women and Leisure in Turn-of-the-Century New York* (Philadelphia, 1986). See also Lois Helmbold and Ann Schofield, "Women's Labor History, 1790–1945", *Reviews in American Labor History*, 17 (December, 1989) and notes 25 and 16 below.

[11] Glenn, "The Dialectics of Wage Work: Japanese-American Women and Domestic Service, 1905–1940" in DuBois and Ruiz, eds., *Unequal Sisters*, pp. 345–72; Joanne J. Meyerowitz, *Women Adrift: Independent Wage Earners in Chicago, 1880–1930* (Chicago and London, 1988); Dana Frank, "Race, Class and the Politics of Consumption: Race Relations and the Seattle Labor Movement, 1915–1929". (unpublished paper delivered at Organization of American Historians meeting, 1991); essays by Hewitt and Janiewski in Baron, ed., *Work Engendered*; Janiewski, *Sisterhood Denied: Race, Gender, and Class in a New South Community* (Philadelphia, 1985); Vicki Ruiz, *Cannery Women, Cannery Lives: Mexican Women, Unionization and the California Food Processing Industry, 1930–1950* (Albuquerque, 1987); Patricia A. Cooper, *Once a Cigarmaker: Men, Women, and Work Culture in American Cigar Factories, 1900–1919* (Urbana and Chicago, 1987). I particularly thank Tera Hunter for sharing a manuscript version of her powerful *Contesting the New South*: *The Politics and Culture of Wage Household Labor in Atlanta, 1961–1920* with me.

one "variable" leads inexorably to a diminished emphasis on the other.[12] Instead class identity and gender identity are so thoroughly interpenetrating that intellectual excitement and understanding come precisely when both are stressed. This example has strongly encouraged a moving away from dead end debates about whether to give priority to race or class identity in the study of labor as well, and a moving toward the difficult, rewarding task of showing how racial identity and class identity have shaped each other. Moreover in giving attention to masculine as well as feminine gender identity, recent labor history has set a vital precedent which can lead to full interrogation of the racial identity of the dominant racial group as well as of the subordinate ones.

The recent outpouring of work on African-American, Asian-American and Latino labor history further signals the possibility that a consideration of race will structure, and not just appear episodically in, new attempts at synthesis in U.S. working-class history. Workers of color occupy prominent places in recent studies of race relations in the unions and among the working class generally, with major contributions made by such scholars as Iver Bernstein, Bruce Nelson, Barbara Griffith, Rich Halpern, Wayne Durrill, Peter Rachleff, Nelson Lichtenstein, Robert Korstad, Robert Norrell, Eric Arnesen, Michael Honey, Roger Horowitz and Nancy Quam Wickham.[13] Much of the finest work in labor history in the past five years has been the result of the partial democratization of the universities. Ronald Takaki, Earl Lewis, Joe William Trotter, Vicki Ruiz, Robin D.G. Kelley and Tera Hunter have written powerful studies which open the possibility that the best of labor history research in the near future will in

[12] Joy Parr, *The Gender of Breadwinners: Women, Men and Change in Two Industrial Towns, 1888–1950* (Toronto, 1990); Faue, *Community of Suffering and Struggle: Women, Men, and the Labor Movement in Minneapolis, 1915–1845* (Chapel Hill, 1991). Boydston, *Home and Work: Housework, Wages, and the Ideology of Labor in the Early Republic* (New York and Oxford, 1990).

[13] Again, the list is quite incomplete, but see Rick Halpern, "Race, Ethnicity and the Union in the Chicago Stockyards, 1917–1922", *International Review of Social History*, 37 (1992), pp. 25–58; Iver Bernstein, *The New York City Draft Riots: Their Significance for American Society and Politics in the Age of the Civil Way* (New York, 1990); Griffith, *The Crisis of American Labor: Operation Dixie and the Defeat of the CIO* (Philadelphia, 1988); Eric Arnesen, *Waterfront Workers of New Orleans, Race, Class and Politics* (New York, 1990); Arnesen, "Rethinking the historical Relationship between Black Workers and the Labor Movement", forthcoming in *Radical History Review* (1993); Wayne Durrill, *War of Another Kind: A Southern Community in the Great Rebellion* (New York and Oxford, 1990); Nancy Quam Wickham, "Who Controls the Hiring Hall? The Struggle for Job Control in the ILWU During World War II" and Bruce Nelson, "Class and Race in the Crescent City: The ILWU, from San Francisco to New Orleans", both in Steven Rosswurn, ed., *The CIO's Left-Led Unions* (New Brunswick, NJ, 1992), pp. 19–68; the essays in Robert Zieger, ed., *Organized Labor in the Twentieth Century South* (Knoxville, 1991); Leon Fink and Brian Greenberg, *Upheaval in the Quiet Zone: A History of Hospital Workers' Union Local 119* (Urbana, IL, 1989); and, above all, Peter Rachleff, *Black Labor in the South: Richmond, Virginia, 1865–1890* (Philadelphia, 1984).

large part be by, as well as about, "nonwhite" Americans. Indeed, the very recent scholarship by Kelley and Hunter comes closer to making real the new labor history's vision of connecting work, community, daily life, consciousness, and resistance than do any other American studies written during the last decade.[14]

Finally, during a period in which every major election has provided reminders that finding a usable past necessitates confronting the issue of white racial identity, scholars have succeeded in raising the questions of when, why, and with what results so-called "white people" have come to identify themselves as white. Making whiteness, rather than simply white racism, the focus of study has had the effect of throwing into sharp relief the impact which the dominant racial identity in the U.S. has had not only on the treatment of racial "others" but also on the ways that whites think of themselves, of power, of pleasure, and of gender. Labor historians cannot claim to have pioneered in this problematizing of the notion of whiteness. That honor belongs to figures in literary and cultural studies, including bell hooks, Coco Fusco, Toni Morrison, and a host of others who sometimes write with rather more postmodernist jargon than we would prefer.[15] But labor historians do have a distinctive and critical contribution to make by historicizing discussions of whiteness and by showing the ways that what DuBois brilliantly termed the "public and psychological wages" of white racial identity varied over time, place, and class location. Moreover, insofar as the new labor history has consistently stressed the role of workers as creators of their own culture, it is particularly well positioned to understand that white identity is not merely the product of elites or of discourses. If some of the most deeply historical work on whiteness and class continues to emerge from English and political science departments, labor historians can at least point with pride to the fact that one of their number, Alexander Saxton, has written the most sweeping and provocative account yet of the pivotal role of

[14] Takaki, *Pau Nana: Plantation Life and Labor in Hawaii, 1835–1920* (Honolulu, 1983); Lewis, *In Their Own Interest: Race, Class and Power in Twentieth Century Norfolk, Virginia* (Berkeley, 1991); Trotter, *Black Milwaukee: The Making of an Industrial Proletariat, 1914–45* (Urbana, IL, 1984) and *Class, Coal, and Color: Blacks in Southern West Virginia, 1915–32* (Urbana, IL, 1990); Ruiz, *Cannery Lives*; Kelley, " 'We Are Not What We Seem': Towards a Black Working-Class Infrapolitics in the Twentieth Century South," forthcoming in *Journal of American History*; Hunter, *Contesting the New South*. Both Kelley and hunter are particularly adept at drawing the literature on slave resistance to inform studies of resistance by later black wage workers. See also Kelley, *Hammer and Hoe: Alabama Communists during the Great Depression* (Chapel Hill, 1990), p. 101. See also Mario T. Garcia's fine "Border Proletarians: Mexican-Americans and the International Union of Mine, Mill and Smelter Workers, 1939–1946", in Robert Asher and Charles Stephenson, eds., *Labor Divided: Race and Ethnicity in United States Labor Struggles* (Albany, NY, 1990) pp. 83–104 and, on slavery, Norrece T. Jones, Jr., *Born a Child of Freedom Yet a Slave: Mechanisms of Control and Strategies of Resistance in Antebellum South Carolina* (Hanover, NH and London, 1990).

[15] Morrison, "Afro-American Presence" and *Playing in the Dark: Whiteness and the Literary Imagination* (Cambridge, MA, 1992); bell hooks, "Representations of Whiteness", in *Black Looks: Race and Representation* (London, 1992), pp. 165–78 with material from Fusco.

whiteness in American politics and American culture in his remarkable *Rise and Fall of the White Republic*.[16]

It would stretch optimism too far to suppose that the study of race, or even of gender, has already established a claim to be central in any revivifying of labor history. Scholarship on race, class, and gender remains in its early stages, and deserves the searching criticism it is sure to receive. The theoretical sophistication of the new scholarship, for example, is at this point far from imposing. New approaches face practical problems in writing and conceptualization which are so daunting as to seem at times insurmountable. Discussing the triad of race, class, and gender would be difficult enough, but that is just the tip of the iceberg. Writing about a single workplace or working-class community might involve analysis of masculine and feminine gender identities formed in concrete material circumstances among workers holding, or developing, or being seen as having, white, African-American, and Chinese "racial" identities. Once we acknowledge that the class identity of, say, an African-American woman worker is influenced not only by her own race and gender identities but also by social relationships with, say, Chinese males (and vice versa), we see the practical difficulties associated with treating race, class, and gender in what Tera Hunter brilliantly terms their "simultaneity".[17]

Too often, and here my own work holds out a revealing negative example, authors settle for treating complex identities in manageable dyads, treating white racial identity and class in one work, for example, and leaving class and gender for a later book, or a later section of the book. In addition, when scholarship on white racial identity focuses, as it sometimes must, on the broad political and cultural forces promoting whiteness, it exists in some tension with studies which take day-to-day relations between white and nonwhite workers or the self-activity of African-American workers as their points of departure. Though such tension is potentially exciting and productive, we should not be blind to the threat of a worst-case scenario in which research on white racial identity and male gender identity becomes yet another way to arrogate to white men the center stage in labor history.[18]

[16] DuBois, *Black Reconstruction*, 700–01; Saxton, *The Rise and Fall of the White Republic: Class Politics and Mass Culture in Nineteenth Century America* (New York, 1990); see also Eric Lott, "That Seeming Counterfeit: Racial Politics and Early Blackface Minstrelsy", *American Quarterly*, 43 (June, 1991), pp. 223–54; Lott, *Blackface Minstrelsy and the American Working Class*, forthcoming; Michael Rogin, "Blackface, White Noise: The Jewish Jazz Singer Finds his Voice," *Critical Inquiry*, 18 (Spring, 1992); Vron Ware, *Beyond the Pale: White Women, Racism and History* (New York and London, 1992); Ruth Frankenberg, *White Women Race Matters: The Social Construction of Whiteness* (Minneapolis, 1993).
[17] Hunter, in her forthcoming *Contesting the New South* urges the examination of "gender, race, and class in their simultaneity, in the way that human beings actually experience these social relations".
[18] See, e.g., the reviews of *Wages of Whiteness* by Iver Bernstein in *Journal of American History*, 79 (December, 1992) pp. 120–21; by Joe William Trotter, in *Journal of Social*

But as crying as the need is for serious critiques of race, class and gender approaches, labor history has not been well-served by recent dismissive broadsides which verge on branding as fraudulent the entire effort to see class consciousness as part of a set of interpenetrating and historically constructed identities. In a recent article in the prestigious *American Quarterly*, for example, Steven Watts characterizes race, class, and gender analyses of American history and culture as merely fashionable "incantations". Within labor history, Judith Stein's recent essay on the work of Joe William Trotter and Robin Kelley sets an equally harsh tone. After perceptively noting that Trotter and Kelley pay substantial attention to gender in their studies of race and class, Stein criticizes their emphases on both race and gender as a historical exercises driven by "current political sensibilities". She charges that by imposing categories and judgments from the present onto the past, Kelley and Trotter lose sight of the relations of class power which shaped the lives and consciousness of both black and white workers. Stein does not very much bother to claim, as more venerable Marxist formulations might, that class relations at the base shaped race and gender relations in the superstructure. She ignores the considerable extent to which white male workers themselves raised the issues of race and gender in fashioning a class identity, and assumes that because it supposedly derives from direct experience in production, class is a more timeless category.[19]

Stein's questionable judgment in choosing to single out for criticism two of the most closely documented and deeply historicized books yet produced by historians attentive to issues of race, gender, and class obviously limits the appeal of her critique. Nor is there much possibility for wide embrace of the chaotic combination of wistful populism with hints of a prolier-than-than Marxism which runs through the essays of both Watts and Stein when they argue that consideration of gender and race detracts from the study of class and power. Nonetheless, and especially insofar as they speak as part of the wider attack on multicultural scholarship, Watts and Stein do succeed in framing issues in a way which historians committed to the development of scholarship on race, class, and gender ignore at their peril. The accusations of fashionability and of present-mindedness must in particular be met head on if we are to avoid apologizing for our successes in producing work which is "trendy" in the sense that it grows out of and engages real trends in the recomposition of the labor force and the labor movement in a way that more nostalgic formulations do not. This need not imply a moralistic lecturing of the dead for their failure to

History, 25 (1992), pp. 674–676 and by Lawrence B. Glickman, in *The Nation* (February 17, 1992), pp. 207–09.
[19] Steven Watts, "The Idiocy of American Studies: Poststructuralism, Language and Politics in the Age of Self-Fulfilment", *American Quarterly*, 43 (December, 1991), p. 653; Stein, "Race and Class Consciousness Revisited", *Reviews in American History*, 19 (December, 1991), esp. pp. 556–559.

live up to the current ideals of egalitarianism. The point of historical studies of racial identities in the working class in such groundbreaking books as DuBois' *Black Reconstruction* and Saxton's *Indispensable Enemy* has never been to mount a facile indictment of white workers as racist. Rather it has been to understand how historicized racial identities dramatically shaped what workers could do and dream in their lifetimes. In a highly emotional atmosphere, this is a point which is as difficult to make as it is vital. For now, the point is best made in an exploration of concrete examples.

If the proof of the value of the study of the racial identity in labor history lies in its ability to open new dramas within that history, it is appropriate to turn in the balance of this essay to instances which illuminate that ability. While DuBois referred to the epic drama of Reconstruction in making the case for the centrality of race to labor history, I offer three very small dramas, hoping to show in each case how they open out into larger dramas and difficult questions which can invigorate study of the U.S. working class.

Drama One: In the early twentieth century, the great African-American author James Weldon Johnson closely listened to white "engineers, machinists, plumbers, electrical workers and helpers" in a smoking room on a large ship. Their conversations convinced him of "how lean a chance" that the black worker had with "his white brothers of the proletariat." Johnson wrote, "The expression which I heard at least a hundred times was, 'Never let a nigger pick up a tool', 'Never let a nigger pick up a tool'."[20]

On one level this is a simple enough vignette providing evidence of working-class racism and of its impact in limiting the economic opportunities of African-American workers and in subverting the prospects for class unity across racial lines. It seems susceptible to a simple explanation, offered by Marxists, by institutionally oriented labor historians and by labor market segmentation theorists alike, which sees white workers' support for racial exclusion as growing out of an economically rational desire to keep African Americans from competing for jobs and from thereby lowering wage rates.[21] But even when we grant such economic rationality as a factor in exclusion, the repeated rehearsing of the need to exclude within the manly confines of a smoking room is striking. Why, in particular, should skilled workers from trades so successful at practising exclusion have been obsessed so consistently about the need to do so?

Part of the answer lies in the dramatic extent to which the class identity of skilled workers took form around the identification with both whiteness and masculinity. the code of manliness, which david montgomery suggestively placed at the heart of the ethos of late nineteenth and early twentieth-century skilled workers undergirded craft union efforts to main-

---

[20] James Weldon Johnson, *Along This Way* (New York, 1933), p. 355.
[21] See Saxton, *White Republic*, pp. 6–7 for acute comments on this score.

tain and extend autonomy and mutuality. But the ideal was to be not only
a man, but a "white man". Those who violated mutuality, and specifically
those who broke strikes, not only lacked "any manhood" but "turned
nigger". Both African-Americans and women were available as symbols
of subservience and of the lack of citizenship rights, and association of
one's craft with either women or blacks constituted a threat to manliness.[22]

Whiteness, masculinity and craft pride mingled in the fashioning of an
identity among skilled workers. In his autobiography, *The Iron Puddler*,
James J. Davis combined gender and craft in writing of the "man of iron"
as a masculine ideal. But Davis added that he wanted "civilization's shock
troops grappling with tyrannous nature" to be specially white "men of
iron". "Some races are pig-iron; Hottentots and Bushmen are pig-iron.
They break at a blow", he added. Others, like the "meek Chinese" let
nature slowly "whip [them] with cold, drought, flood, isolation and
famine". Only his own race could shoulder the manly work of "belting
the world with railroads and bridging the seas with iron boats". The overwhelming resistance to entry of blacks and of females into crafts reflected
how widespread was Davis' conflation of craft, race, and gender. Integration at work would not only make the manly skilled worker associate with
the supposedly servile but also would associate his *craft* with degradation
and weakness. Even the material gain to be realized by excluding blacks,
Chinese, and others was racialized, and expressed in terms of masculine
ideas. As Lawrence Glickman has impressively shown, the workers who
defended the "American standard of living", in the industrializing U.S.
often put their demands in terms of "white men's wages". In "defining
"Americanness" and civilization as against the "other", Glickman adds,
such workers "made consumption as much a terrain of exclusion as production had ever been".[23]

The allegation that blacks threatened the dignity of skilled tradesmen
often found expression in workers' language. Not only was "nigger work"
generally synonymous with servile, *driven* labor, but crafts' occupational
slang reinforced the point that African-Americans would sully the trades.

[22] Mongomery, "Workers' Control of Machine Production in the Nineteenth Century",
Labor History, 17 (1976), pp. 491–92; Freifeld, "American Working Classes", pp. 514–22;
Goldberg, "Beyond Free Labor", pp. 407–12.
[23] James J. Davis, *The Iron Puddler: My Life in the Rolling Mills and What Came of It* (New
York, 1922), pp. 72, 108–09 and 158–59; Michael Denning, *Mechanic Accents: Dime Novels
and Working-Class Culture in America* (London and New York, 1987), pp. 175–77; William
M. Tuttle, JR., *Race Riot: Chicago in the Red Summer of 1919* (New York, 1984, originally
1970), pp. 142–43. See also Colin J. Davis, ed., *Organized Labor in the Twentieth Century
South*, pp. 113–34, on honor and segregation in the shop crafts. For an academic endorsement
of the white craft unions' questioning of African-American manliness, see John R. Commons,
Races and Immigrants in America (New York, 1913), pp. 48–49; Lawrence Glickman,
"Inventing the 'American Standard of Living': Gender, Race and Working-Class Identity,
1880–1925", forthcoming in *Labor History* in Winter, 1993. Glickman takes "white man's
wages" from Montgomery, *Beyond Equality*, p. 254.

For electrical workers, "nigger" was an impurity fouling connections; for cowboys, a saddlesore was a "nigger brand"; for railroaders, "nigger locals' were burdensome short runs. Workers' language further connected mechanization to "niggers", with the logic built on the twin associations of blacks with the kinds of hard work (such as lifting) which was being replaced by machines and with perceptions that machines and blacks both posed threats to whites' employment. Thus Mississippi sawyers termed devices to turn heavy logs "steam niggers". In many trades powerful winches were "niggerheads".[24]

If shipboard machinists had little immediate reason to fear that African-Americans would take their jobs, they had every reason to think that scientific management and mechanization threatened their manly autonomy. The particular precariousness of the worker at sea's patriarchal authority within his family expressed in concentrated form the more general crises in such authority brought by proletarianization and deskilling. As Joy Parr, Paul Taillon, and Patricia Cooper had demonstrated, such crises could generate a strong commitment to what Parr calls "breadwinner unionism"[25] as an expression of both masculinity and class identity. They could also generate fierce assertions of white racial identity which mixed with craft pride in creating an ideal of working-class manliness. In the case of skilled workers, masculinity could not usually be claimed by virtue of doing the hardest and heaviest labor – work that was often left to new immigrants and African-Americans. Therefore masculinity came to be associated ever more closely with craft and discipline and with the avoidance of "nigger work". Indeed the machinists not only tragically saw exclusion of black workers as a critical trade union demand but effected that exclusion precisely through their rituals of brotherhood.[26]

[24] *The American Thesaurus of Slang*, 2nd edn, Lester V. Berrey and Melvin Van Den Bark, eds. (New York, 1962), pp. 724 and 850; *A Dictionary of American Slang*, Maurice H. Weseen, ed. (New York, 1934), pp. 73 and 82; H.L. Mencken, "Designations for Coloured Folk", *American Speech*, 19 (October, 1944), p. 169; A.A. Roback, ed., *A Dictionary of International Slurs (Ethnophaulisms)* (Cambridge, MA, 1944), p. 55; for "niggerhead' as a white miners' term for impure, worthless coal, see Trottter, *Coal, Class and Color*, p. 115; on Mississippi, see McMillen, *Dark Journey*, p. 157; *Dictionary of Americanisms, On Historical Principles* [*DA*], M.M. Mathews, ed. (Chicago, 1951), 2:1117; Roediger, *Wages of Whiteness*, p. 15.
[25] Parr, *Gender of Breadwinners*; Cooper, "Which Workers Built What?" *Labor History*, 32 (Fall, 1991) pp. 570–72; Taillon, "'By Every Tradition and Every Right': Fraternalism and Racism in the Railway Brotherhoods, 1880–1910" (Unpublished paper delivered at the American Studies Association meeting in Baltimore, November, 1991). See also Faue, *Suffering and Struggle* and Ava Baron, "Questions of Gender: Deskilling and Demasculinization in the U.S. Printing Industry, 1830–1915", *Gender and History*, 1 (Summer, 1989), pp. 178–99.
[26] Taillon, "Fraternalism and Racism"; Foner, *Organized Labor and the Black Worker*, pp. 103–07; Stuart B. Kaufman and others, eds., *The Samuel Gompers Papers: The Early Years of the American Federation of Labor*, (Urbana and Chicago, 1987), p. 297 and Paul Taillon, "That Word 'White': Racism and Masculinity in the Debate Over Black Exclusion in the

Drama Two: In *Blood on the Forge*, William Attaway's superb 1941 proletarian novel, Big Mat, a black worker in a foundry, knocks out a "hayseed" who is about to hit an Irishman. Mat becomes the "hero of the morning" to the Irish American foundry workers. He wins praise for being both a model "colored worker" and for being somehow more than black. The boss melter in the foundry, a "big Irishman" in charge of five furnaces, marvels: "Never had a colored helper work better on the hearth [. . .] do everythin' the melter tell him to do and take care of the work of the whole crew if he ain't held back." Other Irishmen on the gang give Mat the title "Black Irish". One allows that "lots of black fellas have Irish guts". Another adds, "The black fella make a whole lot better Irisher than a hunky [Hungarian] or ginny [Italian] "Big Mat does not stay around after work to celebrate his new-found acceptance and his new "race". Instead he finds refuge in the "pleasant thought" of animals "tearing at each other" and hurries off to watch the dogfights.[27]

Perhaps no single passage from a source on labor's past provides quite so exciting a set of reminders of how much historians still have to learn about issues of both power and identity within the American working class. Mat's situation is fraught with both drama and peril. To the boss melter, he seems the very essence of manliness. This masculinity is what underlies his ability to transcend race in a partial way. As the hardest worker and a tough fighter, Mat wins praise and keeps a job. The Irish skilled workers and petty bosses – the line was by no means clear in many workplaces in the industrializing U.S. – accept him not only as an American but as almost an "Irisher". However, the very behaviour which establishes him as manly and American before the Irish on a gang sets Mat apart as an unmanly laborer willing to "work like a nigger' to curry favor from the boss melter, when seen from the point of view of the "hayseed", and "hunky" and the "ginny". We know all too little about the crosscurrents of race and masculinity which black workers navigated in getting and keeping places on work gangs and occasionally in managing to learn a skilled trade from white workers. We have not examined the ways in which everyday life at work reinforced and forged broader cultural images of the African-American male as either supermasculine or docile by requiring that he act both parts.

Nor do we know how manliness and race interacted in instances of biracial mobilizations by labor. Brotherhood of Timber Workers (BTW) organizers disarmed racism in Louisana and Texas just before World War I by arguing that "negro" and white "MEN" joined the union while "nigger [and] white trash company suckers" broke strikes, for example.

International Association of Machinists, 1888–1895" (unpublished paper delivered to the North American Labor History Conference at Wayne State University, 1990). On "nigger work", see Roediger, *Wages of Whiteness*, pp. 144–45 and 180. On physical labor, masculinity and class see Paul Willis, "Shop Floor Culture Masculinity and the Wage Form", in John Clarke, Chas Crichter and Richard Johnson, eds., *Working Class Culture: Studies in History and Theory* (New York, 1979), pp. 185–98.

[27] Attaway, *Blood on the Forge* (New York, 1987, originally 1941), pp. 122–23.

Historians have rightly praised their successes as exemplary reflections of the partial triumph of a common class identity over racial division.[28] But we have been slow to see how fully the questioning of racism by white male workers has rested in such instances on appeals to common manliness.[29] The appeal to values defined as masculine (and even to heterosexism) by the BTW brilliantly reversed the fear that white manliness (and arguably heterosexuality) might be breached – a fear which runs through the obsessive repetition of a line like "Never let a nigger pick up a tool." But we are far from knowing the full dynamics of, or the limits to, historical attempts to build a manly antiracism.

Terms like "black Irish" and "ginny" signal a still more complex set of dramas. Although the supposedly clear distinction between whites and nonwhites underlies racial ideology in the U.S., the history of immigration has constantly mocked that distinction. the use of "black Irish" to register high regard for Mat by the Irish workers suggests the possibility that ethnic Americans at times saw race differently than did the larger U.S. culture. The term "ginny" derived from *Guinea*, a region of West Africa from which slaves were exported. Its application to dark-skinned Italians reminds us that immigrants later categorized as whites often were originally the objects of debate where racial identity was concerned. Referring to the early twentieth-century U.S., the historian of immigration John Higham has observed: "In all sections native-born and northern European laborers called themselves 'white men' to distinguish themselves from the Southern Europeans whom they worked beside."[30] Immigrant workers were therefore often what John Bukowczyk has perceptively called "not-yet-white ethnics" in the double sense that they were still learning (or challenging) the ways of whiteness and still seeing their own whiteness questioned.[31]

Although one of the strongest suits of recent labor history has been its ability to illuminate how immigrant workers constructed their own senses

---

[28] Green, "Brotherhood", is a superb early study which emphasizes class unity in the BTW. For a much cruder version, see my "An Injury to One: IWW Organizing in the Deep South", *Industrial Worker*, 65 9 April, 1988), p. 5. Eric Arnesen's *Waterfront Workers* is probably the best study of race and the labor process in one industry and place, and his current broader project, on black workers, promises to add a great deal to our knowledge in this regard.

[29] For a lengthy attempt to address these questions, see my "Labor, Gender and the 'Smothering' of Race: Covington Hall and the Complexities of Class", in David Roediger, *Up from Whiteness: Essays on Class and Race, Past and Present* (forthcoming from Verso, 1993).

[30] Higham, *Strangers in the Land: Patterns of American Nativism, 1860–1925* (New York, 1963), pp. 173 and 66. On *guinea*, see Donald Tricarico, "Guido: Fashioning an Italian-American Youth Style", *Journal of Ethnic Studies*, 19 (Spring, 1991), esp. pp. 56–57 and Frederic G. Cassidy and Joan Houston Hall, eds., *Dictionary of American Regional English*, Volume 2 (Cambridge, MA and London, 1991), p. 838.

[31] Bukowczyk, as cited in Barry Goldberg, "Historical Reflections on Transnationalism, Race, and the American Immigrant Saga' (unpublished paper delivered at the Rethinking

of ethnicity and Americanity,[32] we know very little about the history of
the not-yet-white ethnic worker and of how the not-yet-white ethnic
became white. The legal requirement, from 1790 until well into the twentieth century, that an immigrant be "white" in order to be naturalized and
the welter of consequent litigation which fully lay bare the biological
fictiveness of race, have scarcely been noticed by labor historians.[33] The
historical tensions between choosing to identify oneself as white or as an
Irish American (fully present in the passage on Big Mat) have not seemed
problematic to researchers used to seeing "white ethnic" as a natural category. The prehistory of the racial identity of "white" immigrant workers,
in attitudes toward gypsies, travellers, Jews, Africans, and others in specific European peasantries and working classes is unexplored territory.
The processes by which less recently arrived immigrants taught racism
(and, I would add, white racial identity) to the more recently arrived have
only recently been prominently identified as subjects for historical research
in James Barrett's fine essay on "Americanization from the bottom up".
Most importantly, historians lack the sense of drama and the appreciation
of immigrant working-class self-activity which runs through the great novelist James Baldwin's seminal work "On Being 'White' [. . .] and Other
Lies". In holding that immigrants "became white [. . .] by deciding they
were white" over time, Baldwin unearths a vital historical process which
not only took place largely in workplaces and working-class communities
but which also shaped those workplaces and communities.[34]

Migration, Race, Ethnicity and Nationalism in Historical Perspective Conference at the New
York Academy of Sciences, May 1990).

[32] Leading recent examples include David Emmons, *The Butte Irish*: *Class and Ethnicity in
an American Mining Town* (Urbana, 1989); James R. Barrett, "Americanization from the
Bottom Up: Immigration and the Remaking of the Working Class in the United States, 1880–
1930", *Journal of American History*, 79 (December, 1992), pp. 996–1020; Cohen, *Making a
New Deal*; Gary Gerstle, *Working-Class Americanism*: *The Politics of Labor in a Textile
City, 1914–1960* (Cambridge, MA, 1989) and Donna Gabaccia, *Militants and Migrants*: *Rural
Sicilians Become American Workers* (New Brunswick, NJ, 1988). Studies which begin to
address the formation of white identity among immigrant groups include Roediger, *Wages
of Whiteness*, pp. 133–63; Dale T. Knobel, *Paddy and the Republic*: *Ethnicity and Nationality
in Antebellum America* (Middletown, CT, 1986), pp. 82–99 and esp. Robert Orsi, "The
Religious Boundaries of an In between People: Street *Feste* and the Problem of the Dark-
Skinned Other in Italian Harlem, 1920–1990", *American Quarterly*, 44 (September, 1992).

[33] Stanford Lyman, "The Race Question and Liberalism", *International Journal of Politics,
Culture and Society*, 5 (Winter, 1991), pp. 203–25; Joan M. Jensen, *Passage from India*:
Asian Indian Immigrants in North America (New Haven and London, 1988), pp. 246–69.

[34] Barrett, "Americanization from the Bottom Up", 1001–002; Baldwin, "On Being 'White'
. . . And Other Lies," *Essence* (April, 1984), pp. 90 and 92. Noel Ignatiev's excellent
"'Whiteness' and American Character", *Konch*, 1 (Winter, 1990), pp. 36–39 alerted me to
Baldwin's article. For useful comments on historicizing "white ethnic" consciousness, see
Barry Goldberg and Colin Greer, "American Visions, Ethnic Dreams" in Louis Kushnick,
ed., *Sage Race Relations Abstracts*, 15 (1990), pp. 29–31. My own unpublished paper "Whiteness and Ethnicity in the History of 'White Ethnics' in the United States' explores the same
issue. Its conclusions will appear in David Roediger, *Shades of Pale: American Whiteness in
the Last Century* (forthcoming from Free Press, 1995).

Drama Three: My great aunt, who recently died at 83, worked much of her life as a telephone operator in the North – South border city of Cairo, Illinois. Assertive, fun-loving and a staunch trade unionist, she exemplified much of the class-consciousness, independence, and willingness to challenge convention of an earlier generation of telephone operators well-described in Steven Norwood's *Labor's Flaming Youth*.[35] Through most of her working life, she in turn employed part-time an African-American domestic worker to whom she related paternalistically in every sense of the word. If her job immersed her in working-class women's culture, her status as an employer of black labor identified her with respectability and with the "better class of people" in Cairo. She fiercely opposed integrating the ranks of telephone operators, drawing on arguments in which whiteness and class defined each other.

Being served, if only for ten hours per week, by a nonwhite woman, influenced my great aunt's daily life, her racial attitudes and her class identity. But little in the historical literature on either labor or women's history helps us to understand how. Although there is abundant evidence suggesting that white working-class families hired black and Mexican American servants, especially in the South and Southwest during the early twentieth century, Tera Hunter is practically alone in making this employment relationship a focus of her historical research. As Hunter keenly observes, the availability of nonwhite servants way a key to both the domestic economy and the political economy of cotton mill villages in the South. Mills gained "progressive" images as havens for white workers by barring African Americans from textile jobs. They paid whites so poorly that whole families had to work, leaving little time for women and children to perform traditional domestic tasks. But since African-Americans could be hired so cheaply, white mill workers could have black servants. Indeed, some gave the "necessity" of having servants as a reason for accepting wage work.[36]

The expectation by workers of service from nonwhite workers was far from confirmed to domestic labor. The rituals of white working-class man-liness, performed at sites as various as barber shops, bars, and brothels, often included service by African-American workers. Eric Arnesen's recent research on the railroad trades suggests that some white engineers

---

[35] Norwood, *Labor's Flaming Youth: Telephone Operators and Worker Militancy, 1878–1923* (Urbana and Chicago, 1990).
[36] Hunter, *Contesting the New South*, forthcoming; David Katzman, *Seven Days a Week: Women and Domestic Service in Industrializing America* (New York, 1978); Janiewski, *Sisterhood Denied*, pp. 43–44 and 127–29; Victoria Byerly, *Hard Times Cotton Mill Girls: Personal Histories of Womanhood and Poverty in the South* (Ithaca, NY, 1986), pp. 99, 125, 147 and 152; Carter G. Woodson, "The Negro Washerwoman: A Vanishing Figure", *Journal of Negro History*, 15 (July, 1930), p. 271; Trotter, *Coal, Class and Color*, p. 91; LeeAnn Whites, "The DeGraffenreid Contoversy: Class, Race and Gender in the New South", *Journal of Southern History*, 54 (August, 1988), pp. 477–78 n.82; H. Roger Grant, ed., *Brownie the Boomer: The Life of Charles B. Brown, An American Railroader* (DeKalb, IL, 1991), pp. 138–39.

preferred black helpers because forms of personal service (and dangerous work) could be exacted from them but not from whites. Thomas Sugrue's fascinating study of the "slave market" through which unionized white construction workers essentially acted as subcontractors employing African-American casual laborers in post-World War II Detroit adds a further reminder that the material benefits of whiteness were not always confined to advantages in terms of labor competition.[37]

In none of these instances can a quick and easy formula be invoked to summarize the impact of buying services from nonwhites on the racial, gender, or class identities of white workers. Mill families, for example, appear to have given up claims to middle-class status by sending their children out to work and using the wages derived to hire African-American servants.[38] My great aunt, childless and widowed after a short marriage, approached middle class status and identity in large part *because* she employed black labor. But whatever the significant variations, for the minority of white workers who hired nonwhites there was no class identity which was not also at once a racial identity.

Much the same can be said for the majority of the white working class which did not hire nonwhite labor. In a recent and provocative essay arguing for "bringing the unions back in" as a key to the future of labor history in the U.S., Howard Kimeldorf maintains that an approach which takes "the job" or "working class culture" as a starting point "holds out the attraction of advancing beyond the narrow 'male and pale' focus of the old union-centred history, but it does so while retreating from the larger questions of social transformation that drew earlier generations of labor historians to the study of unionism in the first place".[39] My own view is that the tactical decision of whether to begin studies with the shopfloor, the union hall or the tavern as a focus is far less important today than the decision to engage fully the interplay of race, gender, and class. Failing that, we will not only miss much in the histories of those workers who were not white men but will also misapprehend the consciousness of those for whom maleness and paleness shaped class identity. By probing small

[37] I am indebted to Eric Arnesen for sharing his parts of his forthcoming study of black railway workers for the point on engineers. On Detroit, see Sugrue, "The 'Slave Market' and Casual Labor in Postway Detroit' (unpublished paper delivered to North American Labor History Conference, Wayne State University, October, 1992).

[38] Hunter, *Contesting the New South*, forthcoming.

[39] Howard Kimeldorf, "Bringing Unions Back In: Or Why We Need a New, Old Labor History", 32 (Winter, 1991), pp. 102–103. Cf. Nell Irvin Painter, "One of Two Things About *The Fall of the House Labor*," *Labor History*, 30 (Winter, 1989), pp. 118–121. The study of racial identity, so profoundly a political as well as a cultural phenomenon, is bound to challenge fundamentally the tendency of labor historians to separate "culture' from (trade union and electoral) politics. See Geoff Eley, "Labor History, Social History, *Alltagsgeschichte*: Experience, Culture, and the Politics of the Everyday – A New Direction for German Social History?" *Journal of Modern History*, 36 (1991), 249–260 for insightful commentary on the tendency to separate cultural and organizational matters in working-class history.

dramas such as those described by James Weldon Johnson and William Attaway, and lived by my great aunt, we may position ourselves to produce eventually a synthesis which makes the role of the whole working class central to the drama of U.S. history.

As the only nation to experience significant formation of a waged working class while a large-scale system of racial slavery continued to prevail within its borders, the U.S. has clearly had a distinctive history where race and labor are concerned. But in pursuing the study of race, U.S. labor historians will not be taking an utterly exceptional course. Racial divisions and racial dynamics within the working class have, of course, become sharply posed issues for historians of recent European labor, but, as the exemplary work of Peter Linebaugh and others have shown, race and slavery also played significant earlier roles in shaping class consciousness and lives or workers in some European port cities. The intimate connections between the slave trade and the rise of capitalism ensured that even in cities with few black workers, maritime workers in the eighteenth and early nineteenth century were well situated to compare their labor and conditions at sea with those of slaves.[40] If the question of how the employing of nonwhite servants shaped class consciousness and gender relations among white workers is an interesting one in the U.S. context, it is a vital one in the South African context. Beyond this, and realizing that race is a social construction rather than a biological fact, we need to ask whether some tensions among so called "whites" were in fact cast as racial divisions. Richard Williams has recently and forcefully suggested that anti-Irish discrimination in Britain, for example, is best seen as a variety of racism rather than of ethnic prejudice. The questions of whether and when anti-immigrant, anti-minority and pro-imperialist ideas and state-sponsored racism created "white" identity among European workers remain open ones.[41] They are far more likely to be sharply posed and aptly answered if U.S. labor historians fully rethink the drama of race and class.

---

[40] See, especially, Peter Linebaugh, "What If C.L.R. James Had Met E.P. Thompson in 1792?" in Paul Buhle, ed., *C.L.R. James: His Life and Work* (London and New York, 1986), pp. 212–19 and *The London Hanged: Crime and Civil Society in the Eighteenth Century* (London, 1991), esp. p. 349; Peter Fryer, *The History of Black People in Britain* (London, 1984). Perhaps the finest history of race and labor in an Atlantic economy is Walter Rodney, *A History of Guyanese Working People, 1881–1905* (Baltimore and London, 1981). See also Peter Fryer, *Staying Power: The History of Black People in Britain* (London, 1989).

[41] Richard Williams, *Hierarchical Structures and Social Value: The Creation of Black and Irish Identities in the United States* (New York, 1990), esp. p. 2. See also Orsi, "Inbetween People", p. 315 and Robbie McVeigh, "The Specificity of Irish Racism", *Race and Class*, 33 (April-June, 1992), pp. 40–43; Clive Harris, "Configurations of Racism: the Civil Service, 1945–1960", *Race and Class*, 33 (July –September, 1991), pp. 1–30; Joseph Bristow, *Empire Boys: Adventures in a Man's World* (London, 1991); Annie Phizacklea, *Unpacking the Fashion Industry: Gender, Race and Class in Production* (New York, 1990).

Gender and Labor History

The nineteenth-century legacy

SONYA O. ROSE

All disciplines and sub-disciplines are defined through a series of inclusions and exclusions.[1] They are based on specific assumptions and conventions that delineate their appropriate objects and methods of study.[2] Historians, like scholars in other fields, including the so-called "natural sciences", do not simply record some objective reality that exists independently of their taken-for-granted ideas about the nature of that reality.[3] Rather, their decisions as to which subjects and events will be objects of study and how they will be conceptualized are shaped both by widely accepted philosophical tenets and common-sense understandings of the nature of human society.

Foundational to the dominant traditions of labor history, I will argue, has been the distinction between public and private as it was delineated in social and political theory, and as it was culturally and socially constructed during the nineteenth century. Thoroughly imbricated in the public–private dichotomy were understandings about the different capacities and rights of men and women. The consequence of these distinctions for history was a limited vision of who and what counts as historically interesting and important.[4] Despite the differences between earlier institutional and political labor history, and "new labor history" conceptualized

The author thanks Ava Baron and Laura Levine Frader for their helpful comments on an early draft of this essay.

[1] Michele Barrett, "Words and Things: Materialism and Method in Contemporary Feminist Analysis", in *Destabilizing Theory: Contemporary Feminist Debates*, edited by Michele Barrett and Anne Phillips (Stanford University Press, 1992), p. 212.

[2] Michel Foucault maintains that through discursive rules, disciplines create their objects of analysis. See *The Archaeology of Knowledge*, translated by A.M. Sheridan Smith (New York: Harper Colophon, 1972); *The Order of Things: An Archaeology of the Human Sciences* (New York: Vintage, 1973).

[3] See Sandra Harding, *The Science Question in Feminism* (Ithaca: Cornell University Press, 1986).

[4] In an important essay, Leonore Davidoff argues that a series of concepts, based on gendered assumptions, came to dominate sociology and history influenced by sociological theory. See " 'Adam Spoke First and Named the Orders of the World': Masculine and Feminine Domains in History and Sociology", in *The Politics of Everyday Life: Continuity and Change in Work, Labour and the Family*, edited by H. Corr and L. Jamieson (London: Macmillan, 1990), pp. 229–255. See also Susan Kingsley Kent, *Sex and Suffrage in Britain, 1860–1914*, (Princeton University Press, 1987), p. 5. As Richard Price notes: "Labour history has always privileged those who organized for and sought power in the public realm, be it industry or politics". See "The Future of British Labour History", *International Review of Social History* 36 (1991), pp. 249–260, esp. p. 252.

International Review of Social History 38 (1993), Supplement, pp. 145–162

as the study of working-class formation, both share this heritage.[5] In short, the public–private dichotomy, with its deeply gendered associations, forms a kind of "deep structure" of labor-history formation.

Most histories of labor and class formation have been centered on productive relations, traditionally defined.[6] The subjects of working-class history have mainly been male artisans and skilled workers.[7] The historical narratives concern how these workers have created formal organizations and working-class movements to press their interests; how various changes in the nature of their work (especially proletarianization and deskilling) have contributed to their politicization; and why these workers have not consistently focused their political energies on changing the production relations in which they were subordinated participants.[8] Moreover, the fount of resistance has been depicted to be "at the point of production".[9]

[5] This is the case, as well, with the so-called "new institutionalism" advocated in British labor history by Jonathan Zeitlin. See: " 'Rank and Filism' in British Labour History: A Critique", *International Review of Social History* 34 (1989), pp. 42–61, and the separate critiques by Richard Price and James E. Cronin, *International Review of Social History* 34 (1989), pp. 62–88. For the United States, see David Brody, "The Old Labour History and the New: In Search of an American Working Class", *Labor History* 20 (1979), pp. 111–126; Howard Kimeldorf, "Bringing Unions Back In (Or Why We Need a New Old Labor History)", and comments by Michael Kazin, Alice Kessler-Harris, David Montgomery, Bruce Nelson, Daniel Nelson and reply by Howard Kimmeldorf, *Labor History* 32 (1991), pp. 91–129.

[6] Mari Jo Buhle, "Gender and Labor History", in *Perspectives on American Labor History: The Problems of Synthesis*, edited by J. Carroll Moody and Alice Kessler-Harris (DeKalb, IL: Northern Illinois University Press, 1989), p. 67.

[7] Leon Fink, "Looking Backward: Reflections on Workers' Culture and Certain Conceptual Dilemmas within Labor History", in J. Carroll Moody and Alice Kessler-Harris, *Perspectives on American Labor History*, pp. 13–14, 20; Michelle Perrot, "On the Formation of the French Working Class", in *Working Class Formation: Nineteenth-Century Patterns in Western Europe and the United States*, edited by Ira Katznelson and Aristide R. Zolberg (Princeton University Press, 1986), pp. 71–110, esp. pp. 71–83; William H. Sewell, Jr., "Artisans, Factory Workers, and the Formation of the French Working Class, 1789–1948", in *Working-Class Formation*, pp. 45–70; Friedrich Lenger, "Beyond Exceptionalism: Notes on the Artisanal Phase of the Labour Movement in France, England, Germany and the United States", *International Review of Social History* 36 (1991) pp. 1–23. For a critique see Jacques Rancière, "The Myth of the Artisan", and responses by William H. Sewell, Jr., and Christopher J. Johnson, *International Labor and Working Class History* 24 (Fall 1983), pp. 1–47, and responses by Edgar Leon Newman and Nicholas Papayanis, and the reply by Jacques Ranciere, *International Labor and Working Class History* 25 (Spring 1984), pp. 37–46. For a study that debunks the idea of an ideal preindustrial artisanal culture, see Michael Sonenscher, *Work and Wages: Natural Law, Politics and the Eighteenth-Century French Trades* (Cambridge University Press, 1989).

[8] For an overview that emphasizes the common themes in European and American labor history, see Leon Fink, "Looking Backward".

[9] For an excellent overview, see Richard Price, "The Future of British Labour History". As several commentators have noted, the presence of a Marxist teleology is lurking within much working-class history, whether revisionist or not. See Richard Price, "The Future of British Labour History", p. 254; Ira Karznelson, "Working-Class Formation: Constructing Cases and Comparisons", in *Working-Class Formation*, pp. 3–46, esp. pp. 3–15; Neville Kirk, "In

Central to these narratives are assumptions about what kinds of conten-
tion are important to class dynamics. Class-conscious action has often been
conceptualized as rationally directed to altering the relations of production. Only resistance that appears to be directed toward the goals of
workers as a collectivity counts as political, and actions undertaken in the
service of family needs or for "immediate gains" are secondary to the
story of history.[10]

Feminist labor historians have attempted to write women into these
narratives, and to show that the social and cultural construction of gender
difference has been a core feature of industrial capitalism. Yet the dominant paradigms in labor history continue to be reproduced as though neither
women nor gender were particularly relevant. As a consequence, numerous feminist scholars have maintained that incorporating women workers
and integrating gender into historical studies of labor and class mandate
a complete revision in the conceptual frameworks of the field.[11]

To make gender a core analytical concept in labor history, we need to
begin by rethinking and then revising the foundational assumptions of the
discipline. In this essay I hope to make a contribution to this project by
exploring the origins of deeply rooted assumptions about gender and the
nature of public and private life in the dominant traditions of labor history.

In what follows I will argue that while the distinction between public
and private with its associated gender means has been a significant feature
of Western thought since the Greeks, how it was understood and elaborated both in Enlightenment thought and in Marxian social theory
influenced the development of the social sciences generally, and labor

Defence of Class, A Critique of Recent Revisionist Writing upon the Nineteenth-Century
English Working Class", *International Review of Social History* 32 (1987), p. 39. For a biting
critique linked to the question of "exceptionalisms", see Dipesh Chakrabarty, *Rethinking
Working-Class History, Bengal 1890–1914* (Princeton University Press, 1989), pp. 219–230.

[10] Joan W. Scott reveals how some of these themes are central to E.P. Thompson's *The
Making of the English Working Class* in *Gender and the Politics of History* (New York:
Columbia University Press, 1988), Chapter 4. For a critique of Scott's reading of Thompson,
see Marc W. Steinberg, "The Re-making of the English Working Class", *Theory and Society*
20 (1991), pp. 173–197.

[11] See Sally Alexander, "Women, Class and Sexual Difference", *History Workshop* 17
(1984), pp. 125–149; Sally Alexander, Anna Davin, and Eve Hostettler, "Labouring Women:
A Reply to Eric Hobsbawm", *History Workshop* 8 (Autumn 1979), pp. 174–181; Ava Baron,
"Gender and Labor History: Learning from the Past, Looking to the Future", in *Work
Engendered: Toward a New History of American Labor*, edited by Ava Baron (Ithaca:
Cornell University Press, 1991), pp. 1–46; Kathleen Canning, "Gender and the Politics of
Class Formation: Rethinking German Labor History", *American Historical Renew* 97, 3
(June 1992), pp. 736–768; Anna Davin, "Feminism and Labour History", in *People's History
and Socialist Theory*, edited by Raphael Samuel (London: Routledge and Kegan Paul, 1981),
pp. 176–181; Alice Kessler-Harris, "A New Agenda for American Labor History: A Gendered Analysis and the Question of Class", in *Perspectives on American Labor History*, pp.
217–234. Joan W. Scott broke new ground in her call to arms to make gender a central
category of historical analysis in her important book, *Gender and the Politics of History* (New
York: Columbia University Press, 1988).

history in particular.[12] Then I will suggest that both the nineteenth-century ideological construction of the private sphere as a feminine domain devoid of political significance, and the constitution of the emerging bourgeois and working-class public spheres as masculine realms of consequential action shaped the boundaries drawn around the subject matter of the field.[13] Finally, I will consider the historiographic consequences of these boundary definitions and will suggest how historians might begin to redraw them in order to incorporate women workers and gender into labor's history.

Despite major differences in approaches to questions of economy and politics in the main paradigms of liberalism and Marxism, both treat the public/private as gendered oppositions. In Enlightenment thought, according to Carole Pateman,

The family is based on natural ties of sentiment and blood and on the sexually ascribed status of wife and husband (mother and father). Participation in the public sphere is governed by universal, impersonal and conventional criteria of achievement, interests, right, equality and property – liberal criteria, applicable only to men.[14]

The subject of Enlightenment political and moral philosophy was not the adult human person, but the male head of household.[15]

---

[12] See Susan Moller Okin, *Women in Western Political Thought* (Princeton University Press, 1979). Nancy Fraser examines the way unrecognized assumptions about gender are embedded in the ideas of Jurgen Habermas. See *Unruly Practices: Power, Discourse and Gender in Contemporary Social Theory* (Minneapolis: University of Minnesota Press, 1989), Chapter 6. Fraser specifically critiques his concept of the public sphere and its necessary separation from the private sphere in "Rethinking the Public Sphere: A Contribution to the Critique of Actually Existing Democracy", in *Habermas and the Public Sphere*, edited by Craig Calhoun (Cambridge, MA: The MIT Press, 1992), pp. 109–142.

[13] See Geoff Eley's important discussion of gender and the construction of the public sphere in nineteenth-century Europe to which some of my ideas about the public sphere are indebted, "Nations, Publics, and Political Cultures: Placing Habermas in the Nineteenth Century", in *Habermas and the Public Sphere*, edited by Craig Calhoun (Cambridge: MIT Press, 1992), pp. 289–339, esp. pp. 309–319. The public–private distinction has been a significant organizing framework for women's historians, although critiques of the idea of separate spheres have also characterized feminist scholarship. For an excellent overview, see Linda Kerber, "Separate Spheres, Female Worlds, Woman's Place: The Rhetoric of Women's History", *Journal of American History* 75 (1988) pp. 9–39. Also see Susan M. Reverby and Dorothy O. Helly, "Introduction: Converging on History", in *Gendered Domains: Rethinking Public and Private in Women's History. Essays from the Seventh Berkshire Conference on the History of Women* (Ithaca: Cornell University Press, 1992), pp. 1–26, and the essays in that volume.

[14] Carole Pateman, "Feminist Critiques of the Public/Private Dichotomy", in *The Disorder of Women* (Stanford University Press, 1989), p. 121. Pateman's work demonstrates that the liberal concept of "the individual", while presented as a universal construct, is in fact, particular – masculine. See "The Fraternal Social Contract", in *The Disorder of Women*, pp. 33–57, and her *Social Contract* (Stanford University Press, 1988).

[15] Catherine Hall, "Private Persons versus Public Someones: Class, Gender and Politics in England, 1780–1850", in *White, Male and Middle Class: Explorations in Feminism and History* (Cambridge: Polity Press, 1992), p. 155.

Ironically, although Marx and Engels were critical of both liberal political theory and the denigration of the private or domestic sphere under capitalism, they also assumed the existence of dichotomous spheres and linked the domestic sphere with women, and the public sphere with men. Engels argued that under capitalism in the "single monogamous family [. . .] household management lost its public character [. . .] It became a private service".[16] As Alison Jaggar has argued, Engels never really defines the difference in social relationships that constitutes public and private work. "He does not explain, for instance, why a man should not be described as engaged in 'private service' for his feudal lord or even for an individual capitalist".[17] Although Engels recognizes that the sexual division of labor in the household was a product of social arrangements, he still described the situation in which women went to work in factories and men stayed at home as depriving "the husband of his manhood and the wife of all womanly qualities".[18] Engels used such images of "unnatural" gender roles as a powerful condemnation of capitalism.[19]

Marx built his concept of class on a view of the "economic" as restricted to the production of food and objects.[20] What this does, of course, is to situate the social relations of reproduction outside of class. As Linda Nicholson has written, "When 'productive' activities [. . .] come to constitute the world of change and dynamism then activities of 'reproduction' become viewed as either the brute, physiological and nonhistorical aspects of human existence or as by-products of changes in the economy".[21] For many scholars influenced by Marx, the relations which define specific forms of the family (the private sphere) are determined by the pmode of production (conceptualized as being in the public sphere).[22] The "motor" of history is located in the public sphere.

[16] Friedrich Engels, *The Origin of the Family, Private Property and the State*, edited by Eleanor Burke Leacock (New York, Monthly Review Press, 1992), p. 137.

[17] Alison Jaggar, *Feminist Politics and Human Nature* (Totowa, NJ: Rowman and Allenheld, 1983), p. 145.

[18] Friedrich Engels, *The Condition of the Working Class in England*, translated and edited by W.O. Henderson and W.H. Chaloner (Stanford University Press, 1958), p. 164.

[19] Linda Kerber, "Separate Spheres, Female Worlds, Woman's Place", p. 13. Also see the discussion of Engels by Eli Zaretsky, *Capitalism, The Family, & Personal Life* (New York: Harper and Row, 1976), pp. 90–97.

[20] For a thorough discussion of the implications of Marx's work for understanding gender relations, see Linda Nicholson, "Feminism and Marx: Integrating Kinship with the Economic", in *Feminism as Critique*, edited by Seyla Benhabib and Drucilla Cornell (Minneapolis: University of Minnesota Press, 1987), pp. 16–30. Also see the important essay by Harold Benenson, "Victorian Sexual Ideology and Marx's Theory of the Working Class", *International Labor and Working Class History* 25 (1983), pp. 1–23.

[21] Linda Nicholson, "Feminism and Marx", p. 25. Also see the discussion by Joan Kelly, "The Doubled Vision of Feminist Theory", in *Women, History, and Theory: The Essays of Joan Kelly*, pp. 54–55.

[22] For a recent review of the debates among feminists on integrating Marxism and feminism in the analysis of gender and labor, see Miriam Glucksmann, *Women Assemble: Women Workers and the New Industries in Inter-War Britain* (London and New York: Routledge, 1990), Chapter 1 and pp. 265–279. See also my *Limited Livelihoods: Gender and Class in*

Marx and Engels appear to have considered the public also as the arena of politics where people engage in collective action to shape the course of history. Marx valorized working men's organization as the active force that would transform society.[23]

Thus, although liberals and Marxists might think differently about the terms "public" and "private", both imagined that sexual and family relations were in the realm of the private. In contrast, rational economic and political action were located in the realm of the public. In both theoretical traditions gender was deeply embedded in the conceptual distinction between public and private, and it was in the public sphere that men acted to shape their history.

It was not just the elaboration of gendered notions of the public and private in formal social theory that influenced the development of the social sciences and history, including contemporary working-class history. Social and political developments peculiar to the late eighteenth and nineteenth centuries were especially crucial. For it was during that period that the ideology of separate spheres came to be central to the world views of both the bourgeoisie and then later, many members of the working class.[24] Indeed, as Harold Benenson has argued, Marx's analysis of capitalism and the historical role of the working class was greatly influenced by this Victorian ideology.[25]

In England as well as in the United States the doctrine of separate spheres became an organizing principle in the lives of the rising middle classes.[26] Increasingly in the nineteenth century, women and men were seen as having essentially different natures.[27] Because of their different

Nineteenth Century England (Berkeley and Los Angeles: University of California Press, 1992), Chapter 1. For a variety of different approaches to the issue of integrating gender and class analysis see the essays in Lydia Sargent (ed.), *Women and Revolution* (Boston: South End Press, 1981).

[23] Harold Benenson, "Victorian Sexual Ideology and Marx's Theory of the Working Class", p. 18.

[24] For an important discussion of the formation of a masculine working class, and its relation to the embodiment of separate spheres in radical discourse, see Catherine Hall, "The Tale of Samuel and Jemima: Gender and Working-class Culture in Nineteenth-Century England", in *E.P. Thompson: Critical Perspectives*, edited by Harvey J. Kaye and Keith McClelland (Cambridge: Polity Press, 1990), pp. 78–102.

[25] Harold Benenson, "Victorian Sexual Ideology and Marx's Theory of the Working Class", pp. 1–23. Also see Joan Scott's discussion of the construction of gender in the writings of nineteenth-century French political economists in " 'L'ouvrière! mot impie, sordide . . . ' Women Workers in the Discourse of French Political Economy, 1840–1860", in *Gender and the Politics of History*, pp. 137–163.

[26] For England, see the pathbreaking study by Leonore Davidoff and Catherine Hall, *Family Fortunes: Man and Women of the English Middle Class, 1780–1850* (London: Hutchinson, 1987). For the U.S. see Mary Ryan, *Cradle of the Middle Class: The Family in Oneida County New York, 1790–1865* (New York: Cambridge University Press, 1981).

[27] For an interesting analysis of changing ideas about the similarities and differences between women and men and their relative status, see Ruth H. Bloch, "Untangling the Roots of Modern Sex Roles: A Survey of Four Centuries of Change", *Signs* 4 (Winter 1978), pp. 237–252.

natures, men were believed to be best equipped to deal with the worldly matters of commerce and politics; women were believed especially suited to providing moral sustenance as well as physical and emotional nurture to family members. These ideas about gender difference and the normative ordering of gender relations comprising the middle-class world view were incorporated into the emerging social sciences, as well as into the biological and medical sciences.[28] Mid-twentieth-century sociology and anthropology reworked these ideas, giving them renewed legitimation.[29]

The impact on the disciplines of the ideology that conceptualized home, family and kinship as a feminine sphere separated from the rest of society has often been noted. However, only relatively recently have scholars begun to appreciate the significance of who constructed the nineteenth-century *public* sphere and how they did it for the development of the concepts used in social analysis.[30]

In the late eighteenth and nineteenth centuries, middle-class men were laying claim to what scholars came to view as the public sphere. Joan Landes has argued that in France the bourgeois public sphere became gendered during the revolutionary era.[31] Geoff Eley remarks,

the very breakthrough to new systems of constitutional legality – in which social relations were reordered by conceptions of right, citizenship, and property and by new definitions of the public and the private – necessarily forced the issue of woman's place, because the codification of participation allowed, indeed required, conceptions of gender difference to be brought into play.[32]

---

[28] There is an enormous literature on how gender, especially as it was worked out in Enlightenment thought, was a constitutive feature of both biology and medicine. For recent work, see as particularly good examples, Ludmilla Jordanova, *Sexual Visions: Images of Gender in Science and Medicine between the Eighteenth and Twentieth Centuries* (Hemel Hempstead, Herts.: Harvester Press, 1989), and Lindsay Wilson, *Women and Medicine in the French Enlightenment: The Debate over Maladies des Femmes* (Baltimore: Johns Hopkins University Press, 1993).

[29] For a discussion of this point, see Jane Collier, Michelle Z. Rosaldo and Sylvia Yanagisako, "Is There a Family? New Anthropological Views", in *Rethinking the Family: Some Feminist Questions*, edited by Barrie Thorne with Marilyn Yalom (New York: Longman, 1982), pp. 25–39.

[30] Barbara Laslett has argued that the gendered concept of separate spheres strongly influences theories of human agency by expunging emotion. See "Gender in/and Social Science History", *Social Science History* 16 (Summer 1992), pp. 177–195. Also see her "Unfeeling Knowledge: Emotion and Objectivity in the History of Sociology", *Sociological Forum* 5 (1990), pp. 413–433. See Leonore Davidoff's exploration of the influence of separate spheres on the development of the social sciences in the nineteenth century: "Adam Spoke First". Also see Leonore Davidoff and Catherine Hall, *Family Fortunes*, p. 29. For an early statement of the link between "representations of gender difference" and "scientific analyses of social and economic life", see Elizabeth Fox-Genovese, "Placing Women's History in History", *New Left Review* 133 (May/June, 1982), pp. 5–30.

[31] Joan Landes, *Women and the Public Sphere in the Age of the French Revolution* (Ithaca: Cornell University Press, 1988).

[32] Geoff Eley, "Nations, Publics, and Political Cultures", p. 310. For England specifically, see Catherine Hall, "Private Persons versus Public Someones".

In Landes' account revolutionary men used Enlightenment discourse, especially Rousseau's ideas about womanhood, to silence woman. Rousseau had depicted men as capable of unlimited rationality and abstract thought. Women were the opposite. The French revolutionaries reworked such Enlightenment ideas and contrasted men's capacity for reason with femininity depicted as passion and frivolity, justifying the exclusion of women from politics.[33] Women's place in the new world order was circumscribed in notions of Republican motherhood.[34]

In England women were actively marginalized as middle-class men dominated the institutions of civil society.[35] Bourgeois men developed a range of formal associations that brought them into contact with one another including their clubs, philanthropic activities, employer associations, and fraternal orders.[36] Social analysts developed their understanding of what counts as agency and of who and what made history using these political and associational activities for their models. In other words, historians took these male-centered activities and institutions as constituting "the social" and "the political" that were their objects of study.[37]

Yet, feminist historians have shown that middle-class women crossed the imagined boundaries of the public and private spheres as teachers, in their religious and philanthropical work as well as in their anti-slavery activities.[38] Moreover, as Davidoff and Hall have shown, many women contributed directly to family enterprises without recognition or reward.[39] Additionally, Davidoff and Hall expose the artificiality of the ideology of separate spheres by showing the many ways that home and family were central to middle-class male identity as well as to their enterprises. Furthermore, a spate of recent studies on the nineteenth and twentieth centuries has detailed the centrality of women's activities in the creation of state

---

[33] Joan Landes, *Women and the Public Sphere*, p. 46. Also see, Joan W. Scott, "French Feminists and the Rights of 'Man': Olympe de Gouge's Declarations", *History Workshop* 28 (Autumn 1989), pp. 1–21, esp. pp. 1–7.

[34] For an account of the construction of the notion of Republican motherhood in the United States, see Linda K. Kerber, *Women of the Republic* (Chapel Hill, University of North Carolina Press, 1980). The American public sphere excluded black men as well as all women.

[35] Catherine Hall, "Private Persons versus Public Someones", p. 152.

[36] See Leonore Davidoff and Catherine Hall, *Family Fortunes*, Chapter 10. For a superb account of the importance of gender and fraternalism for the construction of class formation, see Mary Ann Clawson, *Constructing Brotherhood* (Princeton University Press, 1989). Also see Theodore Koditschek, *Class Formation and Urban Industrial Society: Bradford, 1750–1850* (Cambridge University Press, 1990), pp. 252–319.

[37] For a provocative discussion of creating a history of "the social", see Geoff Eley, "Is All the World a Text? From Social History to the History of Society Two Decades Later", in *The Historic Turn in the Human Sciences*, edited by Terence MacDonaly (Ann Arbor: University of Michigan Press, forthcoming).

[38] Catherine Hall, "Private Persons versus Public Someones", pp. 165–166. Leonore Davidoff and Catherine Hall, *Family Fortunes*, pp. 279–315.

[39] Leonore Davidoff and Catherine Hall, *Family Fortunes*, pp. 279–289.

social policies.[40] However, contemporaries attempted to understand such activities as appropriate to female talents and they saw them as extensions of women's domestic activities.

While these developments in bourgeois society shaped the assumptions of the emerging disciplines that concerned themselves with the social world generally, there were related developments in the working class that were of special consequence for what was to count as labor history. First, the working-class public sphere was created by a distinct segment of working-class men. Second, laboring men and women created a working-class version of the ideology of separate spheres that redefined conceptions of working-class masculinity and femininity.

The emerging working-class public sphere was claimed by male artisans of plebeian communities who stood on speakers' platforms to air their grievances using language that conjured up the images of artisan culture under threat of being dismantled. For example, in England they created the public cultures of collective protest as they fought for their rights as men who had "property in skill", and could claim their independence through pride in their work, their status as heads of households, and their ability to provide a future for their sons.[41] By reworking particular traditions of English liberalism and dissent, these radicals "defined themselves as political agents while their wives, mothers and daughters were primarily defined as supporters and dependents".[42] In Chartism, as Dorothy Thompson has shown, women became marginalized as the movement relied less on spontaneous demonstrations, became more organized, and developed formal rules of procedure and a hierarchy of leadership.[43]

The working-class version of the ideology of separate spheres developed as particular working-class men led their communities' battles for political and social rights. A major strand of radical argument used by the Chartists

[40] For the U.S. see Theda Skocpol, *Protecting Soldiers and Mothers: The Political Origins of Social Policy in the United States* (Cambridge: Harvard University Press, 1992); Linda Gordon, "Black and White Visions of Welfare: Women's Welfare Activism, 1890–1945", *The Journal of American History* 78 (September 1991), pp. 559–590; Linda Gordon (ed.), *Women, the State, and Welfare* (Madison: University of Wisconsin Press, 1990); for England see Jane Lewis (ed.), *Women's Welfare Women's Rights* (London: Croom Helm, 1983); and for a comparative perspective, see Sonya Michel and Seth Koven, "Womanly Duties: Maternalist Politics and the Origins of Welfare States in France, Germany, Great Britain, and the United States, 1880–1920", *American Historical Review* 95 (October 1990), pp. 1076–1108.

[41] On the masculine language of political protest, see Sally Alexander, "Women, Class and Sexual Difference", *History Workshop* 17 (Spring 1984), pp. 125–149. On the notion of "property in skill", see Eric Hobsbawm, *Worlds of Labour* (London: Heinemann, 1984), p. 182, and John Rule, "The Property of Skill in the Period of Manufacture", in *The Historical Meanings of Work*, edited by Patrick Joyce (Cambridge University Press, 1987), pp. 107–108.

[42] Catherine Hall, "The Tale of Samuel and Jemima", p. 84.

[43] Dorothy Thompson, *The Chartists. Popular Politics in the Industrial Revolution* (New York: Pantheon, 1984).

as they agitated for universal male suffrage incorporated ideas of sexual differences derived from Enlightenment thought. By the 1840s the rhetoric of citizenship centered on notions of the independent male head of household with "property in labor" who needed the vote to protect his wife and children.[44] The ideals of domesticity for women and breadwinning for men were deployed as well in the 1840s by skilled male factory workers from Lancashire and Yorkshire as a political strategy to agitate for a Ten Hours Bill in Parliament.[45] Out of these struggles for the vote and for a ten-hour day emerged new working-class ideals of male and female relationships and family life, as well as a limited view of working-class citizenship,

Alternative visions of working-class citizenship based on ideals of mutuality rather than on individualism, and models of equality and cooperation between women and men dimmed during the Chartist period.[46] Their existence, however, further supports the idea that the developing masculine working-class public sphere was forged through contests about competing images of the future in which particular working-class leaders gained preeminence in working-class communities.[47]

What it meant to be an adult man in England changed during the second half of the nineteenth-century from being able to command one's family and provide a trade for one's sons to being a sole family provider. As I have argued elsewhere, this redefined understanding of manhood was intimately linked with working-class respectability.[48]

Working-class leaders promulgated an ideal of "respectable manhood" that emphasized both the family with the male breadwinner at its head,

[44] Anna Clark, "The Rhetoric of Chartist Domesticity: Gender, Language and Class in the 1830s and 1840s", *Journal of British Studies* 31 (January 1992), pp. 62–88. Also see, Catherine Hall, "The Tale of Samuel and Jemima", pp. 90–94.

[45] Marianna Valverde, " 'Giving the Female a Domestic Turn': The Social, Legal and Moral Regulation of Women's Work in British Cotton Mills, 1820–1850", *Journal of Social History* 21 (1988), pp. 619–624. Wally Seccombe argues that the norm of male breadwinning emerged from the ranks of skilled artisans. See his insightful "Patriarchy Stabilized: The Construction of the Male Breadwinner Wage Norm in Nineteenth-Century Britain", *Social History* 11 (1986), pp. 53–76. Also see, Harold Benenson, "Victorian Sexual Ideology and Marx's Theory of the Working Class".

[46] For an important exploration of the moral claims of "mutuality" made by working-class women prior to the Chartist period, see Ruth L. Smith and Deborah M. Valenze, "Mutuality and Marginality: Liberal Moral Theory and Working-Class Women in Nineteenth-Century England", *Signs* 13 (1988), pp. 277–298. For ideals of sexual equality among Owenites, see Barbara Taylor, *Eve and the New Jerusalem* (New York: Pantheon, 1983).

[47] Barbara Taylor, *Eve and the New Jerusalem*. Also see Anna Clark, "Gender, Citizenship and the Making of the British Working Class", in *Gender and the Reconstruction of Working-Class History*, edited by Laura Frader and Sonya O. Rose (Ithaca: Cornell University Press, forthcoming).

[48] See *Limited Livelihoods*, pp. 148–152. Also see Keith McClelland, "Masculinity and the 'Representative Artisan' in Britain, 1850–1880", in *Manful Assertions: Masculinities in Britain since 1800*, edited by Michael Roper and John Tosh (London: Routledge, 1991), pp. 74–91.

and the "self-improved" workman who knew how to conduct himself with proud restraint.[49] These images were key ones deployed in the 1860s as working-class members of the Reform League argued for the suffrage. They were central to the passage of the 1867 Reform Bill through which tax-paying, working-class men obtained the vote.[50] These were the working-class leaders who advocated a restrained style of labor protest, and promoted the harmony of interests between labor and capital.

They were the men who actively built working-class associations for themselves creating friendly societies, cooperatives, and working men's clubs. They also established and became leaders of trade union organizations. For most of the nineteenth century, it was these respectable men who developed the policies of their union organizations, and they were the decision makers in them for much of the period. They used their power to articulate their version of workers' interests often in masculinist terms, even when some of the workers that they represented were women.[51]

Until the rise of the new unions in the 1880s, "respectable men" dominated the working-class public sphere – not all men, and no women.[52] Then early in the last decade of the century there was a struggle for power within the Trades Union Congress, and the language of that struggle was, in part, about competing definitions of working-class manhood (including the kind of clothing that members of one or the other group were prone to wearing). It was also about competing directions for trade unionism, but the important point is that the terrain continued to be mapped by male persons and to be identified as masculine turf.

Labor and working-class historians took as their domain of inquiry these institutions and practices that were not only historically contingent, but were selective ones as well. Instead of understanding their particularity

---

[49] The following discussion of respectable manhood, the suffrage and trade unionism is drawn from Sonya O. Rose, "Respectable Men, Disorderly Others: The Language of Gender and the Lancashire Weavers" Strike of 1878", *Gender and History*, 5(1993), pp. 382–397.

[50] The Reform Act stipulated that in addition to tax-paying householders, lodgers with a year of residency paying 10 pounds rent annually could vote in national elections. Because of those financial and residency requirements, only 30 percent at best of adult males in urban working-class constituencies could vote. For a discussion of the 1867 Reform Act and its role in working-class politics, see Keith Burgess, *The Challenge of Labour. Shaping British Society 1850–1930* (London: Croom Helm, 1980), pp. 34–39.

[51] See my *Limited Livelihoods*, Chapter 7. Also see Patrick Joyce, *Visions of the People* (Cambridge University Press, 1991), pp. 129–130. For the U.S. see Elizabeth Faue, *Community of Suffering and Struggle: Women, Men, and the Labor Movement in Minneapolis, 1915–1945* (Chapel Hill: University of North Carolina Press, 1991), Chapter 3. Keith McClelland suggests that these processes significantly influenced socialist politics and ideas. See "Time to Work, Time to Live: Some Aspects of Work and the Re-formation of Class in Britain, 1850–1880", in *The Historical Meanings of Work*, Patrick Joyce, edited by (Cambridge University Press, 1987), pp. 180–209.

[52] Women trade unionists attended TUC conventions from the mid-1870s, but the male leadership often ridiculed their concerns and arguments, especially in debates concerning hours legislation, and on the subject of female factory inspectors.

and exclusivity, historians took them as *models* for labor activism, resistance, and class identity. In other words, they provided the template for
conceptualizing working-class formation. The consequence was to privil-
ege certain male subjects and their actions as worthy of study and to ignore
what fell outside the mould.

This analysis of the assumptions informing the boundaries of labor and
working-class history helps us to understand why a major argument that
has gone on between women's labor historians and men's historians
is whether or not women were employed in the nineteenth century. In
1979, for example, Sally Alexander, Anna Davin and Eve Hostettler challenged Eric Hobsbawm who wrote that "conventionally women aimed to
stop working for wages outside the house once they got married [. . .]
Once married, she belonged to the proletariat not as a worker, but as
the wife, mother and housekeeper of worker".[53] Alexander, David and
Hostettler argued that Hobsbawm's view of class excluded wage-earning
wives, and denied women any potential for participation in class struggle.[54]
Within the confines of working-class history as he had conceived of it,
women did not fit. In another context Hobsbawm has written; "Insofar as
a conscious working class, which found expression in its movement and
party, was emerging in this period, the pre-industrial plebs were drawn
into its sphere of influence. And insofar as they were not, they must be
left out of history, because they were not its makers but its victims".[55] In
this statement he makes it clear that only some social actors are social
agents and deserve to be counted as historical subjects. Hobsbawm's substantial contributions to social history have helped to formulate what
counts as labor history, and so it is important to recognize that his conception of history has embedded within it the particular (not universal) images
that were the legacy of the nineteenth-century definition of the public
sphere.

Not only have some historians been reluctant to admit the significance
of women's presence in nineteenth- and early twentieth-century labor history, but they not infrequently conflate gender and women. For example,
Brian Harrison's essay, "Class and Gender in Modern British Labour History", is primarily about women.[56] By spotlighting women, Harrison
implies that only women have gender, men do not. When gender is
equated with women, masculinity remains unproblematic, and consequently the actions of male persons are seen either as gender-neutral or

---

[53] E.J. Hobsbawm, "Man and Woman: Images on the Left", in *Worlds of Labor: Further
Studies in the History of Labour* (London: Weidenfeld and Nicholson, 1984), p. 94.
[54] Sally Alexander, Anna Davin, Eve Hostettler, "Labouring Women", p. 175.
[55] E.J. Hobsbawm, *The Age of Empire, 1875–1914* (London: Weidenfeld and Nicholson,
1987), p. 141.
[56] Brian Harrison, "Class and Gender in Modern British Labour History", *Past and Present*
124, (1989), pp. 121–158.

as the standard against which the actions of "others" are to be measured.[57]

Harrison devotes little attention to women's roles as "wage-earner and citizen" declaring in effect that women were mostly housewives, and that their attachment to the home made them apolitical. He argues

housekeeping helped to mould women's political outlook. It could nourish the apolitical response that stemmed from prevailing cultural attitudes. The male's food-getting and fighting roles give rise to a male monopoly of the political process which has only recently and tentatively been challenged.[58]

In short, Harrison "naturalizes" the separation of spheres and their definition, explaining women's political attitudes by their location in the private sphere, and men's attitudes by their location in the public sphere.

The notion that male workers' identities are formed at work while female workers' identities are formed at home has been pervasive in labor history.[59] Ross McKibbin, for example, described a conversation between two women in a World War II machine-tool factory. McKibbin notes: "Girls seemed to derive considerable pleasure from this sort of nattering and [. . .] it substituted interest in time for non-interest in work."[60] Then he described "horseplay and practical jokes" as popular "routine-breaking techniques" for men and states, " [. . .] for men, more than for women, the workplace was an important social institution. Men did not just *work* there, it was in the factory more than anywhere else that they had their social being".[61] Not only does McKibbin conceptualize different forms of social interaction as gender-specific (using the familiar trope of women talking), but he locates that difference in women's and men's supposedly distinct sources of identity.

By uncritically assuming that women (naturally) gain their identities from the domestic sphere while men (just as naturally) gain theirs in the

---

[57] On the latter point and its bearing on public policy, see Martha Minow, *Making All the Difference: Inclusion, Exclusion, and American Law* (Ithaca: Cornell University Press, 1990). For a discussion of the significance for working-class history of examining masculinity, see Ava Baron, "On Looking at Men: Masculinity and Working-class History", unpublished paper. For examples of outstanding work on the construction of working-class masculinity in the U.S. see Ava Baron, "Questions of Gender: Deskilling and Demasculinization in the U.S. Printing Industry, 1830–1945", *Gender & History* 1 (1989), pp. 178–199, and in the U.K. see Keith McClelland, "Some Thoughts on Masculinity and the 'Representative Artisan' in Britain, 1850–1915", *Gender & History* 1 (1989), pp. 164–177.

[58] Brian Harrison, "Gender and Class", p. 126.

[59] In sociology see Roslyn Feldberg and Evelyn Glenn, "Male and Female: Job versus Gender Models in the Sociology of Work", *Social Problems* 26 (1979), pp. 524–538.

[60] Ross McKibbin, "Work and Hobbies in Britain, 1880–1950", in *The Ideologies of Class: Social Relations in Britain, 1880–1950* (Oxford University Press, 1990), pp. 101–138.

[61] Ross McKibbin, *Ideologies of Class*, p. 156. Emphasis in the original. For examples of jokes and other rituals among women workers, see Sally Westwood, *All Day Every Day* (London: Pluto Press, 1984), and for women's expressions of their identities as workers in Germany see Kathleen Canning, "Gender and the Politics of Class Location", pp. 756–757.

workplace, men's labor historians have carried forward nineteenth-century ideology as historical argument. This is "ideological work" in two senses.[62] In the first place, as I have indicated above, it represents labor and working-class history as though it were gender neutral, even though it is primarily about male persons. It does this by ignoring the important links between nineteenth-century constructions of masculinity, workplace identity and politics. In the second place, it is ideological because it mystifies the agency of those laboring women who crossed the boundaries of public and private and implicitly contested their gendered associations.[63]

The dominant mode of labor history ignores how women's identities as workers and their political activities have been shaped at the workplace.[64] On the one hand, women workers are commonly assumed by men's labor historians to be temporary workers. However, as Richard Whipp's studies of the English pottery industry have shown, a generalized "image of the impermanent, young, unskilled, low paid and therefore marginal women worker" is inaccurate.[65] On the other hand, when women have been depicted as politically active, their political identities are portrayed as stemming from their "natural" concern for their families. Such thinking undermines the argument that working-class politics stem from productive relations.[66]

Women's history has also been caught up in the myth of separate spheres, and there is a substantial body of feminist scholarship that has stressed the distinctiveness of women's cultures at work, and the links between their political identities and their family lives.[67] Instead of taking these findings as indicative of the natural proclivities of women, or as

---

[62] I am using the notion of "ideological work" as developed by Mary Poovey in *Uneven Developments*, pp. 2–3.

[63] For an early essay on women in the economy of Britain, see Eric Richards, "Women in the British Economy Since About 1700: An Interpretation", *History* 69 (1974), pp. 337–357. For a recent review see Katrina Honeyman and Jordan Goodman, "Women's Work, Gender Conflict, and Labour Markets in Europe, 1500–1900", *Economic History Review* 44 (1991), pp. 608–628.

[64] For a critique of this assumption in German labor history, see Kathleen Canning, "Gender and the Politics of Class Formation", p. 748.

[65] Richard Whipp, "Kinship, Labour and Enterprise: The Staffordshire Pottery Industry, 1890–1920", in *Women's Work and the Family Economy in Historical Perspective*, edited by Pat Hudson and W.R. Lee (Manchester University Press, 1990), pp. 172–203. Other scholars have also shown that women are not necessarily more temporary and less committed than men are. See, for example, Kathleen Canning, "Gender and the Politics of Class Formation", p. 748; Alison Scott, "Industrialization, Gender Segregation and Stratification Theory", in *Gender and Stratification*, edited by Rosemary Crompton and Michael Mann (Cambridge: Polity Press, 1986), p. 158; Sonya O. Rose, *Limited Livelihoods*, p. 162.

[66] Joan W. Scott, *Gender and the Politics of History*, p. 75.

[67] This is an enormous literature. For an overview for the American case, see Linda Kerber, "Separate Spheres, Female Worlds, Woman's Place", Also see Susan Levine, "Labors in the Field: Reviewing Women's Cultural History", *Radical History Review* 35 (1986), pp. 49–56.

stemming directly from their family relationships, we need to ask why there were these distinctive cultures, how they were formed, and what accounts for the connection between women's family lives and their politics.[68] When women use a rhetoric of family need in supporting political causes, and in labor struggles, we cannot assume that such discourse is a simple consequence either of being born female or their presumed association with domesticity. There is ample empirical evidence that men also used familial rhetoric in political movements and labor struggles.[69] The demand for the family wage is only the most obvious example.[70] By uncritically incorporating a nineteenth-century distinction between public and private that constructed men and women as naturally suited to their respective spheres, labor historians miss both the ways that work was constitutive of women's identities as workers, and family was constitutive of the work and political identities of men. In addition, they fail to explore how family life can be a source of politics and labor activism.[71]

Implicated in these gendered understandings of the significance of work and family in the lives of women and men is the supposition that "interests" stem directly from people's positions in the social structure. When historians adopt such a view they assume that political rhetoric reflects an underlying structural reality, and that consciousness is immanent in social position.

Interests, however, are the outcome of political rhetoric and are generated in the context of struggle rather than simply determining the rhetoric and struggle. This idea is fundamental to the scholarship of those historians

[68] One approach to such questions is taken by Smith and Valenze who argue that women's use of "mutuality" as moral argument stems from their marginality. See Ruth L. Smith and Deborah M. Valenze, "Mutuality and Marginality". Another approach would follow Joan Scott's lead, and examine the discourses that construct women's identities. See *Gender and the Politics of History*.

[69] See Keith McClelland, "Some Thoughts on Masculinity and the 'Representative Artisan' ", pp. 170–174; Keith McClelland, "Time to Work, Time to Live", pp. 206–207; Michael P. Hanagan, *Nascent Proletarians: Class Formation in Post-Revolutionary France* (Oxford: Basil Blackwell, 1989).

[70] On the family wage see Hilary Land, "The Family Wage", *Feminist Review* 6 (1980); Martha May, "Bread Before Roses: American Workingmen, Labor Unions and the Family Wage", in *Women Work and Protest: A Century of U.S. Women's Labor History*, edited by Ruth Milkman (London: Routledge and Kegan Paul, 1985), pp. 1–22; Mary Blewett, *Men, Women, and Work: Class, Gender and Protest in the New England Shoe Industry, 1780–1910* (Urbana and Chicago: University of Illinois Press, 1988), pp. 121–131.

[71] See Joanna Bornat, "Home and Work: A New Context for Trade Union History", *Oral History* 5 (1977) and "Lost Leaders: Women, Trade Unionism and the Case of the General Union of Textile Workers, 1875–1914", in *Unequal Opportunities: Women's Employment in England 1800–1918*, edited by Angela John (Oxford: Basil Blackwell, 1986), pp. 207–234. For the U.S. see Carole Turbin, "Beyond Conventional Wisdom: Women's Wage Work, Household Economic Contribution, and Labor Activism in a Mid-Nineteenth-Century Working-Class Community", in *To Toil the Livelong Day: America's Women at Work, 1780–1980*, edited by Carol Groneman and Mary Beth Norton (Ithaca: Cornell University Press, 1987), pp. 47–67.

who insist on the primary importance of language in social life, and who attempt to move beyond so-called "culturalist" approaches to working-class formation. The work of such historians threatens to displace class and production as the centerpieces of labor history, replacing them with the concepts of politics and discourse. Does the linguistic turn by itself ensure that gender will be integrated into a post-class labor or working-peoples' history?

An examination of such work is not at all reassuring. For example, as Joan Scott has shown, Stedman Jones' focus on the political rhetoric of Chartism ignores the gendered content of the radical rhetoric that he suggests shapes Chartism as a movement.[72] Scott maintains that Jones used a literal view of language, and as a consequence he denies the significance of class and misses how gender contributed to its construction. In a book of essays clearly indebted to Jones' idea about the continuities of radical political rhetoric, that literal view of language and politics is continued and gender as a constituting feature of politics features not at all, even though it was precisely during the period the essays cover that it became possible for working class *men* to vote, and woman's suffrage became a major issue.[73]

Gender does not figure either in Patrick Joyce's provocative new work which focuses on the meanings of "the people". Although Joyce makes an effort to include women in his analysis by indicating women's presence, generally his strategy is to link women and families. For example, in his discussion of community solidarities among the cotton textile workers, he maintains that because the primary idiom in which the factory population was represented by *The Cotton Factory Times* was "the family", its messages appealed to everyone, but especially to women.[74] While Joyce mentions the male domination of the unions and the masculine rhetoric of cotton trade unionists, he does not give this masculine language a role in his story. Rather, he implies that solidarities were created in spite of such rhetoric. His use of Sally Alexander's essay on class and sexual difference is illustrative. After noting Alexander's suggestion that artisan leaders' constructions of community were important for popular politics, Joyce writes:

It was a male construction certainly [. . .] but this does not means that it was not without great effect in the community at large.[75]

Furthermore, in his analysis of custom and the ways that people symbolized order, Joyce says:

[72] Joan W. Scott, "On Language, Gender, and Working-Class History", in *Gender and the Politics of History*, pp. 53–67, esp. 55–60.
[73] See Eugenio F. Biagini and Alastair J. Reid (eds.), *Currents of Radicalism: Popular Radicalism, Organised Labour and Party Politics in Britain, 1850–1914* (Cambridge University Press, 1991). Women appear only in an essay by Pat Thane.
[74] Joyce, *Visions of the People*, p. 135.
[75] *Ibid.*, pp. 98–99.

Sex, age and social status were minutely mapped out by a series of cultural boundary markers, among them sayings, jokes and stories. The overwhelming concern
was thus with the preservation of order. This was reflected in the maintenance
of established gender distinctions even in the Lancashire of the waged woman
millworker.[76]

Joyce maintains that the language of gender reflects an underlying concern
that goes beyond gender – is more universal than gender. He acknow-
ledges gender, but denies its relevance or significance to his project.

It is crucial for historians of labor to appreciate fully the constitutive
role of language in social and political life, because it is only by doing so
that we become cognizant of the cultural construction of social categories
and social processes. Such analyses make it possible for historians to
expose the myriad ways in which gender, race and sexuality have been
imbricated in the intertwined cultural, socio-economic and political formation of modernity. They can show how such constructions worked both to
create solidarities and simultaneously to exclude. However, they do not
guarantee that historians will be attuned to these fundamental dimensions
of modern human existence and their crucial roles in identity formation.

In order to forge a new vision of labor history that both includes women
workers and examines the role of gender in class formation, it will be
necessary to jettison the nineteenth-century legacy of separate spheres.
An important step in transforming the boundaries of labor history is to
examine the relationship between masculinity and male workers' identities. This is crucial as a way of exploring how solidarities among workers
were created, and to understand how male workers dealt with competition
from boys as well as from women.[77] Significant as well is an examination
of the meaning of skill, steady employment, and unemployment for the
construction of manhood. By making the link between masculinity and
work a problem for study, labor historians will begin to appreciate and
assess the possible differences in class identities *among* men as well as
between women and men. By interrogating the gendered language of male
trade union leaders and orators, and by searching for alternative voices of
both women and other men, labor historians will be less likely to confuse
a particular vision of working-class activism with resistance writ large.

This does not mean that labor historians should ignore trade unionism,
and social movements for political and social rights. Rather, we need to
pay greater attention to the question of how allegiances were forged; who
joined and who did not. It is important to recognize that those who were
marginal to those organizations and movements may actually have been
central to the dynamics of labor's history. While the differences among
workers, and the divisions within working-class communities may have
weakened those movements, this is *not* the only reason to study them.

[76] *Ibid.*, p. 155.
[77] Ava Baron, "An 'Other' Side of Gender Antagonism".

The construction of difference, the very creation of "us" as distinct from "them", may have been crucial in the formation of worker and movement identities in the first place. Perhaps the best illustration of this idea is the work of American historian David Roediger that has explored the importance of being white in the creation of white male workers' class identities in the U.S.[78]

It is important, also, to reconsider what counts as resistance and to dissolve the opposition between resistance and accommodation.[79] It is not necessarily the case that resistance only takes place at the point of production, or that it counts only when it occurs in the form of an organized movement. Strikes are effective to the extent that whole communities, not just workers, become mobilized. Consumer boycotts illustrate resistance "at the point of consumption".[80] Furthermore, as the important work of anthropologist James C. Scott has suggested, people use a variety of tactics to thwart wholesale domination by elites.[81] In addition, as he makes clear, there is nothing necessarily apolitical or non-revolutionary about "bread and butter issues".[82] And as this essay has argued, the political sensibilities of men as well as women may be forged by their activities and relations at home.

Finally, I want to consider briefly what differences such an approach will make to the stories we tell about labor's history. The question "so what?" is sometimes asked by those who are sceptical of the significance of gender. Some wonder, for example, given the relative power of capital, if workers would have made greater gains had women and men been united, or if women had been more centrally involved in union affairs. What that question implies is that only victory and its opposite, defeat, are matters of historical significance. Such a view ignores historical process (and paths not taken) in favor of historical outcomes. By integrating questions of gender in labor history, and by attending to how meanings are constructed, and with what consequences, historians will be better able to address how and why events happened the way that they did. By paying closer attention to process, historians will not simply provide fuller accounts. Rather, their stories will be complex and multifaceted explorations of historical contingency.

[78] David R. Roediger, *The Wages of Whiteness: Race and the Making of the American Working Class* (London: Verso, 1991).
[79] Ava Baron, "Gender and Labor History", pp. 27–32.
[80] Dana Frank, "Gender, Consumer Organizing, and the Seattle Labor Movement, 1919–1929", in *Work Engendered*, edited by Ava Baron, pp. 273–295.
[81] James C. Scott, *Weapons of the Weak: Everyday Forms of Peasant Resistance* (New Haven Yale University Press, 1985). Also see his *Domination and the Arts of Resistance: Hidden Transcripts of Power* (New Haven: Yale University Press, 1990).
[82] James C. Scott, *Weapons of the Weak*, pp. 341–345.

Connecting Household History and Labour History

MARCEL VAN DER LINDEN

Labour historians have always shown an interest in working class men and women who participated in strikes, unions, and political parties. However, even when historians are receptive to the importance of family life behind public activism these scholars continue to use the "public sphere" as an approach for studying the family.[1] This approach runs counter to historical logic because the daily life of those who join social movements and organizations involves far more than merely labour activism. To understand the true causes of collective resistance among workers, it is necessary to use the "private sphere" as an approach for studying labour protests as well. While this reverse perspective may not prove a panacea for all problems associated with analysing labour history, it will provide insight into the rather obscure motives of the working class for deciding whether or not to support the development of workers' movements. Furthermore, Jean H. Quataert wrote that examining working-class households makes it possible to keep "in focus at all times the lives of both men and women, young and old, and the variety of paid and unpaid work necessary to maintain the unit".[2]

To the best of my knowledge there has been no systematic effort to establish a link between working-class families and labour movements. While this short paper is by no means an exhaustive discussion of this unexplored field, it does attempt to examine the relationship between labour activism and other strategies for survival and improvement in working-class households.

Principles

Up to this point I have used "families" and "households" interchangeably. The meanings of these terms, however, are not identical, as kinship forms the primary basis for families, whereas households are mainly economic units based on income pooling. The present paper is about *households*.

---

[1] For essays using this approach that are excellent in many other respects, see Harold Benenson's "The Community and Family Bases of U.S. Working Class Protest, 1880–1920: A Critique of the 'Skill Degradation' and 'Ecological' Perspectives", *Research in Social Movements, Conflicts and Change*, 8 (1985), pp. 109–132, and Bruce Scates' "Gender, Household and Community Politics: The 1890 Maritime Strike in Australia and New Zealand", *Labour History*, 61 (1991), pp. 70–87.

[2] Jean H. Quataert, "Combining Agrarian and Industrial Livelihood: Rural Households in the Saxon Oberlausitz in the Nineteenth Century", *Journal of Family History*, 10 (1985), pp. 145–162, 158.

International Review of Social History 38 (1993), pp. 163–173

This concept is rather ambiguous and has been subject to extensive ter-
minological debates.[3] To avoid a digression into this issue, I will use the
description in McGuire *et al.*, which states that households are "those sets
of relationships, historically variable yet relatively constant, that have as
one of their principal features the sharing of sustenance gained from the
widest possible variety of sources".[4] This description is loose enough to
cover a wide variety of situations. It stresses the budget-pooling aspect of
households, an approach that serves the purpose of my project.

The following reservations apply to using the designation of households:
(i) Households do not necessarily consist of two or three generations of
one family. They may include several families, other types of biological
kinship (such as siblings), or members not related by blood or marriage.
(ii) Households do not necessarily entail co-residence, not even according to Donald Bender's definition that calls for "a proximity in sleeping
arrangements and a sentiment similar to that expressed in our folk
concept of home".[5] For example, at least one member in a household
of seasonal migrants is likely to live elsewhere for months at a time and
will nevertheless contribute substantially to the household budget. (In
the absence of co-residence, it is possible to form what I will call secondary households.)[6]
(iii) The focus on economic aspects should not diminish the role of
households as culturally significant units shaped by symbolic processes.[7]
(iv) Rather than being predetermined, the composition of households
is a product of negotiations. Factors affecting the composition of a
household may include income, marriage prospects for men and
women, employment opportunities, and government factors such as
legislation and taxation.[8]

---

[3] It is extremely difficult to provide a generally valid definition of households. Attempts to
find "a precise, reduced definition" have been unsuccessful, as households are "inherently
complex, multifunctional institutions imbued with a diverse array of cultural principles and
meanings". Sylvia Junko Yaganisako, "Family and Household: The Analysis of Domestic
Groups", *Annual Review of Anthropology*, 8 (1979), pp. 161–205, 200.
[4] Randall H. McGuire, Joan Smith, and William G. Martin, "Patterns of Household Structures and the World-Economy", *Review*, vol. 10, No. 1 (Summer 1986), pp. 75–97, 76.
[5] Donald R. Bender, "A Refinement of the Concept of Household: Families, Co-Residence,
and Domestic Functions", *American Anthropologist*, 69 (1967), pp. 493–504, 498.
[6] The Canadian bushworker camps in Ian Radforth's *Bushworkers and Bosses: Logging in
Northern Ontario, 1900–1980* (Toronto, 1987), Ch. 5, are examples of secondary households.
[7] Sylvia Junko Yaganisako, "Explicating Residence: A Cultural Analysis of Changing Households among Japanese-Americans", in: Robert McC. Netting, Richard R. Wilk, and Eric J.
Arnould (eds.), *Households. Comparative and Historical Studies of the Domestic Group*
(Berkeley, Calif., 1984), pp. 330–352, 330.
[8] Yaganisako, "Family and Household", pp. 167–175; David J. Maume and R. Gregory
Dunaway, "Determinants of the Prevalence of Mother-Only Families", *Research in Social
Stratification and Mobility*, 8 (1989), pp. 313–327; Michael Mitterauer, "Faktoren des Wan-
dels historischer Familienformen", in: Mitterauer, *Familie und Arbeitsteilung. Historischvergl-
eichende Studien* (Vienna, 1992), pp. 214–255.

(v) Households should not be considered anthropomorphic entities through being designated as products of collective will. Members do not necessarily work for the common good of the household; on the contrary, they may be driven by selfish motives. Conflicts of interest are also possible, as well as oppression and resistance against oppression.[9] Both dependency and authority may vary according to the member of the household. Laslett pointed out that infants and children have the greatest stake in the household's survival, "since their life chances depend almost wholly on its existence and persistence, on their being accepted and retained as members. But children also have the least power to affect the household's decisions and none whatever to carry them out".[10]

This statement about influencing household decisions implies that while we should not arbitrarily ascribe a collective will to households, members nevertheless try to find (a variety of) ways to control their fate whenever possible. To this end, they negotiate to devise a strategy for generating and allocating the common budget.

In these negotiations, household members must take various aspects into consideration. Contrary to the assumptions of economists constructing models,[11] research in social sciences and history suggests that motives are very rarely purely economic,[12] but are usually based on meaningful orientations. Three of these interdependent motives keep reappearing.

First comes the need for security. Students of the working class[13] have confirmed James Scott's statement that "for those at the margin, an *insecure* poverty is far more painful and explosive than poverty alone".[14] To maximize the size and stability of their budget, members of households may pursue good employment contracts and social benefits, distribution of risks by diversifying their sources of income, and/or earning part of their income through self-employment. These circumstances justify

---

[9] Judith Bruce, "Homes Divided", *World Development*, 17 (1989), pp. 979–991; Diane L. Wolf, "Daughters, Decisions and Domination: An Empirical and Conceptual Critique of Household Strategies", *Development and Change*, 21 (1990), pp. 43–74.

[10] Peter Laslett, "The Family as a Knot of Individual Interests", in: Netting, Wilk, and Arnould, *Households*, pp. 353–379, 370–371.

[11] See Gary S. Becker, *A Treatise on the Family* (Cambridge, Mass., 1981).

[12] Richard Sennett and Jonathan Cobb convincingly argued this point of view in *The Hidden Injuries of Class* (New York, 1972).

[13] Seymour Martin Lipset, *Political Man: The Social Bases of Politics* (Garden City, N.Y., 1959), p. 232; Gaston V. Rimlinger, "The Legitimation of Protest: A Comparative Study in Labor History", *Comparative Studies in Society and History*, 2 (1959–1960), pp. 329–343; John C. Leggett, "Economic Insecurity and Working-Class Consciousness", *American Sociological Review*, 29 (1964), pp. 226–234; Maurice Zeitlin, "Economic Insecurity and the Political Attitudes of Cuban Workers", *American Sociological Review*, 31 (1966), pp. 35–51.

[14] James C. Scott, *The Moral Economy of the Peasant. Rebellion and Subsistence in Southeast Asia* (New Haven and London, 1976), 34.

Rolande Trempé's observation that "The workers of Carmaux preferred to earn less as miners while continuing to do work (whether independently or for an employer) that provided for a substantial portion of their needs and provided some security against hunger during the all too frequent hard times including strikes, unemployment, and periods of deprivation or inflation."[15] A recent study of rural ties among urban workers in Enugu, Nigeria contradicts the theory of modernization by revealing how these ties have become stronger rather than weaker over the past thirty years. This tendency results from the virtual absence of a social security system covering illness, disablement, and old age, thus forcing those with low incomes to continue to rely on their villages for their security.[16]

The second motive for attempting to control the household budget is the drive towards dignity and respectability. People are not mere objects. Rather, their innate value is characterised by its non-negotiability.[17] While social historians frequently limit discussions on respectability to the more affluent workers of nineteenth-century England, a more general application of this term refers to Barrington Moore's "decent human treatment".[18]

The third motive for these household negotiations is a desire for justice, which involves the need for reciprocal relationships with other parties and may apply to "social relationships in the institutional areas of authority and social coordination, production, and distribution, or more commonly in all three".[19] Expressions of this desire for equality may range from a collective struggle for emancipation through individual attempts at self-improvement to envious behaviour designed to drag others down a notch.[20]

These three motives are clearly social constructs subject to various interpretations by different members of a household (especially according to differences in gender and age) and must always be viewed in terms of their specific social, economic, cultural, and political contexts. Furthermore,

[15] Rolande Trempé, *Les mineurs de Carmaux 1848–1914* (Paris, 1971), vol. I, p. 224.

[16] Josef Gugler, "Life in a Dual System Revisited: Urban–Rural Ties in Enugu, Nigeria, 1961–87", *World Development*, 19 (1991), pp. 399–409, esp. 405.

[17] "In the realm of ends everything has either a PRICE or a DIGNITY. Whatever has a price can be replaced by something else as its equivalent. But what is raised above all price and therefore admits of no equivalent, has a dignity. [. . .] but that which constitutes the condition under which alone something can be [an] end in itself, has not a mere relative value, that is a price, but an intrinsic value, that is *dignity*." Immanuel Kant, "Grundlegung zur Metaphysik der Sitten" ["Fundamental Principles of the Metaphysic of Ethics", translated by Otto Manthey-Zorn (Appleton-Century-Crofts, 1938] (1785), *Werke in Sechs Bänden*, vol. IV (Darmstadt, 1983), p. 68.

[18] Barrington Moore Jr., *Injustice. The Social Bases of Obedience and Revolt* (White Plains, N.Y., 1978), p. 326. Also see Elvin Hatch, "Theories of Social Honor", *American Anthropologist*, 91 (1989), pp. 341–353.

[19] Barrington Moore, *Injustice*, p. 455. Cf. Godelier: "[. . .] for relations of domination and exploitation to be formed and reproduced in a lasting fashion, they must be presented as an exchange, and as exchange of services." Maurice Godelier, *The Mental and the Material*, translated by Martin Thom (London, 1986), p. 160.

[20] Helmut Schoeck, *Der Neid. Eine Theorie der Gesellschaft* (Freiburg, 1968).

the three motives are closely intertwined. Reinhard Bendix mentioned the link between self-respect and security.[21] Julian Pitt-Rivers introduced an aspect of reciprocity with his description of honour (dignity, respectability) as "an evaluation of self in the terms which are used to evaluate others – or as others might be imagined to judge."[22] Finally, Oskar Negt and Alexander Kluge convincingly argue that workers are also trying to act on behalf of justice when they go on strike for wage increases.[23]

The existence of a link between the three motives does not mean they are always in harmony with one another. Conflicts may result both from different interpretations by various members of a household and from possible cases of incongruence. Households, like individuals, may for example face a choice between respectability and economic security (if, say, members are forced to do degrading work).

Income and Expenditure

The function of social budget pooling in households entails income and expenditure. This process need not be exclusively monetary: it may also consist of goods and services.

The pattern of *expenditure* in independent households is composed of at least five types of expenses:[24]

—Support of household members involved in productive labour.
—Support of these same individuals during periods of disability or unemployment.
—Support of older household members who used to be involved in productive labour.
—Support of younger household members not yet involved in productive labour.
—Means to make payments to third parties (such as taxes, duties, and payment of debts).

This list includes the possibility of economies of scale arising from common use of certain goods. (Whether a household consists of two members or five, its members can make due with one vacuum cleaner.)

---

[21] Reinhard Bendix, *Work and Authority in Industry: Ideologies of Management in the Course of Industrialization* (Berkeley, 1974), Ch. 7.

[22] Julian Pitt-Rivers, "Honor", *Encyclopaedia of the Social Sciences*, 6 (1968), pp. 503–511, 503.

[23] Oskar Negt/Alexander Kluge, *Geschichte und Eigensinn* (Frankfurt/M., 1981), p. 604.

[24] This distribution is based in part on Claude Meillassoux's three categories of reproduction costs: "The value of the work force is derived from three factors: supporting workers during periods of employment (*retaining* the existing work force), *maintaining* workers during periods of idleness (such as unemployment or illness), replacing workers by providing for their progeny (known as *reproduction*)." Claude Meillassoux, *Femmes, Greniers & Capitaux* (Paris, 1975), p. 152.

The *income* of independent households is derived from at least seven sources:[25]

—Means obtained through labour remunerated in wages or in kind.
—Means obtained through non-commercial labour (directly consumable goods), including homemade clothing, raising domestic animals such as pigs and poultry,[26] and gathering rubbish for direct reuse.[27]
—Means obtained through petty commodity production or petty commerce, including manufacturing cottage-industry textiles, raising livestock for sale, peddling,[28] and professional scavenging.[29]
—Means derived from providing resources such as land, tools for labour, accommodation, and money. These means may include income received from renting out beds or rooms.[30]
—Means obtained through transfer payments received without immediate reciprocal exchange of labour or commodities, including support from friends and acquaintances in times of need, charity, and social benefits.
—Means obtained from theft, including both conventional methods of stealing and, especially pilfering at the workplace.[31]

---

[25] Kathie Friedman listed the first five of these sources of income in "Households as Income-Pooling Units", in: Joan Smith, Immanuel Wallerstein, and Hans-Dieter Evers (eds.), *Households and the World-Economy* (Beverly Hills, Calif., 1984) pp. 37–55, 46.

[26] Bettina Bradbury, "Pigs, Cows, and Boarders: Non-Wage Forms of Survival among Montreal Families, 1861–91", *Labour/Le Travailleur*, 14 (Fall 1984), pp. 9–46; Béatrice Cabedoce, "Jardins ouvriers et banlieue: le bonheur au jardin?" in Alain Faure (ed.), *Les Premiers Banlieusards. Aux Origines des Banlieues de Paris 1860–1940* (Paris, 1991), pp. 249–279.

[27] See James R. Barrett, *Work and Community in the Jungle. Chicago's Packinghouse Workers 1894–1922* (Urbana and Chicago, 1987), p. 104.

[28] John Benson, *The Penny Capitalists. A Study of Nineteenth-Century Working Class Entrepreneurs* (Dublin, 1983); Serge Jaumain, "Contribution à l'histoire comparée: les colporteurs belges et québécois au XIXe siècle", *Histoire sociale/Social History*, 39 (1987), pp. 49–77.

[29] Alain Faure, "Classe malpropre, classe dangereuse? Quelques remarques à propos des chiffoniers parisiens au XIXe siècle et de leurs cités", *Recherches*, 29 (December 1977), pp. 79–102; Chris Birkbeck, "Self-Employed Proletarians in an Informal Factory: The Case of Cali's Garbage Dump", *World Development*, 6 (1978), pp. 1173–1185; Daniel T. Sicular, "Pockets of Peasants in Indonesian Cities: The Case of Scavengers", *World Development*, 19 (1991), pp. 137–161.

[30] Bradbury, "Pigs, Cows, and Boarders"; John Modell and Tamara Hareven, "Urbanization and the Malleable Household: An Examination of Boarding and Lodging in American Families", *Journal of Marriage and the Family*, 35 (1973), pp. 467–479; Franz Brüggemeier and Lutz Niethammer, "Schlafgänger, Schnapskasinos und schwerindustrielle Kolonie. Aspekte der Arbeiterwohnungsfrage im Ruhrgebiet vor dem ersten Weltkrieg", in: J. Reulecke/W. Weber (eds.), *Fabrik, Familie, Feierabend. Beiträge zur Sozialgeschichte des Alltags im Industriezeitalter* (Wuppertal, 1978), pp. 153–174; Josef Ehmer, "Wohnen ohne eigene Wohnung. Zur sozialen Stellung von Untermietern und Bettgehern", in: Lutz Niethammer (ed.), *Wohnen im Wandel. Beiträge zur Geschichte des Alltags in der bürgerlichen Gesellschaft* (Wuppertal, 1979), pp. 132–150.

[31] See Adrian J. Randall, "Peculiar Perquisites and Pernicious Practices. Embezzlement in the West of England Woollen Industry, c. 1750–1840", *International Review of Social History*,

—Means obtained through credit, including billing in instalments, deferred payments, or pawning personal property.[32]

Working-class households (the major focus in this paper) entail households where the first source of income (remunerated labour) prevails in importance. This statement does *not* exclude the role of other sources of income. On the contrary, working-class households usually rely on a variety of sources of income, virtually all members generate some income, and individual members (especially over the course of their entire lives) tend to provide income from numerous sources. While these observations do not imply the absence of a clear correlation between age and gender on the one hand and revenue-producing activities on the other, it is likely that the degree of correlation varies according to the source of income.[33]

Strategies for Improvement

The satisfaction of working-class households with their material circumstances depends not only on whether their income covers basic necessities. Other significant issues include the reliability of the sources of income (the lack thereof may lead to insecurity), the question of whether this income stems from work considered undignified, and the question of whether the acquisition of income involves the acceptance of basic injustices.

All these questions determine a household's strategies for survival and improvement. I will start by examining the means for self-improvement at the disposal of *individual* households. First, they might move to another neighbourhood, city, or country in the hope of finding more satisfactory conditions. Millions have already chosen this option. Second, they can take advantage of better times to take precautionary measures for the hard times that lie ahead. These measures may include saving money[34] or

---

35 (1990), pp. 193–219, and Michael Grüttner, "Working-Class Crime and the Labour Movement: Pilfering in the Hamburg Docks, 1888–1923", in: Richard J. Evans (ed.), *The German Working Class 1888–1933. The Politics of Everyday Life* (London and Totowa, 1982), pp. 54–79. William Freund reveals the possibility of a smooth transition to theft as a collective act in "Theft and Social Protest Among the Tin Miners of Northern Nigeria", *Radical History Review*, 26 (1982), pp. 68–86.

[32] Michelle Perrot, *Les ouvriers en grève. France 1871–1890* (Paris and The Hague, 1974), vol. I, pp. 210–212; Melanie Tebbutt, *Making Ends Meet. Pawnbroking and Working-Class Credit* (New York, 1983); Paul Johnson, *Saving and Spending. The Working-Class Economy in Britain 1870–1939* (Oxford, 1985), Ch. 6.

[33] Joan Smith and Immanuel Wallerstein, "Households as an Institution of the World-Economy", in Joan Smith *et al.*, *Creating and Transforming Households. The Constraints of the World-Economy* (Cambridge, 1992), pp. 3–23, 11–12.

[34] Günther Schulz, " 'Der konnte freilich ganz anders sparen als ich'. Untersuchungen zum Sparverhalten industrieller Arbeiter im 19. Jahrhundert", in: Werner Conze and Ulrich Engelhardt (eds.), *Arbeiterexistenz im 19. Jahrhundert. Lebensstandard und Lebensgestaltung deutscher Arbeiter und Handwerker* (Stuttgart, 1981), pp. 487–515; Jos De Belder, "Het arbeiderssparen 1850–1890", in: August Van Put *et al.* (eds.), *De Belgische Spaarbanken.*

purchasing a house.[35] Third, households may reduce expenses through measures such as living (still more) frugally, not paying their debts, and expelling non-productive members. Fourth, they can change the way they obtain their income, for example by seeking other work or through diversification of their sources of income.

In addition to measures for households to try to improve their living conditions independently, there are several strategies involving help from outside sources. First, households may appeal to *relatives*. Many authors have indicated the value of kinship for household survival. Tamara Hareven wrote that to many American immigrants and urban workers, kin were

the main, if not the only, source of assistance and survival. In the absence of public welfare agencies and social security kin were the exclusive source of social insurance. Kin assistance was crucial in handling personal and family crises (such as child-bearing, illness, and death), and in coping with the insecurities imposed by the industrial system (such as unemployment, accidents, and strikes). [Furthermore . . . s]trategies for kin assistance required both short-term and long-term investments over the life-course. Short-term investments entailed assistance in the workplace, in housing, in loaning money or tools, and trading skills, goods, or services. Among the long-term investments, the most pervasive exchange was that between parents and children, – old-age support in return for childrearing.[36]

Kinship relations *outside* one's immediate surroundings often proved especially important. An interesting method of distributing the risks involves mutual assistance between rural-agrarian and urban relatives. Heidi Rosenbaum described an example of this system when she mentioned the importance "of family support from relatives in the country-side" for workers in Linden (Germany) in the early twentieth century.[37] Jean Peterson showed how the reverse currently holds true for Philippine peasantry by writing that "some families explicitly plan to establish some siblings [. . .] as wage-earners in the city" to generate revenue in cases of crop failure or poor harvests.[38]

A second source of relief lies in *personal communities*. These communities consist of informal networks based on companionship, emotional aid, and

Geschiedenis, Recht, Economische Funktie en Instellingen (Tielt, 1986), pp. 91–119; Johnson, *Saving and Spending*, Ch. 4.

[35] John Modell, "Changing Risks, Changing Adaptations: American Families in the Nineteenth and Twentieth Centuries", in: Alan J. Lichtman and Joan R. Challinor (eds.), *Kin and Communities: Families in America* (Washington, D.C., 1979), pp. 128–129; Barrett, *Work and Community in the Jungle*, pp. 104–107.

[36] Tamara K. Hareven, "A Complex Relationship: Family Strategies and the Processes of Economic and Social Change", in: Roger Friedland and A.F. Robertson (eds.), *Beyond the Marketplace. Rethinking Economy and Society* (New York, 1990), pp. 215–244.

[37] Heidi Rosenbaum, *Proletarische Familien. Arbeiterfamilien und Arbeiterväter im frühen 20. Jahrhundert zwischen traditioneller, sozialdemokratischer und kleinbürgerlicher Orientierung* (Frankfurt/M., 1992), p. 153.

[38] Jean Treloggen Peterson, "Interhousehold Exchange and the Public Economy in Three Highland Philippine Communities", *Research in Economic Anthropology*, 11 (1989), pp. 123–142, 136.

small services in daily life. While the networks may be locally based (neighbourhoods), this restriction is not essential to their operation. Personal communities also include kinship networks and require the same investment as strategies for short-term kin assistance (relatively small and readily available skills and services).[39] Personal communities have always appeared gendered, although their focus varies depending on the time, the place, and the culture.[40] There is often a fluid line between blood relatives and personal communities, as proved by frequent transformations of friendships into fictitious kinship relations, such as with *compadrazgo* (fictitious parenthood usually involving the relationship between parents and godparents to a child) in Latin America[41] and the selection of *Taufpaten* (godparents) among the nineteenth-century German working class.[42]

Acceptance of *patronage* is a third strategy. Whereas the first two forms of social insurance are generally horizontal, (the actors pertained to similar social classes), this approach is clearly vertical. As Y. Michal Bodemann wrote, it involves "a form of class rule and class struggle and at the same time its concealment."[43] Weak subalterns seek protection from higher, more powerful individuals who help them in emergencies in return for material or other types of services. This relationship is not merely economic but sociocultural as well, as patrons receive their clients' loyalty and esteem in return for their protection and help. Forms of patronage may vary from political clientelism to patriarchal enterprise.[44]

A fourth and final strategy for social insurance involves joining or founding *social movement organizations* to bring about overall improvement in the conditions of (segments of) the working class. Examples of this strategy are mutual aid societies, producer or consumer cooperatives, trade unions, political parties, and combinations of these movements.

---

[39] Barry Wellman, Peter J. Carrington, and Alan Hall, "Networks as Personal Communities", in: Barry Wellman/S.D. Berkowitz (eds.), *Social Structures. A Network Approach* (Cambridge, 1988), pp. 130–184, 163.

[40] Compare personal communities in London between 1870 and 1914 in Ellen Ross, "Survival Networks: Women's Neighbourhood Sharing in London Before World War I", *History Workshop Journal*, 15 (Spring 1983), pp. 4–27, to those in Lebanon in the 1970s in Suad Joseph, "Working-Class Women's Networks in a Sectarian State: A Political Paradox", *American Ethnologist*, 10 (1983), pp. 1–22.

[41] Sidney W. Mintz and Eric R. Wolf, "An Analysis of Ritual Co-Parenthood (Compadrazgo)", *Southwestern Journal of Anthropology*, vol. 6, No. 4 (Winter 1950), pp. 341–368.

[42] Hartmut Zwahr, *Zur Konstituierung des Proletariats als Klasse. Strukturuntersuchungen über das Leipziger Proletariat während der industriellen Revolution* (Berlin, 1978), pp. 163–189.

[43] Y. Michal Bodemann, "Relations of Production and Class Rule: The Hidden Basis of Patron–Clientage", in: Wellman and Berkowitz, *Social Structures. A Network Approach*, pp. 198–220, 215.

[44] For a comprehensive analysis of industrial paternalism, see Alvarez Sierra, *El obrero soñado. Ensayo sobre el paternalismo industrial (Asturias 1860–1917)* (Madrid, 1990), pp. 7–164.

At least eight ways exist for households to improve their circumstances, whether they do so independently or with outside help. *How* households devise their strategy is of course crucial. Several factors come into consideration. The preceding description is *taxonomic* in that it covers opportunities that *may* arise over time. The various options are actually limited to specific historical contexts. Paternalism, for example, is less likely in advanced industrial societies than in less developed ones.[45] Each actual situation will therefore present fewer opportunities than those described here. On the other hand, each strategy consists of several options: for example, those who wish to join social movement organizations can sometimes choose from a wide range of possibilities. It is also possible (and even common) to use several strategies at once. Furthermore, the strategies described here are interrelated and can alternatively undermine or reinforce one another. Frequent geographical mobility can work against the establishment of powerful unions in some cases, whereas it might actually form the basis for organizations in other cases.[46] Strategies may even intermingle. Close non-kin relationships can for example be transformed into fictitious kinship relations.[47] Alternatively, kinship and personal communities may provide a valuable basis for a social movement organization.[48]

---

[45] Robin Theobald and Michael A. Korovkin debate historical conditions necessary for patronage in Robin Theobald, "The Decline of Patron–Client Relations in Developed Societies", *Archives Européennes de Sociologie* [henceforth: *AES*], 24 (1983), pp. 136–147; Michael A. Korovkin, "Exploitation, Cooperation, Collusion: An Enquiry into Patronage", *AES*, 29 (1988), pp. 105–126; Robin Theobald, "On the Survival of Patronage in Developed Societies", *AES*, 33 (1992), pp. 183–191.

[46] Joan Wallach Scott, *The Glassworkers of Carmaux. French Craftsmen and Political Action in a Nineteenth-Century City* (Cambridge, Mass., 1974), pp. 68, 83–87; Humphrey Southall, "Mobility, the Artisan Community and Popular Politics in Early Nineteenth-Century England", in: Gerry Kearns and Charles W.J. Withers (eds.), *Urbanising Britain. Essays on Class and Community in the Nineteenth Century* (Cambridge, 1991), pp. 103–153.

[47] The discussion of personal communities provided some examples of this transformation. It may also occur with patronage – patrons and patronesses can become godfathers or godmothers respectively – or self-organizations. Emily Honig's example of female textile workers in Shanghai during the first half of the twentieth century illustrates this point: "After working together for several years, six to ten women would formalize their relationship with one another by pledging sisterhood. Once they had formed a sisterhood, the members would call each other by kinship terms based on age: the oldest was 'Big Sister', the next oldest 'Second Sister', and so forth. [. . .] Often the sisterhoods functioned as an economic mutual aid society". Emily Honig, "Burning Incense, Pledging Sisterhood. Communities of Women Workers in the Shanghai Cotton Mills, 1919–1949", *Signs*, 10 (1984), pp. 700–714, 700–701. Better known than this case of surrogate kinship among women are the countless fraternal organizations that have sprung up in workers' movements over time. For examples, see Mary Ann Clawson, *Constructing Brotherhood. Class, Gender, and Fraternalism* (Princeton, N.J., 1989).

[48] See Zwahr, *Zur Konstituierung des Proletariats*. Furthermore, Bert Altena convincingly argues that "family acquaintance played an important part" in the formation of early working-class organizations in "The Dutch Social Democratic Workers' Party in the Province of Zeeland, 1898–1920", *Tijdschrift voor Sociale Geschiedenis*, 18 (1992), pp. 389–403, 401.

Conclusion

As households clearly have countless means of survival at their disposal, the decision to join a workers movement is far less logical and obvious than is often assumed. Labour activism, in whatever form, is but one of several options.

Historical research shows that at least a portion of the working-class population is more likely to organize *as workers* and resist as the share of wage labour in the household budget increases. Despite increased wage dependency, the involvement of working-class households' in labour activism is always partially determined by other factors, such as the job market, labour relations, state measures, and ethnic and religious cleavages.

Perhaps an analysis of reasons behind and ways of household engagement in labour activities should begin by distinguishing between household, enterprise, and state-centred labour activism. *Household-centred activism* entails measures taken by wage labourers to accomplish more with the material means at their disposal without necessarily eliciting confrontations with entrepreneurs or the authorities. Mutual aid societies, which use a communal fund from several households to provide some protection in cases of unemployment, illness, old age, or death, are one example of this type of activism. Consumer cooperatives that purchase goods for several households at once are another. *Enterprise-centred activism* involves efforts to alter the economic balance of power between workers and entrepreneurs. Changes may occur either through battles against capitalist industry for higher wages or improved working conditions (traditionally the unions' job), or through attempts to establish and maintain producer cooperatives. Finally, *state-centred activism* aims to guide or obtain improvements from the state that would be impossible (or far more difficult) to arrange through household- or enterprise-centred activism. The most obvious organizational instruments for this purpose are, of course, political parties, although it is possible for other organizations to focus their efforts on the state.

Once again, these forms of activism overlap. Mutual aid societies have often become unions, and consumer cooperatives have at times become actively involved in national politics.

The gap between household history and labour history is also made clear by the lack of research on household-centred forms of labour activism. Although many view mutual aid societies and consumer cooperatives as far less heroic than parties or unions, they have nevertheless played a major role in the improvement strategies of working-class households. Bridging the analytical gap between households and workers' struggles can provide valuable new insights into labour history.

Translated by Lee Mitzman

NOTES ON CONTRIBUTORS

Carville Earle, Department of Geography and Anthropology, Louisiana State University, 231 Howe/Russell Geoscience Complex, Baton Rouge, LA 70803–4105, USA.

Gottfried Korff, Universität Tübingen, Ludwig-Uhland-Institut für empirische Kulturwissenschaft, Schloss, D-72070 Tübingen, Germany.

Marcel van der Linden, Internationaal Instituut voor Sociale Geschiedenis, Cruquiusweg 31, 1019 AT Amsterdam, The Netherlands.

Alf Lüdtke, Max-Planck-Institut für Geschichte, Postfach 2833, D-37018 Göttingen, Germany.

David Roediger, University of Missouri-Columbia, College of Arts and Science, Department of History, 101 Read Hall, Columbia, MO 65211, USA.

Sonya O. Rose, University of Michigan, Department of Sociology, LS&A Building, Ann Arbor, MI 48019, USA.

Hartmut Zwahr, Wissenschaftskolleg zu Berlin, Wallotstrasse 19, 1000 Berlin 33, Germany.